HONK!
HONK!

For Charlotte

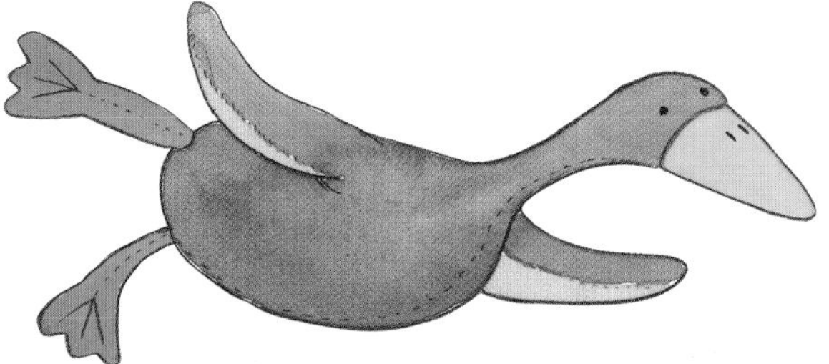

KINGFISHER
Larousse Kingfisher Chambers Inc.
95 Madison Avenue
New York, New York 10016

First edition 1997
1 3 5 7 9 10 8 6 4 2

LIBRARY OF CONGRESS CATALOGING-IN-PUBLICATION DATA
Manning, Mick.
Honk! Honk! / Mick Manning & Brita Granström.—1st American ed.
p. cm.
Summary: A girl takes a journey with a wild goose and her flock as
they migrate to their nesting grounds in the distant, snowy north.
ISBN 0-7534-5103-4
[1. Canada goose—Fiction. 2. Geese—Fiction. 3. Birds—
Migration—Fiction.] I. Granström, Brita. II. Title.
PZ7.M31562Ho 1997
[E]—dc21 97-1427 CIP AC

Edited by Sue Nicholson
Designed by Rebecca Elgar

Typeset in Seagull
Printed in Hong Kong

Honk! Honk!

Mick Manning and Brita Granström

Kingfisher
NEW YORK

A goose landed outside my window
last night, a wild goose, flying north.

I put my arms around her neck,
I climbed on her back, and she carried me away.

We flew above the city lights,

above railroads and highways,

above lakes and fields.

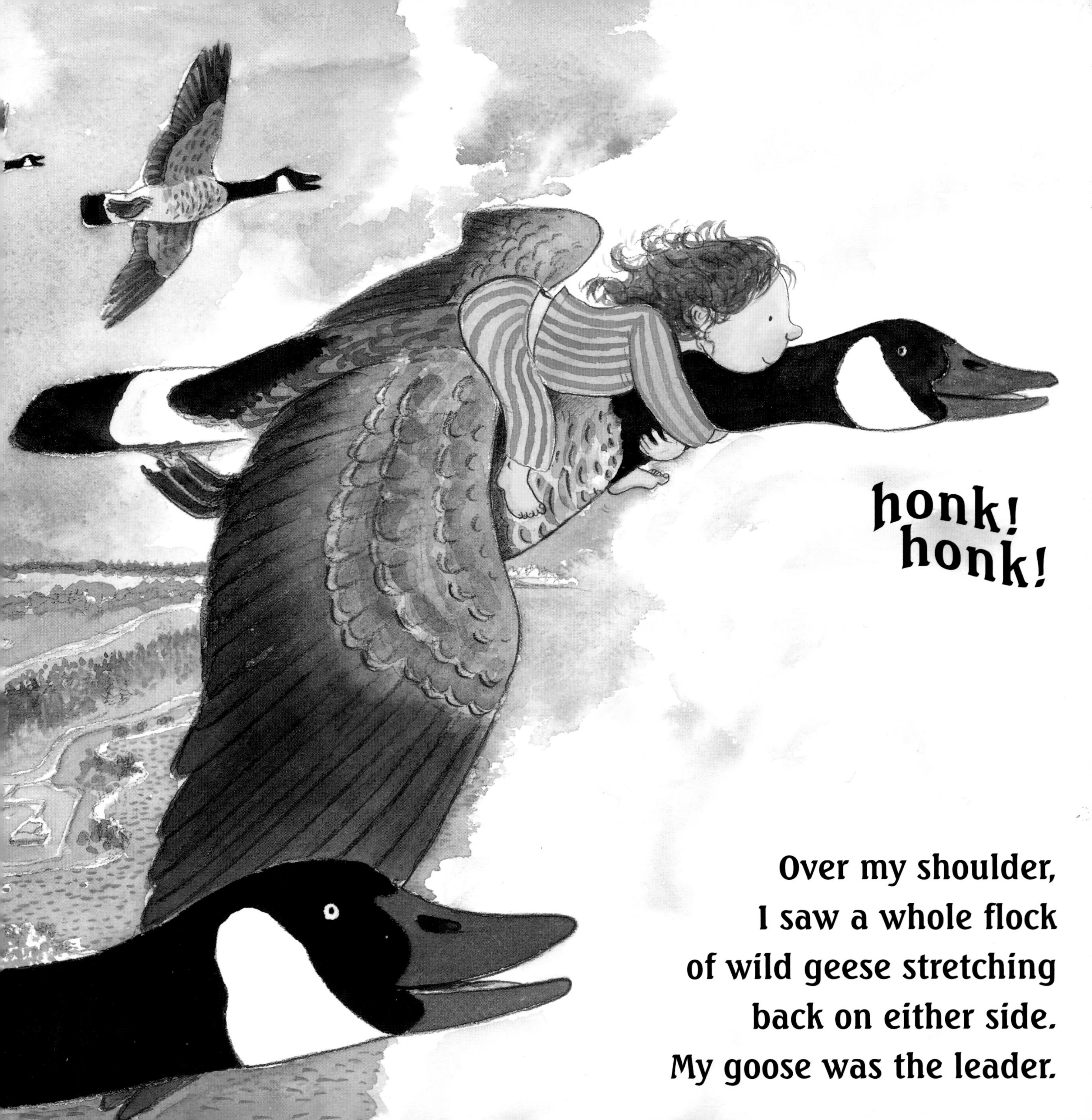

Over my shoulder,
I saw a whole flock
of wild geese stretching
back on either side.
My goose was the leader.

Others joined us.
We became a huge honking flock.
Hundreds of wild geese, all flying north.

North! In wind and rain.

North! By night and day.

North! In sunshine and moonlight.

When we rested,
sentries stood guard.
If one beady eye spotted
a creeping fox, then . . .

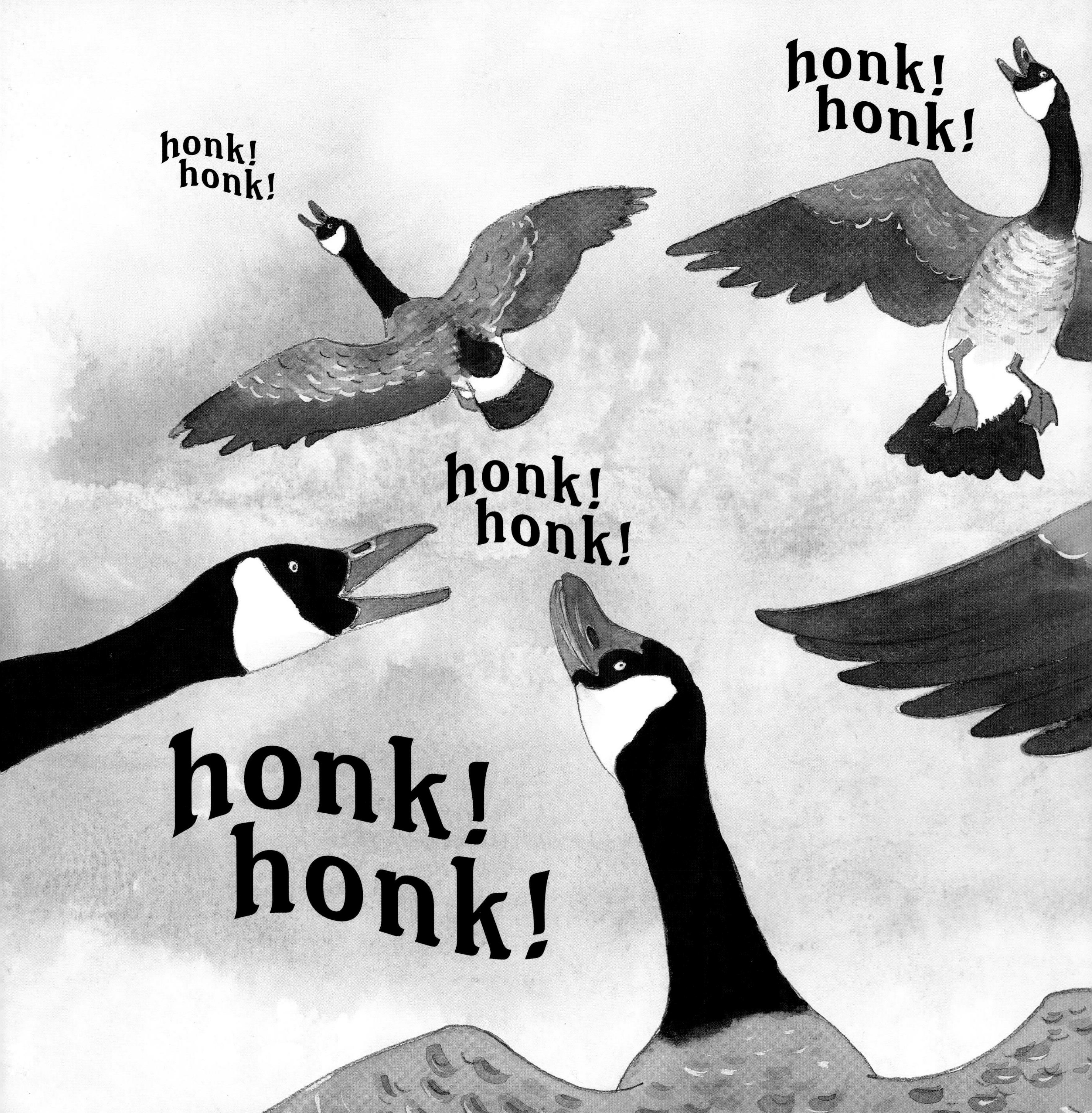
honk!
honk!
honk!
honk!
honk!
honk!
honk!
honk!

. . . we would take off with a WHOOSH of goose wings.

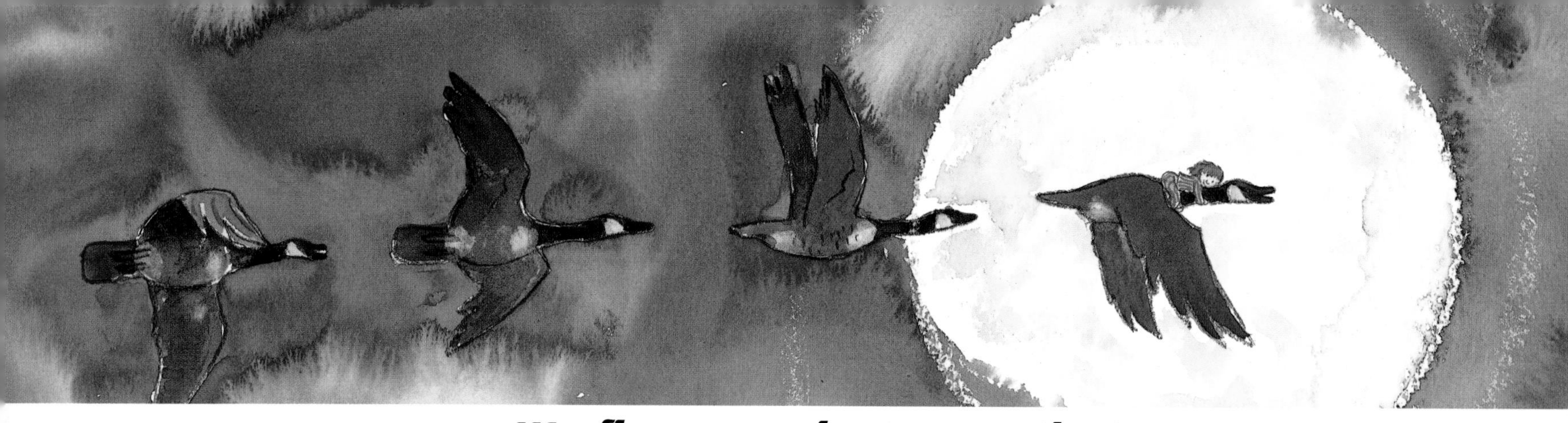

We flew on, always north.

North! Dodging the hunters and hawks.

North!
Over snowy mountains
and icy rivers.
Always north.

We arrived at the nesting grounds.

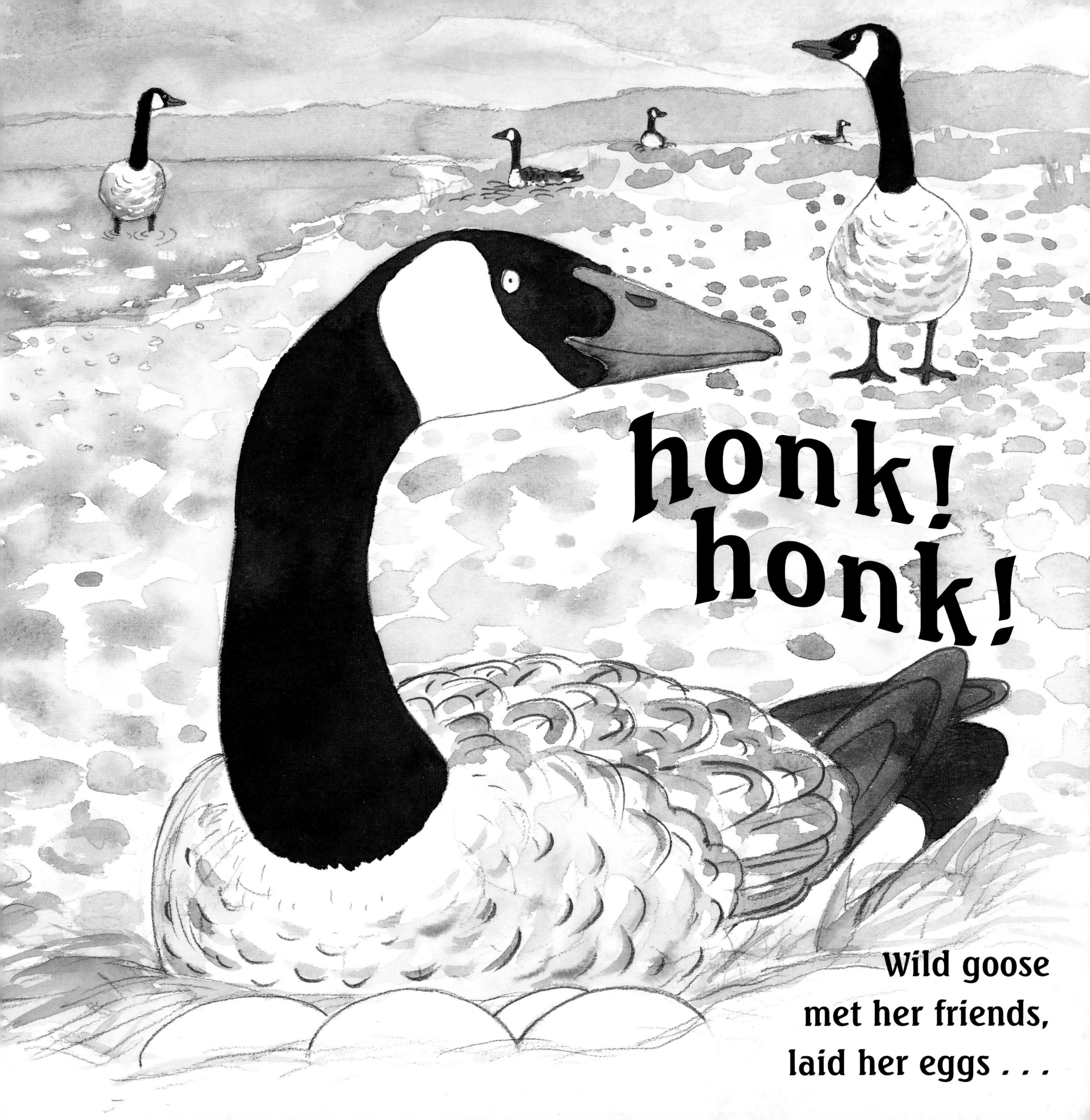
honk! honk!
Wild goose
met her friends,
laid her eggs . . .

. . . and hatched five fluffy goslings.

As the summer ripened, the goslings

grew bigger . . .

and bigger . . .

and bigger.

ho...
hon...
h
h
honk!
honk!
They learned to fly.
They learned to speak.

As the short summer came to an end,
the ice began to creep back over the lake.
The sun sank low in the sky.
Winter was returning.

My wild goose stretched
her wings.
It was time to
fly south again.

I climbed on her back
and we took to the air.
We circled higher and higher,
calling her
family
together.

Then we began our journey home.

South! Dodging the hunters and hawks, foxes, and wolves.

South! Over electric wires and railroad tracks.

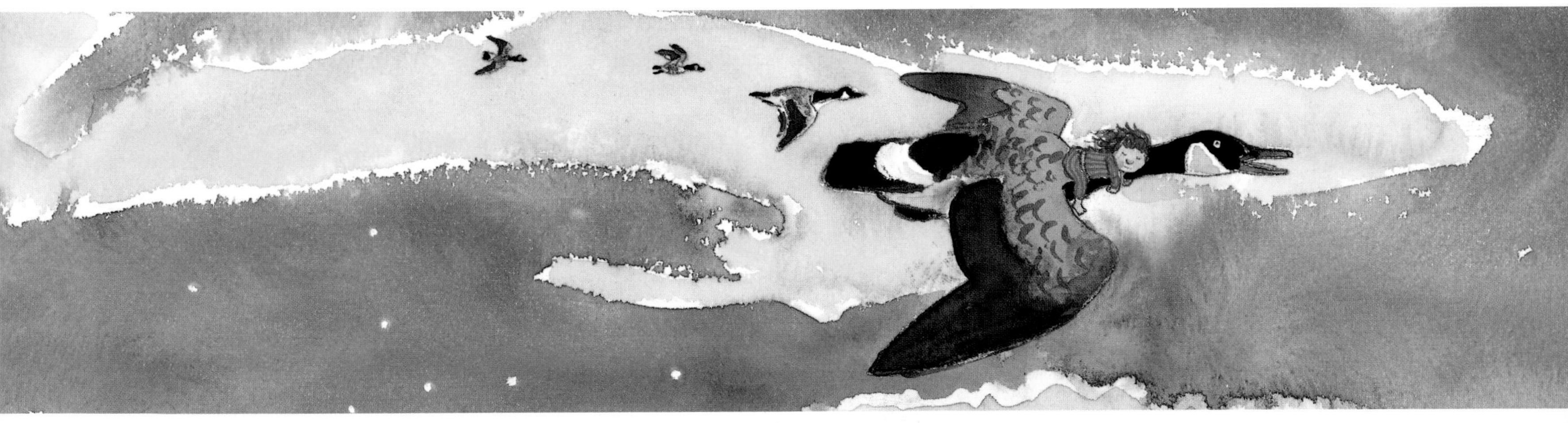

South! In wind and rain, by night and day.

honk! honk!

South! To my window.

Good-bye and good luck, wild goose!

WILD GEESE

Goose Facts

Geese belong to the same bird family as ducks and swans. These birds are often called waterfowl because they live on or near water. Geese have large webbed feet to help them paddle, and oily feathers to keep them dry and warm.

Goose Calls

Most geese make a loud honking sound but some, such as the white-fronted goose, cackle. Others even bark like small noisy dogs.

Living in Pairs

Geese usually live in pairs, especially when they are nesting and raising their young. However, geese often join together for safety, or when traveling. A group of geese is called a gaggle.

Kinds of Goose

There are over 40 different kinds of wild geese. The Canada goose is the most common wild goose in North America. It is also found in parts of Europe and Asia. The domesticated white goose seen on many farms is descended from the greylag goose.

Goose Eggs

Geese usually lay five to six eggs. Goose eggs are different colors. Some are creamy white, some are blue, and some are greenish. Most are about twice as big as a hen's egg.

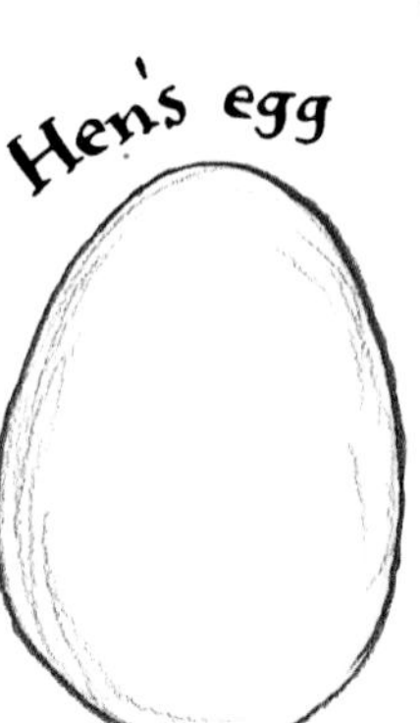

Flying Geese

On long journeys, most geese fly in lines, forming a big V-shape in the sky. Different geese take turns as the leader at the point of the V.

Flying in a group in a V-shape makes it easier for the geese to push through the air, so they don't get as tired and can fly more quickly and for longer. A V-shape of flying geese is called a skein.

Goose Journeys

Most geese spend the summer in the far north, where they nest and rear their goslings, and fly south for the winter when the northern lands get too cold and harsh. This movement of birds and other animals at certain times of the year is called migration.

Other travelers

Butterflies, eels, salmon, and many kinds of bird migrate, too. Every year, monarch butterflies migrate from Mexico and California as far north as Canada. The Arctic tern flies from the Arctic to the Antarctic—a distance of 7,440 miles.

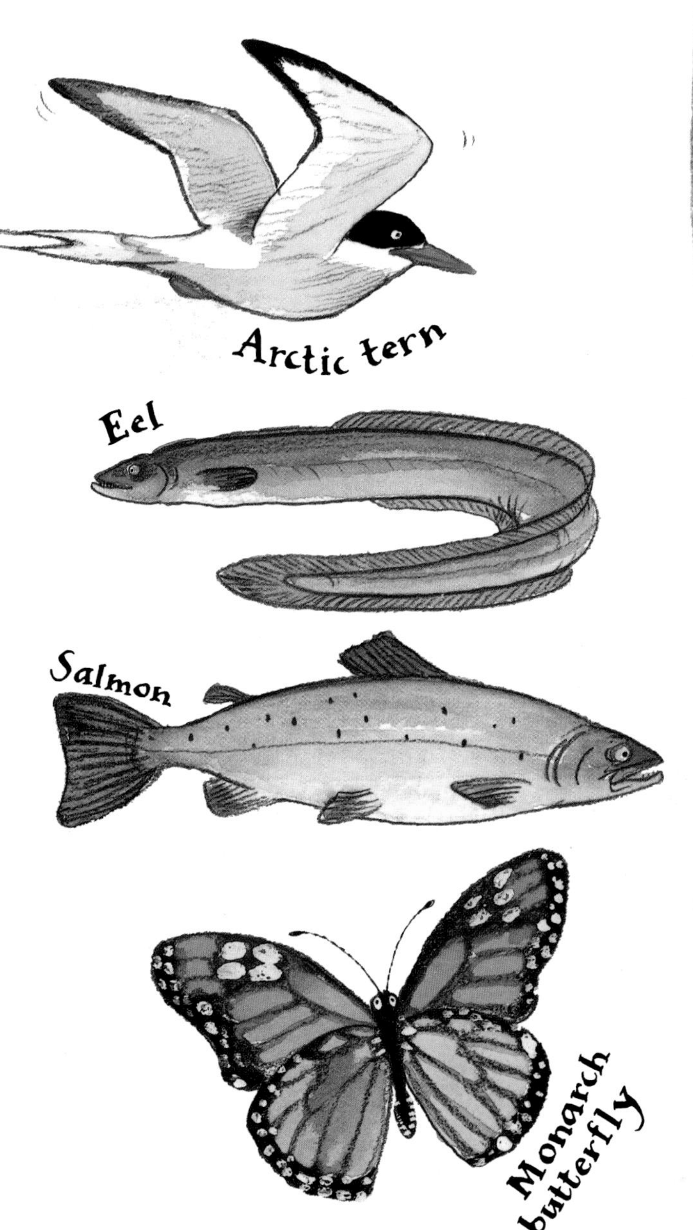

THE NIGHT OF FOUR HUNDRED RABBITS

THE NIGHT

BOOKS BY
ELIZABETH PETERS

The Night of Four Hundred Rabbits
The Dead Sea Cipher
The Camelot Caper
The Jackal's Head

OF FOUR HUNDRED RABBITS

By
Elizabeth Peters

DODD, MEAD & COMPANY · NEW YORK

ISBN 0-396-06323-3
Library of Congress Catalog Card Number: 77-145396

Printed in the United States of America
by Vail-Ballou Press, Inc., Binghamton, N. Y.

TO CAROL

in fond recollection of our joint
Mexican adventures

THE NIGHT OF FOUR HUNDRED RABBITS

CHAPTER 1

I WISH some university, somewhere, offered a course in survival.

Not how to survive when your plane crashes in the jungle, or when you get lost in the woods. Not even how to survive in the jungle-cities of today. Maybe, if I'd studied karate or carried a gun, I would have managed matters more efficiently during my recent misadventures. But I don't think karate or firearms would have helped. What I needed was a course in how to understand human beings.

There are courses in everything else. All of them lead, by some obscure chain of connection, to the acquisition of the Good Life—a nice house in the suburbs, with a nice husband who has a nice job, and a parcel of nice kids. These days they even teach you how to produce the kids—complete with anatomical charts and tests to find out whether or not you're frigid. If my only experience of S-E-X had come from that classroom, I might have decided it would be more fun to set up a workshop and build some nice little robots. You could program the robots to be "nice," which is more than you can do for real children.

But there are no courses in survival.

When you're small, you don't worry about surviving. Other people protect you from danger. They hide the bottles of bleach and the aspirin, and they won't let you ride your tricycle down the middle of the street. Eventually you realize that drinking bleach can make you dead, and so can cars, when you're in the middle of the street.

So what I want to know is: At what age do you learn about people? Your parents can't teach you that; they can't put the bad guys on a high shelf, like bottles of bleach. And one of the reasons why they can't is because they can't tell the good guys from the bad guys either. That's maturity—when you realize that you've finally arrived at a state of ignorance as profound as that of your parents.

I've had my experience, enough to last a lifetime, and all crammed into ten days. I'd like to think that I've learned something from it. But I don't know; if anything, decisions are harder to make now, because so many of the nice neat guidelines I used to accept have become blurred and confused. As I look back on it, I suspect I'd probably go right ahead and repeat the same blunders I made the first time.

If they were blunders. That's what I mean, about things getting blurry. Every action seems to produce a mixture of results, some good, some bad, some immediate, and some so far removed from the original event that you can barely see the connection.

Take, for example, that stupid comment I made the day I arrived home from college for Christmas vacation.

It was snowing outside, and the Christmas tree glittered with colored lights and shiny ornaments; and I looked at the packages under the tree, which were all, by their shapes, dress boxes and sweater boxes and little boxes made to hold costume jewelry and stockings; and I opened my big, flapping mouth, and I said,

"Christmas won't be Christmas without any presents."

It was a feeble attempt at wit, I admit. It was also a tactical error, and I should have known better. I did know, even before I saw my mother's face congeal like quick-drying plaster. Helen liked to reminisce about my childhood, but this was the wrong kind of memory.

The reading aloud—that was George's thing. It went on for years, long after I reached an age when I could read to myself. And *Little Women* was one of our private jokes—George protesting feebly that no male should ever be expected to read *Little Women,* and me insisting that *Little Women* was the greatest book ever written, and that no literary education, male or female, was complete without it.

Helen never did understand those idiotic private jokes of ours. I can remember her standing there in the doorway, with her face wrinkled in an irritable smile, while I lay on my bed giggling and George read solemnly through *Little Women,* word by word, each phrase articulated with the uncertain accent of someone reading aloud in a language he doesn't really understand. . . . Oh, well, I guess it doesn't sound funny. Private jokes never do when you try to explain them. And poor Helen, standing there, with that puzzled half-smile, trying to figure it all out. . . .

She wasn't trying to smile, that afternoon before Christmas. I wondered, disloyally, if Helen realized how much older she looked with that tight plaster mask of resentment. Helen doesn't like being old. She isn't, really. As she is fond of pointing out, I was born when she was only eighteen, and she spends a lot of time and money trying to look ten years less than her real age. More time and money lately, with her fortieth birthday coming up. I don't know why women flip over being forty. I won't mind, especially if I can look like Helen—tall, slim, with a head of reddish-blond hair that shines like the shampoo ads on TV. She has beautiful legs, and she wears the right clothes. Of course she gets them at a discount; she's head buyer at the biggest department store in town, and she looks the part.

"What do you mean, no presents?" she asked sharply. "I'd hate to tell you how near I am to being overdrawn."

"I mean—I meant, I was thinking of the toys you used to get me for Christmas—the dolls and the beautiful clothes for them, the cute little dollhouse furniture from Germany and Denmark. When I was that age, I never considered clothes real presents."

Not like dolls—or books. But I didn't say that. George was the one who gave me the books.

My diversion worked. But as Helen's face relaxed, I felt a little nauseated—at myself. It was a reflex, by now, keeping that look off Helen's face. When I was little, her speechless, white-lipped anger sent me into a panic. Kids learn quickly when they're afraid; I soon realized that the way to keep Helen smooth and smiling was never, ever, to say anything that could remind her of George.

But now there was something contemptible about my instinctive avoidance of unpleasantness. Surely, after all these years, she should have reached the stage of indifference. And surely I was old enough to learn the truth about my father.

"That doll collection," Helen said reminiscently. "It's still in the attic, you know. I hadn't the heart to give it away."

"Save it for your grandchildren."

Helen gave me one of those maternal looks—the suspicious maternal look, not the sentimental one.

"I hope there are none in the offing."

"Oh, Mother, for heaven's sake—"

Helen laughed.

"Sorry, darling, I guess I'm just an old-fashioned mum. that particular worry is completely out of style, isn't it? After all, I should be sure that you know how to take care of yourself."

I looked away. Somehow I hated it when Mother got onto that subject. I suppose I should have been grateful for Helen's handling of the problem; I had been told, in dry, clinical language, all I needed to know, and Helen had even made sure, when I went off to college, that I was supplied with the Magic Potions. The other girls envied me. But there was something about Helen's matter-of-fact briskness that repelled me. I remembered my blank astonishment after The Talk; and my feeling, "Is that all there is?"

It was not late in the afternoon, but the day was dark, pregnant with snow, and Helen had lit the lamps. Outside the window, the lawn lay hidden under a thick white blanket, and the pine trees were frosted along every branch. The bare branches of the big maples by the fence traced dark lines against the lighter sky, as formal and precise as a Chinese drawing. Beyond them were the lighted windows of the Wallsteins' house. There were six juvenile Wallsteins, and I fancied I could almost see the big old house vibrate with excitement. Christmas was only two days away.

My eyes moved from the window to the room itself. It was a big, old-fashioned room which wore its modern furnishings rather awkwardly. The house was too big for the two of us, far too big for Helen, now that I was away most of the time. Yet she had refused to move after George left. You would have thought that since she hated all memories of him, she would not want to stay in the home they had shared. There was not a single object belonging to George in the house—not a stitch of clothing, not a picture, not a book. Perhaps the house represented Helen's triumph. She had survived without him; and she had obliterated him within the physical framework he had once dominated.

It was not a pretty thought. I picked up my knitting, in an effort to improve my mood. The soft blue wool slid through my fingers, and I began to relax. This was the second sleeve; the front and back were already done. I had meant to finish the sweater before I left school, but I hadn't succeeded. So Danny would get a belated Christmas present. I wasn't sure he would wear it; he might think the color too feminine. But it was the same vivid blue as his eyes. That was the reason why I had chosen the wool.

"I'm sorry your friend—Danny—couldn't spend Christmas with us," Helen said.

"ESP," I said. "How did you know I was thinking about him?"

"Logic, not ESP. Seeing you grinning foolishly at that knitting. I'm not that old, darling; I can remember a time when one young man or another filled all my waking thoughts."

"Mmmm."

"You're purring," Helen said accusingly. "How serious is this boy, anyhow?"

"Pretty serious."

"You mean my fears about incipient grandchildren are not without foundation? And don't say, 'Oh, Mother!' "

"You leave me speechless, then."

"No. Really."

My hands slowed to a stop, but my eyes remained fixed on the knitting needles and their banner of blue wool. I wanted to talk seriously to Helen about Danny; actually, I didn't want to talk about anything else but Danny. Yet in a perverse way, I didn't want to talk about him, I wanted to hug my feelings to myself, keep them safe and secret. I was afraid of laughter.

"Well," I said slowly, "he mentioned getting married."

I hadn't meant to put it that way. I felt my cheeks redden, and braced myself for a smile or chuckle.

"He's supposed to come and ask my consent," Helen said.

"Oh, Mother!"

I looked up and met Helen's twinkling cynical eye, and then we both laughed, together. That kind of laughter I didn't mind. A wave of affection swept over me as I watched Helen's mouth curve and her hazel eyes narrow with amusement. She could be such fun when she wanted to be.

"I certainly don't mean to rush you," Helen said, reaching for a cigarette. "And I'll be honored if you so much as mention the date of the wedding to me; I guess, these days, I should be relieved that you even plan to marry. But I'd like to know more about Danny."

"You know everything important."

"That he's blond, blue-eyed, handsome, and brilliant? All that is undoubtedly important, but there are other considerations."

It was almost dark outside; the lighted windows of the Wallstein house shone bravely through the gray twilight, and small white flakes of snow drifted against the pane.

"What is his full name?" Helen persisted. "You must have told me, but I've forgotten."

"Linton. Daniel Cook Linton the Third." I took a deep

breath; might as well get it over with. "His mother has remarried, to someone named Hoffman, he's a stockbroker or something in New York. Danny has a stepsister, much younger than he, no other brothers or sisters. He really is brilliant; Professor Marks said his last paper—"

"Hoffman." Helen took a deep drag on her cigarette. She was always trying to quit smoking and never succeeding. "The name sounds familiar."

"Maybe you've seen it in *The New York Times.* His mother is some big deal in society."

Helen blew out smoke. Her face was peaceful, but I wasn't fooled. Helen was thinking.

"What is Mr. Daniel Whatever the Third doing at a second-rate cow college, instead of one of the Ivy League schools?"

"You would," I said. "You would think of that. He did go to one of the fancy prep schools, but he—well, he got into a little trouble. Just jokes, nothing serious . . . His mother decided that a nice healthy midwestern school would be good for him."

"You mean Harvard wouldn't take him," Helen said. She put out her cigarette. To my relief, I saw that she was smiling. "Well, that's not too important. A few wild oats . . . I gather that what they call his 'prospects' are good."

I was saved by the bell from the sort of answer I would probably have regretted. It was the doorbell.

"Who can that be, on a night like this?" Helen wondered. As she moved across the room toward the door, her hands were busy, brushing back her hair, straightening her skirt.

"Don't be such a ham. Your boyfriends don't let sleet or snow or dark of night or—"

"Boyfriends, indeed. How vulgar."

We had time for one quick, conspiratorial grin—mother and grown-up daughter—before Helen opened the door and admitted a flurry of snow and the distinguished lawyer who was her latest conquest. He was carrying an enormous parcel, wrapped in gold paper adorned with ribbons and sprigs of mistletoe. I suppressed a grin as I rose to greet him. Mistletoe, I thought; silly old man.

II

So it was a lovely Christmas, complete with snow and mistletoe and old friends dropping in for punch, and dozens of presents, and more old friends dropping in for Christmas brunch, and sledding with the Wallstein kids, whom I had baby-sat, singly and in bunches, over the years. It was a lovely Christmas vacation. Up till the last day.

III

The balding salesman in the seat next to me was sulking. I didn't feel guilty; he had asked for it. Some of them won't give up till you're rude. What gets me is how they have the conceit. I mean, he had too much stomach and not enough hair, and he must have been at least forty. A man that age looks silly chasing college girls—unless his conversation runs to remarks more scintillating than "Come on, honey, a little drink won't hurt you."

Momentarily, though, I wished I had accepted the offer. My thoughts weren't very good company.

The weather was unusually clear. Far down below, I could see the plane's shadow skimming over the snow-covered fields. The view, which was so rich and green in summer, now had the stark beauty of a Wyeth painting; the pale symmetrical squares of fields and pastures were cut by India-ink lines of highways and broken by the black shapes of fir trees. Another hour, I thought. Another hour before I can see Danny.

Tall, blond, blue-eyed, and handsome; it was like describing mountains as big stony things with snow on top. His hair was a silvery gilt color, as fine as floss; he kept it cut short because it wouldn't stay flat otherwise. Against his fair skin his eyes stood out with startling vividness—an electric, vibrant blue, like sapphires, like a lake with the sun on it. . . .

The plane window reflected my own features dimly, like a clouded mirror. It wasn't much of a face, even in a good light—too broad through the forehead, narrowing down to a pointed chin. Helen kept telling me I ought to do something about my hair. A rinse, to give its dishwater-blond color some highlights; a haircut, for heaven's sake! My eyes are my only good feature, big and dark against my pale complexion; but now they looked like empty eyesockets. I look like my father. Even though there wasn't a picture of him in the house, I knew what he looked like. I would have recognized him instantly if I had met him on the street.

For those first few months, after he went away, I kept expecting to meet him. Helen and I left town too—on vacation, she said, but I knew it wasn't an ordinary vacation, so suddenly, between night and morning, with no note to my teacher, no cancellation of piano lessons and dentist's appointments. I hadn't learned my lesson then, I kept asking questions. Finally she broke down. I'll never forget what she said—shouted, rather.

"He's gone, gone for good! He's deserted us. You'll never see him again—never ever! Don't ever mention his name. Don't ever talk about him."

Which was enough to discourage even a brash twelve-year-old from asking any more questions.

I was never brash, I was bookish and shy, and the news, with the shock of its telling, stunned me so badly that I was just now beginning to appreciate the depth of the shock. It pushed the whole subject of my father back into some deep recess of my mind, behind a mental door which I locked and bolted. Helen's prohibition was unnecessary. I was literally incapable of hearing anything about George. There must have been gossip, I must have heard things; I knew, without knowing where the information had originated, that George had left the college where he taught as an Assistant Professor, under a cloud. There was something about a woman; or was that only my maturing imagination, reaching for the obvious reason?

Yet in those years I played a secret, pathetic game, usually late at night, when I was supposed to be asleep. I explained my father.

Some nights he was a Secret Service agent, compelled by the urgency of the special mission which he alone could accomplish, to abandon his beloved family lest he bring them into danger. Sometimes he was the long-lost heir to a kingdom, whose dedication to his people required that he marry a haughty princess. (That was when I was very young and still under the influence of *The Prisoner of Zenda*.) Later, more grimly and realistically, I imagined accidents, amnesia, or kidnapping. But whatever the excuse, he was always the knight on the white horse, the Good Guy in the white sombrero, who would one day come riding back into my life, bearing the gift of an explanation.

There were clouds outside the window of the plane now, clouds and the early darkness of a winter afternoon. I could see my features more clearly. My mouth had an ugly twist as I recalled my youthful stupidity.

How could I have been so stupid, even at that age? Other men deserted their wives and children. Other men copped out; most of the time the women they left were as bitter as Helen had been. But I didn't care about Helen, then. I only cared about me. And I had been so smug—even before I knew the meaning of the word—because my daddy was different, my daddy really liked to play with me. Not like the other fathers, who were openly bored, or hideously jovial. He invented games. He told me all the old stories, and made up new ones, stories that went on for weeks and brought in all the beloved familiar characters, the Scarecrow and Frodo and Pooh and Water Rat. . . .

I don't know when the dreams finally died. I guess it was when I admitted, finally, that not once during all those months had he attempted to communicate with me. I used to come straight home after school, and look on the hall table, where Helen left my mail. When Christmas came and went without so much as a card—I think I knew, then. But the dreams took a long time to die.

Maybe they weren't dead yet. After what happened this morning, the last day of my vacation . . .

I came downstairs in time to see Helen close the door on the mailman. There was a package, that was why he had knocked instead of leaving the mail in the box. I was barefoot, as usual; Helen didn't hear me coming. After one quick glance at the package she put it down and began to shuffle through the envelopes. There were quite a few of them, mostly late Christmas cards. And then . . . That sudden, furtive movement as Helen, seeing me, half turned away, clasping the letters to her breast with greedy hands.

She recovered herself at once, with a light, "Heavens, you startled me, sneaking up like that," and continued sorting through the mail, handing over the letters addressed to me as she came to them.

I don't know why the dirty, distorted suspicion should have struck me. Except—for a second she had looked guilty. Like someone preparing to read a letter that wasn't meant for her.

Was it possible that Helen could have intercepted mail for me, mail from my father?

I knew the answer. Helen was perfectly capable of doing just that. Not out of malice; she would have some neat rational excuse: a sharp, merciful break, much kinder than prolonged hope. . . . Parents do things like that—"for your own good."

I didn't voice my suspicion, not directly, but the incident was the catalyst, the final ingredient in the explosive mixture of my mind. Right then and there, standing in the hall in my bathrobe and bare feet, I brought up the forbidden subject.

God knows it was long overdue for discussion. I was too old now to be sent out of the room when the big people talked about important things. And Helen had carried her burden of hate long enough. After all, what did she have to complain about? She had been a career woman, making good money, when George walked out. Since he left she had climbed spectacularly in a job she loved. If her ego had been damaged by George's desertion, it had had ample medication since; there were always a couple of men hanging around, taking Helen to dinner, to the theater—taking me to circuses and movies, as part of the deal. They were all nice, respectable men, widowers or bachelors—nothing shady or disreputable, not for Helen. Some of them had been fairly nice guys. No; if Helen had wanted to, she could have remarried within a year.

Certainly it had occurred to me that she might still be in love with George. I wasn't so naïve as to believe that people over twenty-five can't be in love. But for ten years? That isn't romantic, it's just silly.

I pointed some of these things out to Helen; and Helen, looking at least sixty, told me to shut up.

She walked out of the room without another word, leaving me standing there. Later, when she drove me to the airport, neither of us referred to the incident.

Rain beating against the window dispelled my hateful memories. We were in the clouds now, descending; and the stuff pounding on the window was sleet, not rain. A nice, typical Great Plains winter day. When we broke through the cloud blanket I craned my neck eagerly, seeing the airport below—the tiny toy planes, the lines of the runways, the white-roofed terminal building. . . . I imagined I could even see the small red dot that was Danny's car. I didn't need to look for it. I knew he would be there.

The car was a small, warm, enclosed world. The windshield wipers fought the sleet, ticking busily; the headlights cut a bold path through the gloom. Curled up on the seat, shoes off, feet tucked up, I watched Danny's hands on the wheel. They made small, effortless movements, responding expertly to the movement of the car over an icy surface. Big strong hands, a little too faded and white after the sunless months of winter.

I looked up at Danny's profile. He was pale; a little too pale, I thought anxiously. As if he felt my gaze, Danny's mouth curved in a smile, but he did not take his eyes from the road. He was a good driver.

"Warts?" he inquired. "My other head starting to show? I'm sorry about the face, but it's the only one I've got, and you must have seen it somewhere before. . . ."

"I just like to look at it," I said.

His smile broadened.

"Weird," he murmured. "You're really weird, you know that?"

"You look like the underside of a fish, though. I thought you were going to Bermuda with your mother."

"Changed my mind."

"What did you do?"

"Nothing much."

"Studying?"

"Who, me? I never study; how can you accuse me of such a filthy thing?"

"With semester finals only three weeks away—"

"Love, I tell you it's all set. Straight A's, no sweat."

"How do you do it? Blackmail?"

"Watson, darling, you know my methods. I don't give a damn about those little letters on a sheet of paper, but Hermie does. And we must keep Hermie happy. Happy Hermie, that's my goal in life." He was still smiling, but there was a different quality in his smile now, the same tautness that always followed the mention of his stepfather's name. He added, in the same light voice, "The system stinks, we both know that, but why fight it? Any good, social or personal, has to be measured against the amount of effort necessary to attain it. Save your strength for the important issues. Grades, for God's sake, aren't that important compared with—"

His hands jerked the wheel. The car slid sickly, caught itself, and went on, whipping neatly around the big trailer which had suddenly loomed up out of the sleety darkness, its brake lights scarlet.

"War," Danny calmly finished his sentence. "Pollution, injustice."

I let my breath out.

"Those are major issues," Danny went on, "but there are so many others—abortion, narcotics. . . ."

I wouldn't have said it, except that I was still shaking after the near-collision.

"You aren't high, are you, Danny? Not now?"

His long, sensitive mouth—my barometer for measuring his moods—tightened, and then relaxed.

"Honey, you are so hopelessly square. I don't get high on pot. Nobody gets high on pot, they just get a happy glow. If you'd try it yourself . . . You know I don't smoke when I'm driving. Which is more than can be said for the users of the socially acceptable drug."

I knew his disapproval of alcohol wasn't purely ideological. His mother had lost her license for drunken driving.

"I'm sorry," I said humbly.

"Don't be sorry. Don't ever be sorry."

He didn't look at me, or take his hand off the wheel. He didn't have to. The feeling between us filled the air, as piercingly sweet as perfume. I felt dizzy with it.

"Want me to slow down?" he asked, after a moment. His voice was back to its normal pitch. He seldom let his emotions show; that was why their rare expression shook me so.

"Maybe a little . . ."

"Like they say, your wish is my command."

"Then couldn't we . . . stop for a little while?"

"Why, Miss Farley!"

"You know what I mean."

"How well I know." He gave an exaggerated sigh. "Why I put up with your Victorian hang-ups I do not know. I must be, like they say, in love."

"You haven't even kissed me properly."

"I have my hang-ups too, and making out in public is one of them. It gives the old fogies such a chance to feel superior. Wait till we get onto the campus, honey. It isn't safe, stopping along the highway."

After a time I said quietly,

"Maybe we shouldn't stop at all. It isn't fair to you."

"We've been over all this before. What I told you still goes. No pressure. Whatever you want, whenever you want it. It's up to you."

I felt the same paradoxical mixture of relief and disappointment.

"You're a slightly wonderful guy."

"Glad you realize that."

He began to whistle softly.

When I came into my room several hours later, flying high on love, the first letter was there, waiting for me.

CHAPTER 2

SITTING cross-legged on the floor, surrounded by books, notes, and papers, I leaned forward and covered my aching eyes with my hands.

Under the bright glow of the reading lamp the air looked as thick as fog. It was three o'clock in the morning, the deadest hour of the twenty-four. I had been studying for eight hours without a break. That damned psych exam . . .

I opened stinging eyes and blinked. Sentences swam up at me from the open books. "The narcissistic component of the castration complex transgresses its original scope and becomes one of the principal sources of male narcissism." "Ideas of persecution frequently exist in the closest connection with the delusion of sin." "For decades this patient lay in bed, she never spoke or reacted to anything, her head was always bowed, her back bent and the knees slightly drawn up."

I rolled over, back bent, knees slightly drawn up. What a heavenly thing it would be to lie in bed for decades, never speaking or reacting. . . . Nothing I had read seemed fixed in my mind. If my brain was still working like this at 10 A.M. tomorrow—oh, God, today—I would flunk the exam. At that point, I didn't care.

Across the room, in the shadows, my roommate was a huddled shape of sodden sleep. Only her snores attested to the fact that she was alive. I stared at her with dislike. The snores were keeping me awake. Sue and her damned pep pills; she had been popping pills all evening, and just look at her now.

Uneasiness pierced through my fatigue and I crawled to where Sue was lying, cursing under my breath. But when I shook her by the shoulder I saw that she was breathing normally. Prolonged shaking produced a groan and a flicker of swollen eyelids. I stood up and went to the window.

When I threw it open the blast of icy air felt great. I leaned on the sill, enjoying even the needle darts of sleet that scored my face, drawing deep breaths of clear air into my lungs. There was no sign of life down below; the lamps in front of the dormitory shone feebly through the slanting lines of icy rain. Through the branches of the elms which were the campus pride and tradition I could see lively patterns of lighted windows in the buildings that formed the other sides of Dormitory Square. Most of the kids stayed up half the night anyhow, now that the old rules had been suspended, but tonight the number of lighted windows was greater than usual. Exams tomorrow.

Behind me, Sue's soft southern voice let out a string of expletives.

"I'm freezing! Shut that damn window! What're you trying to do, give me pneumonia?"

"Trying to get some of the poison gas out of this place."

"So I'll stop smoking after exams." Sue rolled over and grabbed at the edge of the bed, trying to pull herself up. "God. I feel awful."

I closed the window.

"No wonder, with all that junk you've been taking. Go

to bed, you'll be okay in the morning."

"Gotta study some more. Where—where's the dex?"

"You idiot, you can't take any more of that stuff."

"Gotta have—"

"Go to bed." I crossed the room and gave Sue a shove. She toppled over, across the bed, and buried her face in the pillow.

"Sleep a l'il bit," she muttered. "Wake me up. . . ."

The words trailed off into snores. I stood looking down at my roommate with mingled affection and exasperation. Sue was a good kid, and a lot of fun; but Sue wasn't going to graduate this June if she didn't manage to pass a couple of courses, and if she didn't graduate her parents would send her off to a nice quiet convent school instead of letting her get married. Getting married, for Sue, meant a big church wedding and that cute little house in Nashville, all furnished and decorated by her doting parents. Doting, that is, up to a point. Parents, I thought, are weird. Poor Sue.

There was no point in trying to study any longer, my brain was saturated; anyhow, I didn't have Sue's worries. Or Sue's incentives; nobody was offering me a furnished house and a husband as a reward for a B.A.

But instead of collapsing onto my own bed, I sat down at my desk and reached for my philosophy textbook.

The letters were tucked into the flap formed by the plastic book cover. My fingers dealt them out, like cards, onto the top of the desk—as if the neatness of the display could clarify their meaning.

I knew all about anonymous letters, not only from mystery stories but from my psych courses. I had learned to think of them with academic tolerance, knowing that they were one manifestation of mental disturbance, and that their pattern of obscenity was only a pathological symptom.

I wouldn't have been shocked by obscene or threatening letters. These communications were worse.

The first one, the one I found waiting the night I got back from Christmas vacation, wasn't a letter at all. It was a clipping from a newspaper, a picture, indistinct as newspaper reproductions are. It showed a number of people at a meeting or a party. Staring at it that night, in absolute bewilderment, I decided that the occasion must be a party. The men wore tuxedos, the women's shoulders were bare; one man in the foreground was holding a champagne glass.

The shock of recognition hit me so hard that I could feel the blood draining out of my face. The man holding the glass was my father.

His hair was gray. It had been dark, with only streaks of white, when I saw him last. But I recognized him without a second's doubt, despite the changes of time and the poor quality of the photograph—knew him, in my blood and bones, as I had always known I would.

Since that night I had looked at the clipping a dozen times. I had examined every face in the photograph, every word of print in the caption underneath, and in the news items on the back. I had theorized and guessed and speculated. I had squeezed out every bit of information and every possible implication from the envelope and its enclosure. I was still doing it. I couldn't believe that my conclusions were correct, that I hadn't, somehow, missed a vital point.

The caption referred to an affair called the Valentine Ball, and gave the names of the people in the photograph. George's name leaped out at me, as his face had projected itself from the photograph. Dr. George Farley—"and his lovely companion, Señora Ines de Alarcon Oblensky."

to the same theme: warning. The doctor's bill might be meaningless in itself, but as a symbol of illness or physical injury it reinforced the subtler suggestion of the photograph, with its implacable little black cross. X marks the spot. The target.

Which was absurd, silly, childish, and all the other contemptible adjectives I could think of.

I reached for my purse and took out another envelope. No anonymous message, this one; it had the familiar postmark and Helen's firm handwriting. I didn't read the letter, I knew its few lines by heart. Once again I drew out the long pink slip of paper and studied it thoughtfully. My mind was almost made up. First, of course, I had to talk to Danny. As soon as that grubby psych exam was over.

II

"Now that," Danny said admiringly, "is what I call bread." He held the check up between his fingers. "Not prepackaged vitamin-enriched mush, real home-baked loaves. A thousand bucks! I didn't know I was marrying into the capitalist class."

"That's the trouble," I said. "That's what doesn't make sense."

Danny tore his eyes from the check.

"Something's bugging you, I've seen it for a couple of weeks. What's the matter?"

"It's a long story."

"Aren't they all? Let's find a place to sit and you can tell me about it."

We found a bench under one of the barren elms. It was a clear, windless day. The weak sunshine felt good, after the days of rain and snow, but it added no beauty to the land-

There were three women in the photograph, but I had no trouble finding Señora Oblensky. Lovely, for once, was not a society reporter's exaggeration. Oval face, dark hair swept up into a formal coiffure, one magnificent shoulder bare above the drapery of a long gown—the woman was beautiful, and the face turned toward my father. . . . No, it wasn't her expression, that was not clear in the photo. It was the tilt of her head, the position of her hand on his sleeve, that gave her away.

The clipping almost ended up in the wastebasket, crumpled and torn.

The impulse was fleeting. It scared me a little, though; I didn't think I could still feel that strongly about my renegade parent. Another emotion replaced the quick, sharp stab of jealousy—curiosity. Why would anyone send something like this to me?

On the back of the clipping was an advertisement for a restaurant in Mexico City, and a mutilated story about the meeting of the Friendship Club of Mexico. The envelope had a Mexican stamp. The postmark was too blurry to read, but the origin of the letter was obvious. Yet the language of the clipping was English. An English-language newspaper, published in Mexico City—for only a large city could support a newspaper designed for tourists and expatriates. So now I knew where George was living.

Was that why the unknown correspondent had sent the letter, to give me George's current address? The desire to communicate information is the usual reason for sending mail. But I knew the motive for this communication couldn't be so simple. In the first place, the address wasn't even a current one. A Valentine Ball must take place around the middle of February. It was now January. So the clipping must refer to last year's ball, and the unknown had painstakingly searched through old newspapers in order to extract this particular clipping. A clipping that showed George with a beautiful woman.

So, I thought, what else is new? Presumably there had been some female in the picture when George left home. This might be the same woman, or it might not. What difference did it make? And what was I supposed to do about it? I certainly wasn't going to rush off to Mexico and throw myself at George's feet, begging him to return to the arms of his loving family. His loving family didn't want him back. And, after seeing the Oblensky woman, I was pretty sure George didn't want to come back.

Malice prompts most anonymous letters, the desire to hurt without risking one's own reputation or safety. But ten years is a long time, after ten years no one would expect me to care that much. And why me? Anyone wishing to cause pain might more reasonably have sent the clipping to Helen.

Perhaps the letter was sent by a kind friend, who thought it was time for Daddy and daughter to be reconciled. If so, kind friend wasn't very tactful. A picture of white-haired old Daddy patting an orphan, or stroking a cat, the sole comfort of his old age, might have moved me. If Señora Oblensky was the comfort of his old age, he didn't need any sympathy.

I couldn't believe in the kind friend. There was an air about that anonymous communication—its very anonymity, for one thing—something about the stiff, black block printing on the envelope—that was stealthy, sneaking, unhealthy.

In the smoky lamplight, with Sue's bubbling snores the

only sound, I looked again at the tiny detail which had almost eluded my attention that first night.

George had been facing the camera. His outstretched arm, holding the glass, pulled his coat back and exposed a stretch of white shirt front. On this whiteness, in the center of his chest, a small cross had been printed, in the same black ink that had been used on the envelope. At first glance I had taken it for a blot on the paper, or a shirt stud; but when I examined it closely, the shape was clear, deliberate.

Since that first letter, there had been four others. They lay before me now, on the desk: four envelopes, identical in shape and penmanship; and four enclosures. Three were clippings from the same newspaper—*The News,* it wa called, the name had survived on one of the clippings. Tw of the excerpts simply mentioned George's name as hav been present at a lecture or meeting. The third comm ated with him on having sprained his ankle. There w friendly small-town chattiness about the style; no dou foreign community was relatively small.

The last enclosure was a bill from a doctor.

There was no mention of the treatment that h given, only George's name, and the amount, $10 quite a lot of money, enough for a minor operatic thought, until I just happened to pick up a b Mexico and found that the dollar sign is used One hundred pesos is only about eight dollar visit, then, possibly a house call—not a serio for eight dollars.

I thought I had given up melodrama wit *of Zenda.* Yet, in searching for a motive be tle group of communications, I found mys

scape, only illuminated its stark ugliness. Melting snow bared patches of dead brown grass and red mud. Along the street the mounds of snow raised by the snow plows were gray hills streaked with the same rusty mud.

I put my books down on the bench and brought out my collection of envelopes.

Danny was fascinated. He heard me out without speaking, his candid, intelligent face reflecting his interest as clearly as words could do.

"Now you see why that check bugs me," I finished. "We don't have that kind of money, Mother never saves a dime. Especially with my school expenses. She's always complaining about being broke."

"According to her letter, she got an unexpected inheritance. Must have been a tidy sum, if she sent you this much."

"Not necessarily. She's pretty fair, as mothers go; she'd share, half and half. In fact, I'm sure it wasn't much because of what she says—that she's going to squander the rest of it on a winter cruise. If it amounted to a lot of money—say, fifty thousand dollars—she'd invest it. But to Helen a few thousand isn't capital, it's just fun and games."

"Okay, I'll buy that. So what's the problem?"

"It's the timing."

"You mean the money right after these letters?"

"Right. Look, doesn't it seem obvious to you, or am I cracking up? Somebody wants me to go to Mexico."

"Yes, but . . ." Danny thought. "You're assuming a connection between your anonymous letters and your mother's check. You don't think she sent the letters, do you? She could arrange to have them sent, through a friend in Mexico, but—"

"No. Helen wants me to forget him. She turns green if I so much as mention his name."

"Okay. So the converse may be true; that the person who sent the letters somehow arranged for the inheritance. I guess it wouldn't be that hard to arrange."

"So we're back to where we started. Someone wants me to go to Mexico."

"So why don't we?"

I swiveled around to face him, the seat of my jeans scraping the damp wood.

"Would you?"

He grinned. The sunlight showed the fresh coloring of his skin and reflected off his close-shaven jaw, making little prickles of light. He was wearing the sweater I had given him; he had worn it almost every day, firmly denying my stricken discovery that the sleeves were about four inches too long. At least the color was right; it made his eyes an even deeper blue.

"What could be greater? Sunshine, exotic nights, guitars strumming, señoritas with roses in their teeth—after this?"

His hand moved out in a comprehensive sweep, taking in cold air, bare trees, muddy ground, and the red brick halls of academe.

"Besides," Danny said, "they really dig blondes in the Latin countries. You don't think I'd let you go wandering off alone, do you?"

"My hero," I murmured, touching his cheek.

"Your gigolo. I don't have a dime."

"Oh, stop that."

"What's mine is yours, what's yours is mine?"

"Of course. I thought we agreed that money was the lousy root of all evil."

"Right. The thing to do is spend it fast before it can corrupt you. Only . . ."

"What?"

"I'll pay you back in February when my allowance comes due."

"Don't be silly."

"I can't help it, I was born that way."

"You know what I mean."

"Sure. But . . ." Danny grinned sheepishly. "Funny, how hard it is to get rid of the complexes you learned at Mamma's knee. I can lecture about the equality of the sexes, but I can't take money from a girl. I wouldn't even borrow it if I didn't think you needed an escort."

"Why do I need an escort?"

"Don't ruffle your fur." Danny patted me on the head. "What I meant was, you need somebody to keep reminding you that you're taking a vacation, not charging off on a private sentimental quest."

"What makes you think—"

"Because," Danny went on inexorably, "there is no proven link between the two separate chains of circumstances. The anonymous letters may be the work of a harmless busybody—there are half a dozen nonsinister, if slightly neurotic, explanations for them. And your mother's inheritance may be just that. In fact, to expect any other explanation is a little melodramatic, isn't it?"

"You think I'm pretty childish. That's what you mean."

"I wouldn't love you if you were wrinkled and middle-aged."

He put his arm out, but I twisted away from it. The heat of my body had melted the slush on the bench; the seat of my jeans felt damp and uncomfortable. I stared down at the tips of my muddy boots.

"You don't have to go with me."

"What are you trying to do, chisel me out of a free vacation?"

I turned on him in a sudden burst of anger.

"Why can't you take anything seriously? Do you have to make sick jokes about everything?"

His face changed. For a moment it was that of a stranger, years older, lined and frightened.

"If I took the world seriously I'd cut my throat. Or set fire to myself; that's in, these days."

"That's not even slightly funny."

His face altered again; I might have imagined that stranger's mask.

"No?" he said lightly. "I thought you liked melodrama. Don't take everything I say so seriously, will you? The world is a bucket of worms, a prolonged sick joke, that's the only way to think about it. But watching the worms wriggle is interesting at times. If I cop out, it won't be permanently."

"Danny. What—did anything happen, over vacation?"

His mouth hardened. For a moment I thought he was going to retreat into the stiff silence that frightened me even more than his fits of depression. Then he shrugged.

"Hermie is laying down ultimata."

"About your grades?"

"No, he's got no gripe there. That nosy Jenkins wrote to him."

"Tony? But he's one of your best friends."

"That's why he wrote." Danny's mouth twisted ironically. " 'For Danny's own good—because he is so fine, so worth saving . . .' Ever since Tony decided to study divinity he's taken on the souls of his ex-pals. And he thinks grass is the devil's weed."

"Oh," I said helplessly. That was about all I could say. Any hint of "I told you so" would have enraged Danny.

"That was all Hermie needed. He wouldn't care if I got stoned on Scotch every night—so long as it was the best Scotch. But pot! No, no, bad boy!"

Suddenly Danny laughed, and I looked at him in surprise. It was a carefree, youthful laugh, and his face was alight with amusement.

"Hermie read me the funniest damn thing you ever heard. Out of some John Birch pamphlet. All about dope fiends, and the evil weed, and how pot leads straight to heroin and makes criminals and rapists out of people. It rots the brain, too."

"What did you say?"

"I burst out laughing. I couldn't help it."

"That didn't improve Hermie's mood, I don't suppose."

"Not much." Danny's amusement died. "Honest to God, though, it's the stupidity of cats like that that really bugs me. Why don't they find out what they're talking about before they start lecturing?"

"I suppose you tried to enlighten him?"

"Well, I pointed out some of the obvious contradictions. Such as the fact that my grades are as high as ever. My brain obviously hasn't rotted."

"No, but—well, I mean, it is illegal. Pot."

"Thank you," Danny said, with ominous gentleness. "Hermie has already mentioned that."

"What would they do to you—the administration here, I mean—if they knew?"

"Do, to me? Shake their fat fingers at me and sign me up

for a course with the local headshrinker. I told Hermie that."

I sighed.

"You seem to have pointed out a lot of things to Hermie. Oh, Danny, couldn't you have—well, said you were sorry, and you wouldn't do it again, and like that? It's only a few months till graduation, and then—"

"Why bother? It was just an excuse; Hermie is about fed up with darling mum, I don't think he can stick it with her much longer. I don't blame him, in a way; she's a lush, always has been, always will be. But—he didn't do much to help her."

Neither did you.

The thought was as unexpected and as unpleasant as a slimy beetle landing suddenly on my arm. My brain shook it away, as my body would have flung the insect off, with a spasmodic jerk.

"Hermie probably doesn't understand," I said quickly. "About alcoholism being a disease . . . Danny, I'm so sorry. I wouldn't have bugged you if I had known."

"That's okay. It feels kind of good," Danny said, with some surprise. "To talk about it. Cathartic, like they say. I'll tell you something else, while I'm baring my soul. I called—while I was in Manhattan, I called Frank."

"Your father?" I knew Danny hadn't seen his father for years. "What did he say?"

"Said how was I doing at school; swell; we'll have to get together sometime."

"Oh, Danny."

"Real nice and polite, he was." Danny stood up suddenly. "My God, I feel as if I'd been sitting in a pond. Come on, Carol, let's go get some coffee."

His hand pulled me to my feet, and we stood looking at one another.

"So," Danny said, "shall I see about the plane tickets?"

"If I go to Mexico, I'll try to see him."

"I know. I know you will. All I'm trying to say is—don't expect too much. Don't expect anything, from anybody."

"Not from you?"

"Oh, me, I'm perfectly reliable," Danny said extravagantly. "I'm still under thirty. And I'm not a parent."

III

My generation is sometimes accused by the Establishment of having a limited vocabulary. I will admit that the word that came oftenest to my lips that first afternoon in Mexico City was not very original.

"Wow," I said, staring out of the window of my hotel room. "Double wow, in fact."

Danny came across the room to join me. I didn't have to move over to give him room, the window went from floor to ceiling and covered half of that side wall. The window matched the room, with its wall-to-wall carpeting, modern furniture, and ultra-fancy bathroom, and the room suited the hotel, which was one of the most expensive in Mexico City. The view was part of the expense. It was not a vista of mountains or gardens, just a main street. But what a street. There were six or eight lanes, with small access roads on either side. The lanes were divided by a wide expanse of grassy park, with towering pine and palm trees, and bright flower beds. There were walks and benches under the trees. But the *pièce de resistance* of the view was the monument that stood in the center of the traffic circle beyond the hotel. It was a tall column surmounted by a large gilded statue, the statue of a winged girl. Her robes flowed out and her bright pinions were lifted, as if she were just about ready to rise into the air.

"Wow is right," Danny said, putting his arm around me. "What a monstrosity."

"The Angel? Danny, how can you? She's beautiful."

"Hideous."

"You're impossible, you don't like anything that was sculpted outside the borders of ancient Greece. Who is she, anyway?"

"Independence, I guess. That's the Independence Monument. The boulevard, in case you don't know, and I expect you don't, is the Paseo de la Reforma. It is reputed to be one of the most beautiful streets in the world."

"I believe it."

"Oh, you believe anything. Don't you know it's dangerous to stand in a high place and look down? Gives people vertigo, it does."

He turned me neatly into his arms and kissed me.

His kisses always made me giddy. But even as my arms circled his neck and my mouth responded, I felt a prickle of warning. There was a new demand, and a promise, in this embrace.

When the newspapers preach about the loose morality of the university crowd, they are not talking about Mid-Victorian U., as Danny calls it. We're small-town stuff, hick stuff, squarer than square. A lot of the old rules have been relaxed, like the "Lights Out" rule, and having to sign in and out all the time; but it still isn't easy to find an ideal setting on or near campus where two people—of opposite sexes, that is—can be alone for any length of time. Danny had a catlike fastidiousness about the obvious places. There are two motels—count 'em—within easy driving distance. Not only are they crummy, they are practically university annexes, with both managers under the thumb of the administration.

But that was just an excuse. The real reason why we had never made love together was me. My neurosis. Danny said I was hung up on the subject, and that it all had something to do with George. Apparently a nice normal Electra complex gets all confused when Daddy departs unexpectedly, leaving the budding girl with nothing to hang her neurosis on. Danny was very sweet about it. Take it slow, he always said; take it easy, don't push; someday . . .

So now maybe the day had come. I can understand why people run wild when they're away from home, on a cruise or something. The old rules don't seem to apply any longer, out of the familiar setting. And there was nothing grubby about this hotel; its smooth luxuriousness glamorized conduct that might have seemed sordid at the Shady Rest Motor Hotel.

I pulled myself away from Danny, so abruptly that our parting lips made a silly, popping sound. I giggled nervously.

"Hey. We just got here."

For a minute I was afraid I'd gone too far. Then Danny took a deep breath, and the flush in his cheeks subsided.

"Yeah. We just got here. So what do we do now?"

"Let's go for a walk. We haven't seen anything of the city yet."

"Okay, we'll go for a walk. Anything to keep you from reaching for that telephone directory."

He went to the door, moving with short, angry strides. Then he turned, and his face softened.

"Sorry, love. I'll unpack, be back in ten minutes. Okay?"

The door closed as I stood there, speechless and ashamed.

He had reserved two single rooms, without even mentioning the alternative. I was grateful to him for not mentioning it. This way was better, just in case . . .

In case I located George, and he was glad to see me.

It was childish, and it was foolish; but I had to admit the truth. I was still hoping.

My eyes went across the room to the telephone. The directory was there, on a shelf of the bedside table.

It took Danny half an hour, instead of ten minutes. He was always late. He had changed into the blue-striped shirt I liked best, with navy slacks and sandals. I don't remember what I was wearing. I had changed, and hung up my clothes, and put on fresh lipstick, but I don't have the faintest recollection of what I put on. Danny looked at me, and under his direct, unblinking stare I felt the blood rise up out of the neck of my dress, clear up to my hairline.

"Did you find it?" he asked.

"It was there, in the book. His real name."

"What did you expect, an alias? His real name was on the clippings." Danny took my arm. "Let's go. We can ask at the desk about the address. Or do you plan to telephone before you go rushing out to find him?"

"I don't know. I hadn't thought that far ahead."

"There's no hurry, you know. We'll be here for over a week. I didn't realize you were so . . ."

His voice died away as we walked down the hall, our footsteps muffled by the thick carpeting. The soft, subdued lighting and the quiet of the place had a well-bred reticence which inhibited conversation of a private nature—especially the nature we were working up to.

When we reached the elevator, the red "down" arrow was lit up; another guest, gray-haired, swarthy, with a narrow black moustache, was waiting. He stepped aside to let me precede him into the elevator, and the operator, a cute boy who looked about fifteen years old, gave me a big white smile and a *"Buenos días."* I returned the grin and the greeting, which constituted almost my entire Spanish vocabulary. Danny didn't say anything. He was in a bad mood, and I didn't blame him. Here we were on our glamorous vacation, complete with everything except the señoritas with the roses in their teeth, and I was being about as much fun as a melancholy grandmother.

I couldn't help it. The closer we got to the problem geographically, the more it obsessed me. Now that we were actually in the same city, I was twitching with nerves. The anonymous letters, which had always had a faintly sinister air about them, now seemed diabolical. The anonymous sender was here, in the city; I knew it had several million inhabitants, but I felt his unknown presence among them all. He was like a shadow—featureless, undefined, a black outline without identity.

What if my wild theories were right after all? What if the messages were meant as a warning?

We passed through the lobby and were out on the street before I remembered.

"I thought we were going to ask at the desk."

"About the address? I decided not to. If you want to go straight there, a taxi driver is more likely to know the location than a hotel clerk. We'd have to take a taxi anyhow."

"Okay."

I was obscurely relieved. The first meeting with my father was beginning to take on the ominous proportions of a visit to the dentist; it had to be done, sooner rather than later—but not too soon. I drew a long breath and looked down the street, with its tree-lined shade and its crowds of pedestrians.

"It's so pretty," I said. "Funny, this isn't what I expected Mexico to be like."

"Dirty peons squatting in the dirt," Danny said sarcastically. "Emaciated dogs and scrawny chickens in the same dirty huts with the lousy people . . ."

"So I'm stupid. Don't rub it in."

"An effete snob, that's what you are."

"But it's so modern and so clean. And I'm not making comparisons between the reality and my effete imagination, I'm thinking of the U.S. cities I know. This puts them to shame. No bottles, candy wrappers, cigarette butts . . ."

"It's safer than any U.S. city too," Danny said. "At least the downtown area is. You could walk these streets at night. You'd be propositioned and pinched, but you wouldn't be dragged into an alley."

His voice had the old familiar note, and I knew he was going into one of his Jeremiah moods, when all he could talk about was the sins of the world. I reached for his hand and said impulsively,

"Let's have a real vacation. Not think of the terrible state of the world, or what's going to happen next year or next week. Let's just enjoy this."

"Nothing lasts."

"All the more reason to enjoy it while it does."

"Hedonist," Danny said. But he was smiling.

We walked on in silence, holding hands, while the golden

light deepened into the soft blue of a southern night.

The mood lasted longer than moods generally do, through a long, aimless ramble and into dinner, which we ate at a little place Danny found by accident. A fountain bubbled softly in a brick-floored courtyard, and the walls were hung with flowering vines whose scent pierced sweetly through the darkness. By the light of the flickering candle on the table we ate spicy things like tortillas stuffed with ground meat, which Danny had ordered from the menu. His Spanish produced politely suppressed grins from the waiter.

"I thought you spoke six languages," I said accusingly.

"I do. Apparently Spanish isn't one of them."

"It's your pure Castilian accent," I said, and we both laughed.

By the time we reached the coffee stage we were more subdued, drugged by fatigue and excitement and heavy food. Danny's attempts at communication improved. The waiter hovered, correcting Danny's pronunciation and offering suggestions about food. He was young, about our age, and he told Danny that he was the son of the owner, learning the business. At this Danny insisted that he join us and drink a toast to "beautiful Mexico, the land of freedom."

I leaned back in my chair, drawing my sweater around my shoulders. The air had sharpened with the fall of darkness, but it felt wonderfully warm in comparison to the winter nights on the prairies. The temperature and flower-scented air reminded me of a May evening at home. I listened lazily, not trying to understand the words of the conversation between Danny and the young waiter, just enjoying the soft musical flow of the voices and the fine-boned facial planes brought into relief by the candle flame. Handsome young men's faces, very different in coloring and shape, yet oddly alike in the tautness of skin and muscle, and the alert life that shone in the two pairs of eyes, one blue, one dark.

Danny stood up, so quickly that I started.

"Gosh, I'm falling asleep," I said apologetically. "Are we ready to go?"

"You can't go to sleep, it's the shank of the evening here."

Danny pulled out my chair and handed a wad of peso notes to his newfound friend. The young man pocketed them without counting them or returning any change. He followed us to the door.

"I didn't introduce you," Danny said. "Carol, meet Jesus. Jesus, Carol. It's a common name here," he added.

"I know."

I started to put out my hand and then thought better of it as Jesus made me an elegant bow.

"He's going to walk a way with us," Danny went on.

"That's nice."

The sidewalk was too narrow for us to walk three abreast. Most of the shops were closed, but restaurants and bars were still open; the customers spilled out onto the sidewalk, and small groups stood on corners, talking and arguing animatedly. Jesus led the way, threading an expert path through gesticulating arms and moving bodies.

Gradually we passed out of the populated district, entering a street that was comparatively deserted. Some of the shop windows displayed lovely merchandise, furniture and clothing and jewelry. When we reached the next corner Jesus said something to Danny, who stopped and took my arm.

"Hey, look at the stuff in that window. How about taking one of those mirrors back for our hope chest?"

The mirror was a baroque papier-mâché fantasy. Red and pink and cerise flowers, as big as cabbages, writhed in a vinelike circle around the mirror surface.

"I love it! Let's buy it."

"It's me or it," Danny said darkly.

"But I could just slip it into my suitcase . . ."

"If you have a suitcase four feet square."

I turned, alerted by a movement in the darkness, not realizing until I saw Jesus returning that he had gone. His hand came out, and something was transferred from him to Danny. He gave me another bow, and a charming smile, and then melted away into the night.

"Oh, Danny," I said. "Couldn't you wait?"

I must have sounded like a mother scolding a greedy child for eating sweets before a meal. Danny looked sheepish.

"It seemed like too good a chance to pass up, meeting Jesus that way."

"By accident," I said slowly.

"Of course it was by accident; what do you mean? I just happened to mention it to Jesus, and he said his friend had some good stuff."

"Acapulco gold," I said. "The Piper Heidsieck of pot."

My tone was sharp, and Danny looked at me in surprise.

"It isn't Acapulco gold, he never claimed that it was."

"He just handed it over to you—a perfect stranger?"

"We aren't in the good old fascist U.S.A."

"Oh, cut it out," I said irritably. "Are you trying to tell me marijuana isn't illegal here? Are you sure?"

Danny didn't answer, and his silence increased my irritation. I knew it wasn't the purchase of marijuana that had destroyed my giddy mood. Danny and I had never argued about pot before, I had accepted his reasoning, which seemed to me to be proved by his own conduct. Pot hadn't hurt his grades or his brain, or lowered what the over-thirty generation refers to as his moral standards. It was another, deeper worry which made me persist.

"If it isn't illegal, why did you have to go through all this pussy-footing around to get it? I read somewhere that the Mexican police are cooperating with U.S. customs on narcotics control, so that certainly implies—"

"Shut up," Danny said savagely.

I stared at him in shocked surprise. He went on, more calmly,

"You're yelling, Carol. Look, if you didn't object to pot back in the old country, why are you raising such a stink about it here? Be consistent, will you?"

"I'm sorry," I muttered. "But . . . well, back home we were breaking our own laws. It was our country. Here, it just seems like . . . I mean . . ."

"Rudeness to your host?" Danny laughed softly. "That's cute. You are a cute, sweet nut, you know that?"

"I just don't want to get thrown out of the hotel. It would be so embarrassing."

"Thrown out of the—what is the matter with you? Hotels don't give a damn what you do so long as it doesn't make a loud noise or damage the furniture."

"You learned that in your long cosmopolitan life abroad, I suppose."

"Cosmopolitan, hell. We wouldn't be in that overpriced hotel if you hadn't wanted to show off for your old man."

I hated what I was doing, but I couldn't seem to stop. It

was as if some perverse, malicious imp had seized control of my tongue.

"It was your idea to live it up. That's just what you said, 'Let's live it up while we can.' If you hadn't—"

"Carol." Danny took me by the shoulders and shook me, not too gently. "Stop it. You sound like a shrewish wife. If that's the way you're going to act—"

We stared at one another in mutual horror. Then Danny's scowl smoothed out.

"I get it," he said softly. "Sure. That's it. What is that address?"

"That's ridiculous. It doesn't have anything to do with . . . It's too late. We can't go out there at this time of night."

"It's ten o'clock. That's early in Latin countries. You wrote the address down, didn't you? I thought you would. Okay, give it to me. We're going to settle this, right now."

It took me a while to find the paper, in the depths of my purse. Danny took it from me, and, without even glancing at it, started off down the street, pulling me with him.

As we turned the corner, the tall trees and open spaces of the Reforma came into sight. Danny headed toward it. I tried to keep up with him, but my feet felt as if they had gone to sleep. The dark street was like a tunnel, and the shrouding trees at its end did not suggest escape but rather a dark forest in some old legend, filled with witches and wolves, and phantoms of the night.

CHAPTER 3

THE TAXI stopped again. Danny leaned forward to expostulate with the driver.

We had been stopping, and arguing, for what seemed to me an interminable period of time. The first argument began before we got into the taxi, back on the Reforma, when Danny saw that it didn't have a meter. He started bargaining about the price, and my stretched nerves made me want to scream: "What difference do a few pesos make? If we're going to go, let's go, and get it over with."

I knew better than to interrupt Danny when he was in the middle of a discussion, friendly or otherwise, so I stood twisting my hands together in unconscious echo of the twisting sensation in my insides. Despite its acrimonious sound, the argument ended to the satisfaction of both parties. The driver grinned as he leaned out to open the back door and Danny's head had an unmistakably cocky tilt. He struck a match as soon as the taxi started, and I recognized the sweetish smell of the smoke from his cigarette.

The taxi driver started off confidently, driving with dash and bravura. But when we reached the quiet, dark streets of the distant suburb, he had to stop to get directions, or to debate, with Danny, over the map the latter produced. When we stopped again, I resigned myself to another prolonged discussion. But almost at once Danny turned to me.

"This is it."

I looked out the window.

The street might have been in a ghost city for all the signs of life it displayed. Except for a dim street light some distance away, it was dark, lined by high structures that were blank and windowless. The structures were walls. Here, in this older section of the city, the houses, with their patios and gardens, were enclosed for privacy. The section of wall illumined by the headlights of the taxi was built of stone, covered with an adobelike plaster; on its surface were graffiti and advertisements and a few of the caricatures children will scribble onto any flat, blank surface.

Where the taxi had stopped, there was a gate, big enough to admit a car or a carriage. The wooden double doors were closed.

I drew back as Danny opened the door of the taxi.

"How do you know this is it?"

"He says it is."

"How does he know? There isn't even a street number."

"That last guy we asked knew the place; he described it in detail. This is the back door; the guy said nobody ever uses the main entrance anymore. Come on, Carol, get out."

"They've all gone to bed. There aren't any lights."

Danny sighed with exaggerated patience.

"The house is back there somewhere. You couldn't see lights behind that wall."

He got out of the car and went up to the gate. The driver gunned his engine suggestively; he was anxious to get out of this deserted area, back to the profitable streets of the center. Obstinately, I continued to sit. The gate looked as blank and unwelcoming as a barn door, and I wondered how Danny planned to notify the occupants of the house of our arrival. Then his arm moved; and after a moment he came back to me.

"I rang the bell," he said. "It's a weird thing, just a big iron chain with a loop on the end. When you pull on the loop it rings a bell, somewhere inside."

"Great," I said. "They may be asleep, or out of town, or . . . I'm not getting out of here. If I do, the taxi will go away and we'll be stuck out in the middle of noplace, and what if no one is home, or this is the wrong address, or . . ."

Superbly tolerant, Danny patted the hand I had placed on the ledge of the open window, and addressed the driver. The engine, which had been reverberating like a steel drum, died.

"He'll wait," Danny said. "I promised him the same fare to take us back, plus something for his time. Now come on. Get out, you can't hide in there as if it were a friendly womb. Life is real, life is earnest, and you asked for this."

There was no warning—no rattle of bolts nor creak of hinges. The big gates did not move. Within their rectangle a smaller aperture opened, a door the size of an ordinary house door. I had not seen its outline in the poor light. I froze, halfway out of the taxi, my hand still in Danny's.

A man stood framed in the oblong of darkness where the door had opened. He was only a shadowy shape, but I knew him, by the unforgotten outline of shoulders and head, by his stance—those characteristics which are harder to disguise than the features of the face, and which change so much more slowly. I knew him.

The taxi driver, sensing drama, had his head and shoulders out of the window and was frankly staring. Danny's fingers contracted, squeezing mine until I could have squealed with pain. My mind formed sentences and rejected them; it was impossible to imagine an appropriate greeting. But I had to say something. He wouldn't recognize me, not after all this time. . . .

"Carol," the man said.

He moved forward, out of the darkened doorway. The pale light shone off his gray head and gave a luminous glow to his white shirt. He was still broad-shouldered, tall—unchanged except for his hair. Unlike so many of childhood's memories, he had not shrunk with the passage of years. Tongue-tied, I struggled for a response.

"Carol?" he said again; this time there was a questioning lift to his voice. He took another step forward. "It is you, isn't it? You look just as I expected you would."

In those days I was still a sentimental fool. I was so moved that I didn't stop to wonder how on earth he could possibly see what I looked like, in the poor light.

I didn't show my emotion; I was afraid of it.

"Hello," I said, and held out my hand.

He had made an abortive movement, half raising his arms; but if he had intended to put them around me, my stiff, outstretched hand stopped him. There was an awkward fumble before our fingers met, and the clasp of hands was brief, by mutual consent.

"I know we ought to apologize, sir, for coming at this hour," Danny said—it being obvious that I was not about to contribute any sensible remark. "My name is Daniel Linton. I'm a friend of Carol's."

"George Farley," my father said unnecessarily. They

shook hands. "Well. Won't you come in, both of you?"

"I told the taxi driver to wait," Danny said.

"Good. It's not easy to get a taxi out here at this hour."

We followed him through the narrow doorway. I suppose it isn't surprising, considering my state of mind, that it looked to me like a slitlike mouth, waiting to gobble us up.

I won't try to describe the terrain as I saw it that night. I was in no condition to observe closely, and I had an opportunity, later, to see it by daylight. We seemed to walk for hours, I remember that; first across an open space, then among trees. There was a light in the distance, a yellow, smoky light that flickered like that of a torch. Very little of the illumination penetrated the thick foliage. Trees and shrubs leaned in on us, branches plucked at my skirts. I was grateful for Danny's warm, steadying hand as I stumbled along a rough path. My father preceded us.

Finally we emerged from the trees into a patio, walled on all four sides and paved with stone. I saw the source of the light: a lantern, hung high on one of a series of pillars that supported a roofed arcade along two sides of the patio. Its exquisite tracery of wrought iron made a black pattern against the flame within. There were trees here too, tall ones, and the shapes of tables and chairs and benches. In the center was a structure that looked like a fountain, though I heard no sound of water; an elongated, squarish column stood in its center.

George did not pause, but led the way through the patio and under the arcade, to a door that led into the house.

The door stood open. We went through, into corridors as dark and confusing as a maze. The silence was getting on my nerves; I could hear my own heart beating, and its rhythm was too fast. When at last we emerged into a brightly lit room where several people were sitting, the light almost blinded me. Then I heard George's voice.

"This is my daughter, Carol," he said, in a tone which was insanely matter-of-fact. "And her friend, Mr. Linton. Carol, I'd like you to meet . . ."

A jumble of names, none of which registered then. A group of faces, unfamiliar—all except one.

She came across the room toward me with the air of a hostess greeting guests in her own home—unwanted guests, who will receive courteous treatment not because it is their due but because rudeness is a mark of bad breeding.

She was as beautiful as her picture, and I resented her beauty all the more because it was a beauty of middle age that was untouched and unadorned except for the thick layer of powder many older Mexican ladies use. Helen was a good-looking woman, but Helen worked at it. This woman must be five years older than Helen. The comparison made me feel disloyal and disgusted, but there it was; if this woman had walked into a room where Helen was sitting, no one would have looked at Helen again.

Her thick black hair was streaked with gray, pulled straight back, without artifice, into a heavy chignon. Her eyes were so big and dark that I thought at first she must be wearing makeup, but she wasn't; as she came closer I could see the papery skin under her eyes and the wrinkles around them. She was too thin. Her black dress was old. It had never been an expensive dress. I had the impression that she had considered all the standard beauty aids and dismissed them with amused contempt. These days Black is Beautiful; so is Young. But here was a woman who was beautiful and who had rejected youth. It was almost an insult.

Ines Oblensky.

She was holding out her hand, so I took it. I felt the callouses, the roughened skin, and I knew that her air of aristocratic delicacy was misleading. This woman worked, and worked hard, with her hands. But the thought didn't give me any satisfaction, I wasn't that mean. All I wanted was to make as good a showing as she was making, display the same gracious control. It couldn't be easy for her, either—meeting, without warning, the grown-up daughter of her lover.

I made myself think that word; it's a wonder I didn't say it out loud. Danny's hand was pulling me down, so I sat, without looking to see whether there was anything under me, I was still that shaken up. There was something—a sofa or divan. And Danny was sitting right beside me, his eyes meeting mine reassuringly, his right lid quivering in a barely perceptible wink. Of course, to him this was only a play and he was a detached observer. He was carrying the conversational ball, giving me time to collect myself.

I took a deep, shaky breath, hearing Danny making the conventional answers to the conventional questions. When did you arrive? How was the flight? And how do you like Mexico, Mr. Linton? Ines was the perfect hostess. She offered refreshments, and Danny refused a drink, for both of us, and accepted coffee, ditto. She excused herself and left the room; and then, finally, things began to get back into focus.

For all its splendid size, the room was rather shabby. The floor was made of beautiful old planks, hand-pegged and dark-stained, but it was dusty and almost bare. The few rugs were worn. The furniture resembled old Spanish pieces I had seen in a museum—heavy, dark, ornate. But there wasn't enough furniture for that big room, and it was scarred with time. The big stone fireplace occupied one entire end of the room; it ought to have blazed with a log fire instead of adding chilly gusts, from its gaping black mouth, to the already chilly room. In spite of its shabbiness, the room had the same kind of beauty that Ines had. It made no effort, no pretense.

It all takes longer to tell than it did to see. Danny and George were still talking about airlines when I turned my attention from the room to its occupants.

There were only two of them after all, not counting George and Ines, and us, the intruders. One was an elderly man. He sat so still, a solid, motionless mass hunched up between the arms of the big overstuffed chair, that I thought he had gone to sleep. He was almost bald. The lamplight reflected off his bare head and the few strands of white hair arranged across its dome. It was innocent and pathetic, the arrangement of that scanty hair, and so was the bright serape wrapped around his bowed shoulders. It made me think of tremulous old age, swathed in shawls against the chill of the room.

Then the massive head lifted, and I saw a face which wasn't at all pathetic. It was round, fat and brown, much browner than the bald head. The creases and lines in it were lines of conviviality, not old age. He had tiny little black eyes, as bright and shiny as the pieces of jet in an antique brooch Helen had. I stared, shamelessly, and wasn't conscious of being rude; he was staring right back, and the stare seemed to me a perfectly natural and friendly interest. But those squinty jet eyes held mine; I don't think I could have looked away if I had wanted to. And when his eyes finally shifted, it was as if they led mine on, to the next point of interest.

I saw the other man for the first time—really saw him, I hadn't noticed anything at first except Ines. I wondered, in the first dazed moment, how I could have been aware of anything but him.

It's hard to describe the impact he made without sounding silly. If I say, "He was the most perfect specimen of masculinity I've ever seen," then I sound like an old lady in pince-nez inspecting Greek statues. If I mention the word "sexy," I sound like a teeny-bopper drooling over Tom Jones. There was more resemblance to Apollo than to Tom Jones, but he was no Greek god. He had the same kind of physique, though—slender, perfectly proportioned, with no bulging muscles or misshapen shoulders. His thin brown face would have been too fine-drawn for some tastes. The nose was almost too sharp, the mouth too tight, the black brows straight, thick lines. But there was a stinging, keen quality about his looks.

He was sitting on a rug in front of the fireplace, half-turned, one leg extended and the other drawn up, with one careless arm resting on his knee. He was wearing dark slacks and an open-necked white shirt, with sleeves much fuller than shirts usually have. The costume brought back memories of that same old *Prisoner of Zenda,* and Zorro, and a lot of other romantic fiction. On Ivan's lean body, against his polished brown skin, it looked just right.

Ivan. The name came back to me, from that half-heard introduction, and I thought, my God, what a name for a Spanish nobleman. Obviously there was a Slav somewhere in the family tree. Oh, but obviously again—Oblensky. His father, Ines's husband. An expatriate, perhaps a descendant of a White Russian refugee? He looked like an aristocrat, every beautiful inch of him.

This was my night for staring. Unlike the old man, Ivan wasn't looking at me. His profile, long-nosed and precise, was pointed toward George, as if he were following the inane conversation. But gradually the feeling came over me that he was quite well aware of my fascinated stare; and as a slow smile began to curve his mouth, a smile which nothing in the conversation could account for, I looked away.

George and Danny had progressed from airplanes to the sights of Mexico City. George wasn't doing awfully well. If it hadn't been for Danny, who could carry on a conversation on his way to be hanged, there wouldn't have been a conversation. He was telling George all about the religious customs of the ancient Aztecs when Ines came back, and I'm sure he was as relieved as I was. He didn't know much about the ancient Aztecs.

Ines was empty-handed, and for a minute I thought she had decided not to break bread with us after all. Then I saw that someone was following her.

The distant doorway through which they had come was in relative darkness, and at first I saw only a hunched dark form and heard a shuffling that sounded like the progress of something not accustomed to walking on two feet. Then I saw that the shrouded form carried an ordinary tray, loaded with cups and coffeepot and a plate of cookies; and I relaxed.

She was so old. I don't know; I guess I just never had seen anyone that old. She looked like the girl at the end of that old movie, *Lost Horizon,* that appears on the Late Late Show sometimes—when she leaves the enchanted valley which has preserved her youth, and suddenly, horribly, shows the hundred-odd years of her real age. But this old mummy was walking, in a fashion. Her black, shapeless gown was so long you couldn't see her feet move; she trundled along like one of those squared-off wooden dolls that have no feet under their skirts.

If I'd thought about it, I'd have sat still. I didn't think, I just got up and went over and took hold of the tray.

I might as well have climbed onto a table and started taking off my clothes. Ines stopped short, turning toward me. From somewhere in the background came a soft, quickly stifled sound of amusement—I knew, without looking, that it came from Ivan. The poor feeble old lady didn't give me any help either. She clutched the tray as though she thought I wanted to steal it. She was awfully fierce-looking for someone so small. I'm only five five myself, and I had to look down on her, but the expression on her face didn't restore my failing self-confidence. I guess it wasn't any more malevolent than any old face is, but she didn't smile, she didn't say, "Thanks, I can manage." She didn't say anything. She just stood there, tugging at the tray.

"You are thoughtful, Carol," Ines said. "But María is a very old family servant, and rather resents any suggestion that she can no longer do her work."

Maybe that was meant to make me feel better. Or maybe it was meant to do what it did—reduce me about three feet in size and ten years in age. I crawled back to the couch without looking at anybody. Danny took my hand and squeezed it, and I didn't look at him either. He meant it to be kind, but it irritated me, as if I were a child who needed consoling.

The old lady bent over, jerking like a badly animated puppet, and put the tray on the table. She came back up in the same fashion; she looked as if her arms and legs were about to fall off. I wished they would. Just before she left the room, she turned and poured out a long string of rusty syllables which didn't sound at all like the lovely liquid Spanish I had heard, and which clearly had me as its subject.

"She says that you must watch out for the *aires*. They like the young, tender, innocent girls."

The voice was a mellow baritone, with hardly any trace of accent. It was as attractive and as masculine as Ivan's other qualifications. I turned. He was sitting up, arms folded around his bent knees. His smile was dazzling.

"What are *aires?*" I asked. "Local cannibals?"

Ivan's grin broadened, but it was George's voice that answered me. I thought he sounded a little embarrassed.

"They are small dwarflike spirits, some say the survivors of the pagan rain gods. If anyone wanders around at night, the *aires* may afflict him with various unpleasant physical ailments."

"That's fascinating," Danny said eagerly. "The old beliefs still linger, don't they?"

"Only among superstitious peasants like María," Ines said coldly. "She is an ignorant old woman."

"And a *curandera,*" Ivan said. "You had better stay in her good graces, Carol, for if the *aires* do catch you, María can cure you of the illness they cause."

"A witch?" Danny said. He was delighted; his eyes shone like sapphires.

"*Curandera* means healer. *Bruja* is the word for witch. But it is true that the categories overlap. The servants of our neighbors are very, very polite to María."

I seemed to be cut out of the conversation, so I leaned back and looked at the only other person who wasn't talking. The old man. His eyes were waiting for me, and I wondered how long he had been watching me. His wide mouth smiled. It was a funny smile, his lips didn't part, but just curved up in the half-moon shape little kids put on the faces of stick figures when they want them to look happy.

Danny was interested in witchcraft and black magic; we all dabbled in it, just as we played around with Zen and meditation and a lot of other things. Ivan answered his questions with charm and accuracy. But it became obvious, after a while, that the two of them were carrying all the social graces. Nobody else said anything. The coffee was gone and Ines didn't suggest refills. George had slumped down in his chair, his face in shadow; maybe he'd gone to sleep, I didn't know. I only knew that he had hardly addressed a word to me all evening.

Since that night I have felt hurt, and horror, and fear. But I have never felt quite so humiliated. The thing that made me cringe internally was the memory of my melodramatic theories. Danger, warning—visions of George lying pale and wan on his deathbed, yearning for his long lost daughter . . . I could have endured that more easily than the reality—indifference, poorly masked by an intolerable courtesy.

I nudged Danny. I wasn't subtle about it, I didn't care who saw me.

"It's late," I said. "And the taxi is waiting. I hope."

George wasn't asleep, he got to his feet so fast I felt a little sick. He was so anxious to get rid of us. His farewell address didn't help.

"It was good to see you," he said. "Give my—my regards to Helen."

I don't suppose he meant to say that; at least he had the

grace to flush slightly under my incredulous stare. He added, with even less conviction,

"I'll—er—call you one day before you go and we'll have lunch."

"Great," I said. I turned to Ines. "Thank you, señora, for your hospitality. It was a pleasure meeting you."

She acknowledged the remark with an inclination of her head. I thought that, before her lowered lids veiled her eyes, there was a flash of something like pity in them.

Ivan said something I didn't hear, but I didn't say good-bye to him, I didn't speak to the old man. I knew I had to get out of there, fast, fast, before I did something stupid. Like cry.

The taxi was still there. The driver's snores were audible from inside the gate.

"He's so happy," Danny said. "I hate to rouse him to the cares of the everyday world."

"Rouse him," I said.

"I guess I'd better. It's a long walk. We've got to get up early, you know. Ivan is coming at nine."

"Coming at—"

Danny opened the back door and shoved me in. I sat there with my mouth opening and closing while Danny woke up the driver, commiserated with him on being awake, and suggested that we depart.

As the taxi lurched off, I tried again.

"Why is Ivan coming?"

"Taking us sightseeing."

"I didn't hear you arrange that."

"You didn't hear much." Danny put his arm around me. "I'm sorry, Carol."

"What for? I was just curious, that's all. I mean, he made

it pretty clear how he feels. Why should I expect . . ."

I cried halfway back to the hotel. The driver was so sweet; he stopped along the way and brought me a glass of some awful-tasting stuff, from a café that was still open, and gave me all kinds of advice which Danny translated, probably not very accurately. When we finally got to the hotel, Danny and the driver were deep in a theological discussion, the best of pals; and I was about two thirds stoned. I never can drink, I've got no head for it. But since that night I can understand why some people do.

CHAPTER 4

IF IT hadn't been for Ivan, I'd probably have taken the first available flight back to the States. He made that day one of the shining days, the sort that stands out in your memory like a diamond in a long string of pebbles.

It didn't start out very well. I woke up with what I guess must have been a hangover; it was the first and only time I've ever felt like that. My head was splitting and my stomach was disconnected. Danny said I sounded just like his mother on one of her mornings-after.

"On one glass of tequila?" I croaked.

"It's an unjust world," Danny agreed. "There's one advantage to being related to a lush, though. You learn useful recipes. Hold on, I'll be right back."

I held on, literally, to my head, which felt as if it might go rocketing off into outer space at any minute. The room was gloomy. The maid had drawn the draperies the evening before, and I hadn't been in any condition to pull them back. I hadn't even undressed; I was lying on top of the bed, and my clothes were horribly wrinkled.

Danny came back with a glass of poison, which he made me drink. There was an imminent moment of upheaval, like Popacatapetl getting ready to erupt; and then miraculously my stomach began to make connections with the rest of me. I looked up at Danny out of one eye; he was holding my head over the edge of the bed, just in case.

"Hey," I said.

"I told you it works." His cheerfulness was almost bearable now. "The next step is a cold shower. Shall I . . . ?

"Thanks just the same." I rolled to my feet, staggered, and righted myself. When I got out of the shower Danny was tactfully absent, but I heard him whistling outside the door and I got dressed as fast as I could.

We went to the coffee shop in the hotel for breakfast. It was a cheerful room, filled with sunshine and with plants standing around in pots. The waitresses were cute and young and didn't speak a word of English, but the menu was in both English and Spanish. I toyed feebly with a boiled egg while Danny devoured a grisly dish called eggs ranchero. It looked, and smelled, like fried eggs in tabasco sauce.

Ivan found us there. My back was to the door, but I knew when he came in, from the waitress's face. She froze like a bird dog getting ready to point.

Ivan gave her a friendly pat on the shoulder—he seemed to know everybody in the city—and joined us for coffee. In broad daylight he was almost too much. He wore a black shirt and dark slacks, his favorite costume, and his hair shone like black satin. The exaggerated sideburns and long-in-the-back cut didn't look mod, not on him; they suggested a Spanish hidalgo out of the last century. There was nothing in the least Slavic about him except for his name; even the high, broad cheekbones, which gave distinction to a face that might otherwise have been too severe, could have come from the Aztec strain that is present in many Mexican families. The sons and daughters of Montezuma married into noble Castilian houses.

"Where are we going?" Danny asked.

"That depends on you." Ivan sampled his coffee and smiled at the waitress, who looked as if she might swoon at his feet. "You are interested in antiquities, you say. So, perhaps we might go first to our great Museum of Anthropology. We are proud of it; it is the most beautiful museum in the world. It would give you a general background in pre-Columbian history. Or, since it is a beautiful day, we might go at once to the most impressive ancient site in this part of Mexico—the pyramids of Teotihuacan."

"You sound like a guide," Danny said.

"But that is what I am. Did I not tell you? Six days of the week I work for our finest tourist bureau, guiding the visitors. So you are in good hands, believe me."

"That's not fair," I said. "Asking you to spend your day off showing us the sights. Busman's holiday."

"Ah, but work is only work when one has to do it, eh? To do the same thing for choice, that is pleasure. So where shall we go?"

"The pyramids," Danny said. "Carol needs some fresh air. She's a little under the weather this morning."

I braced myself for a joking comment, but Ivan's dark eyes were sympathetic.

"The *turista,*" he said, nodding. "Most visitors succumb to it sooner or later; they say it is the result of the altitude, or the change of food and water. But it only lasts a short time, you will be better now."

I did feel better as we drove out of town. The car was a beauty, a big black Chrysler, which Ivan said he had borrowed from the agency. Unknown to the agency, I suspected, but who was I to complain?

It was a gorgeous day, cool and bracing and sunny. The air had a bite to it. I remembered that Mexico City has an altitude of six or seven thousand feet. It's hard on some people, I guess, but I found it exhilarating. I wanted to flap my arms and take off, like a bird.

Ivan was in great spirits. He kept up a running spiel as we drove through town, burlesquing a guide's lecture. We went so fast that I didn't see much; it was like watching a movie run at double speed. Then we were out of the city driving through the countryside, and Ivan went even faster. Danny loved it. I could see that he was dying to take the wheel. We were all jammed together in the front seat, so I closed my eyes and let them have their fun. I was still groggy and was dozing when the car came to a stop.

That was the beginning of a love affair, one which is still in full bloom. I don't know why I should have fallen for Teotihuacan the way I did. Sure, the site is magnificent, impressive, and all that, but people don't usually get emotional over architectural grandeur. Especially when it's in ruins. And heaven knows my later associations with the place were bad enough to cancel out my initial fondness. But I loved it at first sight, and I still do, in spite of what happened there.

The surroundings weren't romantic. The Pyramid of the Sun is a national monument, so it's all tidied up, and crowded with tourists, and there's a gaggle of souvenir shops right at its foot. I didn't see any of the modern distractions. I saw the slopes, dusty gold in the sunlight, lifting up in steep steps like a giant child's building blocks.

They had to pull me out of the car and lead me down

the bare earth path. We came around to what I still want to call the "front"—the face with the huge ceremonial staircase, where the great processions mounted up toward the temple on top; priests and nobles in their colorful feather cloaks and plumy headdresses rich with golden ornaments.

Ivan reeled off some statistics, to which I paid no attention. Feet and inches don't mean anything to me. It was big.

It wasn't a true pyramid, like the ones in Egypt that I've seen pictures of, with smooth slopes all the way up to a pointed top. Instead it ascended in a series of giant steps, five of them, each sloping inward. The top was flat; that was where they built the temple; the pyramid was only a kind of platform.

I started off.

"Where do you think you're going?" Danny grabbed my hand.

"Up there." I gestured.

"Hey, wait a minute. That slope is about forty-five degrees, kid."

"You don't have to come. I'll see you later."

I pulled like a fish on a line. Danny, laughing, held on to me.

"My little unathletic violet," he said to Ivan. "Her normal idea of exercise is turning the pages of a book. She's flipped."

"You like it?" Ivan said to me.

I nodded.

"Can't I go up there? Please?"

"Of course, why else have we come but for you to climb the Pyramid of the Sun? But go slowly, the slope is very steep, and the stairs are uneven. If you slip, there will be nothing behind you."

"Except me," Danny said resignedly. "We'll all go together when we go."

"But of course we will all go," Ivan said.

He went first, and Danny followed me; they acted as if we were climbing Mount Everest, but I didn't mind; I adore having lots of big strong men assisting me. About halfway up I heard Danny wheezing behind me. His idea of exercise was taking a long drive in the car, but of course I didn't point that out. We may be as smart as the opposite sex, but we aren't as big; and tact is the strongest weapon the little guy has.

In spite of my exhilaration I was wheezing myself by the time we reached the top. But the view was worth it. The countryside stretched out like a panorama, dusty gold and brown under a hot sun, with patches of bright green where a stream cut the treeless uplands, or where beds of the big sprawling cacti were located. To the north were the carefully restored remains of the ancient ceremonial center, with the long avenue and the facing Pyramid of the Moon, only slightly less tall than its mate.

Danny promptly collapsed onto the rubble-strewn surface, but Ivan stood beside me. The wind ruffled his dark hair and his voice was soft when he spoke.

"In 1519, when the Conquistadores came, all the Valley of Mexico was wooded, covered with fertile fields and gardens, with lakes and fair cities shining in the sun. And the fairest of all, a jewel on the bosom of the lake, was Tenochtitlan, the city of Montezuma. A city of gardens and canals, waterborne like Venice, with the great teocallis lifting up their shining temples above the tiled roofs of the palaces of emperor and noble. Gone, now. Vanished. The temples destroyed, stone by stone, the treasure stolen and lost, the priceless manuscripts burned by fanatical priests who saw in them the devil's hand."

His voice wasn't bitter; it was calm and reflective, even faintly amused. I wondered with whom he identified himself—with the ruthless, courageous Spanish adventurers or the equally ruthless Aztecs whom they had conquered.

"I wish I knew more about it," I said, half to myself. "When we study 'American' history, we get George Washington and the Civil War over and over and over again. Mexico is 'American' too. Why don't they skip the Pilgrims one year and teach us about the Aztecs and Cortez and the Mexican Revolution? Maybe we'd understand each other a little better."

"But for you, this place is more than history, is it not? You need not tell me, I have come here with many visitors and seen many reactions. Perhaps it is true, this business of reincarnation, hmmm? Five hundred years ago, in another life, you were an Indian princess, leading the dance of the Virgins of the Sun, up these very slopes."

He was joking, but there was something in the words that made a shiver run up my spine.

"When people talk about reincarnation they always picture themselves as kings and princesses," I said. "More likely I'd have been a slave or a peasant, and my memories of this pyramid wouldn't be so pleasant."

"You are thinking of the terrible tales of human sacrifice, I suppose. But that was not necessarily done here."

"No?" Danny tugged at my hand. "Sit down, you two, you make me tired standing there. Sit down and tell me all about human sacrifice. That's one of the few things I do remember about the Aztecs—that gory bit about cutting out the heart of the victim as an offering to the gods."

"The Aztecs, certainly." Ivan sat down, as neatly as a cat. "Twenty thousand sacrifices a year, the records say." He shook his head with a kind of fascinated admiration. "But these people at Teotihuacan were not the Aztecs. They are the mystery people of Anahuac; even today archaeologists call them only by the name of the site. They were not Toltecs; they were here, in their splendid city, when the Toltecs came. And when the Aztecs followed the Toltecs down from the north, the Teotihuacans were gone, vanished into the limbo of lost races."

Danny listened intently.

"I'd like to read about it," he said. "Can you suggest some books?"

"Certainly, I will give you a list. But you must talk with George, this is his hobby—the pre-Aztec peoples of Mexico. Particularly their art."

His voice was perfectly casual. Neither Danny nor I said anything. Ivan added,

"George does not care for the Aztecs. I presume he does not approve of human sacrifice."

"Who does?" Danny reached in his pocket. "Smoke?"

I felt myself stiffening. Ivan glanced unconcernedly at the clumsy brown cigarettes and shook his head.

"Marijuana? No, thank you, I do not indulge."

"Why not?" Danny lit his cigarette. He wasn't usually that blunt, and I knew that Ivan's indifference irked him.

"Oh, I have experimented, of course, when I was young." It was not a tactful comment, and Ivan must have sensed it, for he added, almost apologetically, "It has always been available here, so perhaps, for us, the novelty has worn off."

There were bright red spots on Danny's cheeks. Sunburn? Maybe, but I hadn't noticed them before.

"You think that's the only reason for its use in the States? Novelty?"

"Oh, but surely you are too intelligent to be unaware of that factor." Ivan smiled at him. "With your young people it is a symbol of rebellion, a way to slap the parents in the face. It is also the 'in' thing to do. Cool, as you say. Groovy? A wonderfully expressive language, English."

I don't know how he did it. In their analytical detachment, the words were almost insulting. But his smile, his tone, implied that he wasn't talking about Danny; that he and Danny were both sophisticated enough to see how ridiculous these motives were.

Danny nodded thoughtfully.

"Sure, those are factors," he said. "But they aren't the only reasons."

"No, of course, there is the 'high,' the euphoria. It is a pleasant enough feeling, as I recall. So mild, compared with other methods of intoxication, that I find myself wondering why there is such a fuss about it."

"That's just my point," Danny said eagerly. "If they legalize pot—" He broke off, and his eyes narrowed. "You mentioned other forms of intoxication. Which ones have you tried?"

"All of them."

"Acid?" Danny said incredulously. "Snow?"

"These are your terms for LSD and heroin, are they not?" Ivan sounded a little bored. "Yes, I have sampled LSD, also badoh negro, the seeds of the morning glory; teonanacatl, the sacred mushroom; and peyote. Heroin, no. I had no ambition to become a sedentary vegetable. The hallucinogens at least promise mind expansion; heroin leaves the user with no mind at all."

"So does LSD," I said.

I didn't like the look on Danny's face. I had got worried about acid, after all the scare stories started coming out, about people who kept tripping involuntarily. I mean, the right-wing press puts out a lot of nonsense about drugs, but this sounded as if it were for real. Danny promised me he'd never try LSD. I don't believe in premonitions. But in the sunshine, perched on top of my pyramid with the landscape spread out below me like a vision, I felt as if a thunderstorm were building up.

Ivan turned to look at me.

"So you know."

"Everybody knows," I said, not quite understanding what he meant. "Everybody who reads the newspapers."

His eyes were very big, very dark. They remained fixed on my face, and I stirred uncomfortably.

"Of course," he said, after a moment. I relaxed, knowing how a suspect must feel when the police finally turn off the spotlight. "The reports have been alarming. That was one of the reasons why I decided not to make a career out of hallucinogens."

"What other reasons?" Danny asked.

"Why, vanity, perhaps. The need to produce my own visions of grandeur, instead of sharing them with every fool who has a few pesos to spend on marijuana."

His eyes were fixed on the horizon; and under the thin shirt his chest lifted as he took a long, deep breath, the kind of breath a diver takes before he goes down. I thought he'd never let it out. Then his eyes came back to me, and he smiled. He stood up and held out his hands; I gave him mine, and he swung me to my feet, laughing down at me.

"Here, in the form of woman, is the subtlest intoxicant of them all. Marijuana is a poor substitute."

It sounded very gallant, offhand. I was halfway down the pyramid before I decided that, after all, the comparison wasn't very flattering.

II

There are a couple of nice restaurants at Teotihuacan, but Ivan wouldn't let us eat at either of them. Instead we had *guisado,* a kind of stew simmered with tomatoes, with a friend of his. The friend's name was Carlos Mendoza—the Mexican equivalent of John Smith or Robert Jones. Carlos looked like something straight out of one of those enormous Rivera murals, brown and broad-faced, with a big, drooping moustache. He even wore a straw hat and a serape.

The costume, he explained, was for the benefit of the tourists.

"I am the local color," he said, his floppy moustache vibrating as he grinned. "This way, when the tourist come to my shop, she think, 'Ah, so picturesque! Here is the true Mexico, the pride of the local craftsman.' She buy much, much more. You will drink coffee now?"

We were served by a silent woman in dusty black, who said not a word the whole time. She looked old enough to be Carlos's mother. She might have been his mother—or his wife, or a servant, or his girlfriend. He didn't introduce her, and I didn't ask. He was a cheery rascal, Carlos, but there was something about him which made me think the word "rascal" might be euphemistic. I felt sorry for any woman who worked for him—in any capacity.

After lunch we went to his shop, which was in front of the living quarters. It was quite a cut above the souvenir stands, and some of the things were really great—the silver rings and bracelets, the straw bags with designs done in bright-colored straw, and the pottery. There were bowls and ashtrays and mugs and, occupying a large section of the shelves, copies of pre-Columbian statues.

"These I make," Carlos explained. He touched one of the figurines, which was eight or ten inches tall—a squatting woman with flat, Mayan features, who held a stiff bundle of baby across her knees. "The jewelry I buy to sell for more money than I pay. But the statue, they are true copies, like statues in the great museum. A good thing I am honest man, eh? I could sell for real, for antiquity. Make much, much money."

When he laughed, the rich oily chuckle seemed to come from far down below his sagging belt. Laughter made his moustache flop up and down and deepened the long parallel lines in his cheeks till they looked like the scars of a surgical operation. The laughter lines should have given him a merry look, but they had just the opposite effect. Life really wasn't all that funny, you found yourself thinking; and you wondered what sort of jokes Carlos found so amusing.

He showed us the workshop where he made his statues. It was among a group of scattered outbuildings, behind the house-shop. The operation struck me as amazingly primitive, till I remembered that the basic process of pottery making hasn't changed that much in thousands of years. There were molds for the figures—he only made about a dozen different types—and some simple tools for incising the final details. Open bowls held the powder for the different colored glazes. It was hard to believe that the drab material would change, as it was fired, into the glowing clear oranges and green-blues that decorated the bowls.

When we left, Carlos presented me with a pretty little silver ring. I still thought he was the meanest-looking man I'd ever seen.

I have been told that my face is an open book. Ivan certainly could read it easily.

"Carlos is a great villain," he said, smiling at me. "But at least there is no pretense. You know he is not to be trusted and you make your arrangements accordingly. My arrangement with him is profitable to us both."

Danny caught on before I did.

"You get a cut?"

"Oh," I said. "For steering your tourists to his place, you mean?"

"It is the custom," Ivan said gently.

"I know."

"You do not approve."

Danny gave me a meaningful scowl; it meant, "Don't be gauche." I said quickly,

"Approve, disapprove. It's none of my business."

"One must live," Ivan said.

I felt sorry for him. I remembered the proud shabby old house, and my father sitting in the middle of it, with no visible means of support.

For once I had sense enough to shut up and not make matters worse by apologizing or explaining, and after a minute Ivan brightened up. He led us through the long lines of stalls near the pyramid, and I poked around and bought a silver thimble for Helen—she never sewed, not even a button, if she could help it, but the thimble was so pretty, with little incised flowers on its top. And I bought some beads made out of unpolished semiprecious stones, lovely soft, pale colors, and I bought Danny an enormous sombrero, which he promptly put on—and took off, with a flourish, to every lady he met. And then I bought some little wooden boxes that opened up and ejected carved wooden snakes, with fangs that stuck your finger, for the kids next door; and I bought a guidebook and some postcards; and then Danny led me gently but firmly out of the stalls.

Under the shade of the trees many cars and buses were parked. Ivan led us toward them. The shade was grateful; it was midafternoon and hot. I kept reminding myself that it was February back home, with snow up to here and icicles down to there, and the broiling sun felt marvelous.

As we crossed the road, a big bus pulled away in a cloud of dust, and another one promptly took its place. Danny sneezed as the dust got into his nose, and Ivan said,

"Come and meet some of my colleagues."

The men were clustered around one of the cars, some sitting on the car seats, with the doors open for air, others leaning against trees or sitting on stones. Ivan greeted them as we came up and they hailed him with good-natured jeers. I gathered that they were kidding him about the way he spent his day off, for Ivan turned to us with a smile.

"A busman's holiday," he said, in English. "Today I guide my friends."

He introduced us. The men were all guides or drivers from the various tourist agencies in town. They were an amazing mixture of types, ranging from a tall, tow-headed boy who might have come straight from Minnesota to a very black, very fat little man with grizzled gray hair.

They were talking shop talk, as professionals will. One melancholy gentleman, who looked like a deeply tanned Noel Coward, told of his adventures with a little old lady from Schenectady—his pronunciation of that was wonderful to hear—who insisted that he was her long-lost son, who had run away from home at the age of fifteen. She was determined to take him back to Schenectady with her.

Most of the stories were funny stories, told with a tolerance and goodwill that I found rather touching. Danny seemed to find it unbelievable. After listening for a while, he burst out,

"How do you stand it? Don't you have to put up with sneers, insults . . . ?"

There were shrugs. The elderly black man said,

"Most people are kind, señor. That is the beautiful lesson we learn from this dull trade of ours; that people are alike, wherever they come from, and that most of them wish to be kind. Oh, there are some. . . . Do you know the insult we resent most? The patronizing remark, that is the worst. 'Yes, indeed, you people can be proud of what you have done here.' It makes us feel like intelligent chimpanzees."

"I suppose you get that sort of thing from American tourists—what do you call us? *Gringos? Yanquis?*"

"It depends on how we feel about you when we are speaking," the blond boy said slyly. There was a general laugh; and then the black man said,

"In general you *yanquis* have fairly good manners. No, it is the Argentinian we resent, of all the national types."

A gloomy murmur of agreement rose up.

"Always they tell us how much better things are in their country," said the melancholy man. He grinned. "One of them said to me, 'Ah, the Pyramid of the Sun? Yes, if it were in Argentina, it would be very impressive.' "

"They are misers," said the blond boy. "They give nothing, not even a smile."

"Well," Danny said—with a smile—"it's nice to hear some other nationality being abused for a change. When I was in Europe, everybody hated Americans."

"We have toward the United States a love-hate relationship," said another man amiably. "When we think of the colonialist imperialist wrongs inflicted on Mexico by the United States, our blood boils! But we also admire the United States and wish to be as rich, as powerful, and as imperialistic."

There was a chorus of disagreement; and the black man said, with the most gracious bow in my direction,

"The hatred, if it exists, is only theoretical. For individuals we have only love."

I would have left it at that; I don't enjoy being abused personally, or as a member of a group. But Danny was all agog to find out how people *really* feel about Americans, and I had a feeling that the gentlemen would express themselves more freely in my absence. Besides, I had been away from my pyramid long enough.

"Would you all excuse me?" I said. "I want to take a walk."

"Oh, for God's sake," Danny groaned. He was sitting with his back up against a tree and his sombrero tilted at a cocky angle, trying to look ethnic. "Can't you sit still a minute?"

"It's been a lot of minutes. You don't have to come."

"I will come with you," Ivan said.

"No, really. I'd like to go by myself."

"Of course." He smiled at me. It was a confidential

M

smile, as if we shared a secret.

"I'm going to walk down the Avenue of the Dead," I muttered, flipping through my guidebook. "Down to the Pyramid of the Moon. And then I'm going back to the other end of the Avenue, to the Citadel. And then I'll come back here."

Danny groaned again, and Ivan laughed.

"I would not for the world dissuade you. But do not walk back from the Citadel, believe me, you will not wish to. I will take the car to the Museum, near the Citadel. You will find us there."

"Okay," I said, poised for flight.

"Stay here," Danny said, from under the sombrero. "Take a nice nap, like me."

"You are sure you know how to go?" Ivan asked, reaching for my guidebook.

"Yes, sure, there's a map." I said impatiently. My feet were twitching. "Good-bye."

I went bounding back up the dusty slope that led to the path around the Pyramid of the Sun. As a rule I like being by myself part of the time, but I've never felt the urge so strongly as I did that day. As for getting lost, that didn't worry me a bit, I knew exactly where I was going. I have a good sense of direction. And there was that feeling . . . Oh, well, I might as well say it. That strange feeling that I'd been here before.

When I got around to the front of the pyramid, there was a high wall ahead of me. On top of it, like magnified crenellations, was a series of small, flat-topped pyramids. There were steps at intervals, steep steps, leading up to the top of the wall. I went up.

There was the Avenue of the Dead. It was stone-paved

and quite wide; don't ask me how wide, I never know things like that. Wide as a two-lane highway, maybe. On the other side of the avenue, opposite me, was another wall like the one I was standing on top of. Off to right and left the stately avenue stretched, culminating, to my right, in an open space before the Pyramid of the Moon. Farther off to the left was another ceremonial area, the Citadel, with pyramid and temple ruins.

They called it the Avenue of the Dead, the early archaeologists, because they thought the buildings along its length were tombs. It turned out they were temples, in fact. But the name stuck, and as I went down the precipitous stairs onto the Avenue, I could understand why. Even in bright sunlight, with the rubble and weeds cleared away and gabbling tourists in shorts and camera bags all over the place —there was still an atmosphere. I suppose an architect could explain the impression these ruins give in strictly aesthetic terms. The lines are almost all horizontal, parallel lines; even the pyramids are a series of platforms, one on top of the other. So you get a feeling of repose, dignity, heaviness.

In front of the Pyramid of the Moon the Avenue widens out into a handsome plaza, lined with buildings. I decided I would not climb the Pyramid of the Moon. One pyramid per day is enough; I didn't want to get blasé.

According to the guidebook I was supposed to inspect the buildings on the left side of the plaza. I climbed another of those wide, steep staircases—the ancients couldn't seem to build anything without putting a platform under it—and there on top was a long roofed hall. A doorway at one end led into a courtyard. It was open to the sky, but all around it there were beautiful pillars, carved with intricate reliefs, which supported a roofed walkway like those found in cloisters. I don't know what it was about the place—the graceful proportions, perhaps, or the traces of rosy pink paint on the walls and pillars—but it fascinated me, just as the pyramid had done, so I sat down on the floor with my guidebook and found that I was in the Palace of the Quetzal-butterfly.

The palace and the adjoining buildings were like a maze. Back in the roofed vestibule you could go through another door and down some more stairs, and there was an alleyway with more rooms, and another courtyard, with more rooms still, and a platform with another stairway. A passageway led from the courtyard, with more rooms, and a tunnel going way down under the Quetzal-butterfly Palace to some really old rooms. The guidebook mentioned more tunnels and an ancient drainage system.

As I have said, I don't believe in premonitions. The reason why I don't is that I never have them at the right time. By all the rules, I should have been prickling all over, that day at Teotihuacan, from the moment I laid eyes on the pyramid, up till the very end. Even if my sixth sense were out of order the rest of the time, it ought to have come alive in the lovely little temple courtyard, with its surrounding maze of rooms and corridors.

Not a single prickle of warning. I gamboled like a carefree sheep; they don't have premonitions when they pass the butcher shop, either. I didn't think about anonymous letters or anonymous letter writers or a father who had turned out to be even less satisfactory than I had expected. I walked and read my guidebook and walked again, down the impressive stretch of the Avenue of the Dead, toward the Citadel area and the museum. I poked into all the corners and explored all the rooms. I flushed a couple of pretty birds, with bright-red heads, and a pair of black-haired lovers, who went right on with what they were doing. And after I had finished investigating the Pyramid of Quetzalcoatl, there was the museum, in front of me, and the sun was far down the western sky, and I was absolutely bushed.

I found my two escorts in the restaurant, drinking lemonade. They didn't see me at first. I stood in the doorway watching the two heads, one jet black, the other bleached fairer than blond, bent together as if they were having a confidential discussion. I was glad they were getting along so well. All the same . . . What good were the two handsomest men in Mexico to a girl if they were going to concentrate on each other?

When they saw me, they greeted me amiably, but as casually as if I'd been gone for five minutes instead of almost three hours. I accepted their offer of a drink. I didn't realize till I saw the frosty glasses in front of them that I was dying of thirst. And then, because I was still a little miffed at not being missed, I said,

"I do hope you had a jolly time. What have you been talking about?"

"Nothing much," Danny said.

III

"Why the rush?" I asked.

Ivan had just dropped us in front of the hotel. I felt grubby and disheveled as we walked toward the big glass doors and the uniformed doorman. I had shaken a couple of pounds of dust out of my hair and my clothes, but my bare toes and once-white sandals were coated with the gray-brown powder. Worst of all, my nose was red as a beet and my shoulders were beginning to ache.

"What do you mean, rush?" Danny asked.

He was carrying his sombrero. After his restful afternoon he looked pink and sleepy-eyed, like a big, overgrown kid.

"I mean from Ivan. All day today and now this party tomorrow night. He's taken quite a fancy to you."

Danny laughed and squeezed my shoulder. I said "ouch" and he laughed again.

"I told you you should have taken a nap instead of walking around in the hot sun. As for Ivan, you're the one he has his eye on. Nothing queer about that lad."

"You don't mind?"

"I don't mind his looking," Danny said. "And suffering. If he goes any farther, I'll have to take steps."

"What kind of steps?"

"Oh, I'd probably beat you up, for encouraging him."

We had to wait at the desk to get our keys; it was a busy time of day, with people coming back from tours and shopping. While Danny pushed his way through the mob I stood off a few paces, waiting. That was when I saw the man.

I wouldn't have noticed him if I hadn't caught him staring at me. There was nothing particularly distinctive about him, at first glance. He had one of those faces friends describe as "clean cut," because even a friend couldn't call it handsome, and his clothes were equally unremarkable—a light-gray, lightweight suit which needed pressing rather badly, and a wrinkled white shirt. He wore a tie—a boring tie, blue with light-blue spots—but it was dragged down to the base of his throat and his shirt collar gaped open. He was as deeply tanned as Ivan, but for some reason I was sure he came from north of the border. There's something unmistakable about Americans, the way they wear their clothes, or the way they stand, or something. He had dark eyes but his hair wasn't black, it was a dusty brown, sun-bleached in places.

On second glance, I was struck by his physique. He had enormous shoulders, so broad and heavy that they made him look shorter than his actual height of about six feet. Something about his nose, too—it wasn't actually crooked, but there was a kind of curve which suggested that it might once have been broken.

An ex-football player, I thought—and a boor. He didn't look away when my eyes met his, but stared harder. The corners of his mouth began to turn up. If it was meant to be a friendly smile, it was a failure; I didn't like the shape of his mouth or the boldness of his stare. I looked away.

Just then Danny came back with the keys. As we went toward the elevators I tried to resist the impulse, but I couldn't. I looked back. He was still there, and he was still staring. I realized that his hair actually was dusty, and that the dust was the same color as the stuff I had shaken out of my hair on the way back from Teotihuacan.

Maybe that was why he was staring. He could have been at the site that day. I didn't remember seeing him, but I wouldn't, there had been so many people.

I forgot about him in the elevator, when Danny handed me an envelope.

"It was in your box," he explained.

I didn't recognize the elegant, slanting handwriting, but I had a pretty good idea whom it was from. It was a woman's hand, and I didn't know that many women in Mexico.

I was right. Ines Oblensky was brief and businesslike. She was coming into the city next day; would I care to meet her for lunch? There was an unpretentious but pleasant restaurant at the Museo de Antropologia; I might like to visit the museum in the morning and meet her at the restaurant at one o'clock. No reply was necessary; she would be there in any case, and if I didn't show up she would assume I had not been able to make it.

I was still brooding over this amazing epistle when we arrived at my door, and Danny had to open the door for me and push me in. I handed him the note.

"Hmm," he said, after he had read it. "I am not mentioned, I see. Sounds like a family conference, kid."

"Maybe I won't go."

"Maybe you should."

"Why?"

"Honey, don't be parochial." Danny crossed the room and came up behind me; I was standing in front of the big window, staring at the Reforma and the lovely gilded shape of the Angel. He took me gently by the shoulders. "Ivan really knocked himself out trying to show us a good time; it was damned nice of him. Now his mother wants to talk to you. Isn't it obvious that they're trying to make up for your father's coolness? Hasn't it occurred to you that there might be reasons for that coolness, that it may have nothing to do with his feelings for you?"

"Such as what?"

"How the hell should I know? Maybe he's got an incurable disease. Maybe he's planning a revolution and doesn't want you to get involved. At least Señora Oblensky is being decent. Give her a chance."

"Okay," I said, and gulped audibly.

"Don't let it get you down," Danny murmured into my hair.

"I'm not."

"Then what are you crying about?"

I let go; the tears splashed down like summer rain.

"Because my sunburn is killing me," I wailed.

Danny couldn't have been sweeter. He went down to Sanborn's, the "American" drugstore, which is just across the way from the hotel, and got some sunburn oil and came back and smeared it all over my back. I couldn't stand the idea of putting anything thicker than oil on my shoulders, so we splurged on room service and had a hilarious supper in my room, finishing up with some Kahlua, a divine coffee-flavored liqueur, and not really booze, as Danny explained, because you don't drink much of it. It went straight to my head, though, after my exertions in the sun.

"A fine thing," Danny said, as he tipped me over into my bed. "Soused for the second night in a row. What am I going to do with you?"

There was one thing he obviously couldn't do—not with sunburn all over my back. So that took care of that.

I don't know why I woke up later. The walls were soundproof, but his room was right next door. It seemed to me, though I couldn't be sure in my drowsy state, that I heard a door open and close, and footsteps that I knew went tiptoeing off down the hall.

CHAPTER 5

I REMEMBERED the Kahlua as soon as I woke up next morning, and I opened one eye at a time. The caution was unnecessary; I felt fine. I was alive, the sun was shining, and I didn't have a hangover. What more could anyone ask? I brushed all my teeth, even the back of the back ones, and put on a pink dress and went and hammered on Danny's door.

It took him a long time to answer. I was sorry to see that he wasn't as bright-eyed and full of vim as he usually was in the morning. The room was gloomy; the draperies were drawn against that heavenly sunshine. When I started to pull them, Danny staggered back to the bed and fell on it. "Let the sunshine in," I said heartily, continuing to pull. "Like the song says."

Danny put a pillow over his head.

"Are you always like this early in the morning?" he inquired suggestively.

"If it bugs you that much—"

"Sorry, kid. I only had about an hour's sleep."

"What were you doing all night?"

"Reading." He was still under the pillow and I had a hard time understanding him. "I went out and bought some books at the drugstore. That's a great place, they sell everything."

"Including pot?"

In my initial *joie de vivre* the smell had escaped me. Now it seemed to permeate the room, and I didn't feel quite so cheerful.

"Come back in half an hour," Danny said.

"Where else did you go last night? Back to your pal Jesus?"

"Any reason why I shouldn't?" His voice was quiet, but there was a note in it I had learned to recognize.

"I guess not."

"Then stop nagging, okay? Look, I'll meet you at Sanborn's in half an hour. You can have a cup of coffee and browse around till I get there."

Sanborn's is a landmark in Mexico City—Mexico, as the inhabitants call it—and a haven for English-speaking visitors. There are several Sanborns, actually, scattered all over town; the most famous one is the House of Tiles, whose facade is covered with blue-and-white glazed squares. This Sanborn's wasn't so fancy outside, but like the other, it sold just about everything. I would have bought a few souvenirs, but I didn't have much cash. Danny was carrying the traveler's checks. So I limited myself to some postcards. I adore postcards. I don't like to send them, I just like them. And this trip there wasn't anyone I could send them to. Helen thought I was in Nashville, with my roommate.

I browsed among the books and finally bought a guidebook, one of those slick, quick synopses for the semiliterate, with lots of colored pictures. Then I went up the stairs to the coffee shop and settled down in a booth with my book.

I don't know where men get off talking about women being slow. I could have tried on every dress I owned, and set my hair and taken it down, in the time it took Danny to get shaved and dressed. The guidebook was arranged alphabetically; I had finished the "Historical Sites" and was well into "Museums" by the time he appeared. It was after eleven o'clock.

Danny was in hilarious high spirits, to make up for his earlier grouchiness. He wouldn't take his sunglasses off, even in the soft light of the coffee shop; he said my rosy frock and golden locks dazzled him. He offered to go to the museum with me and then tactfully disappear when it was time for me to meet Ines. First he wanted to tell me all about the museum, so we had another cup of coffee while he lectured.

Maybe he was trying to prove to me that he had been reading most of the night. If so, he hadn't read much about the Anthropological Museum. My little guidebook had already given me most of the information he repeated.

When we got up to leave I saw that the gray-haired man in the next booth was reading a guidebook too; I recognized the glaring technicolor cover. It struck me as a little odd. He was the same man I had seen that first night, waiting for the elevator on our floor at the hotel. I had assumed, if I thought about it all, that he was Mexican. Of course he could be from Peru, or Brazil, or even from another part of Mexico.

It was getting late, so we decided to take a taxi—not one of the regular taxis, but another kind Danny had read about in the guidebook. You can spot them by their color, green and white, and by the fact that the driver has one arm sticking out of the window, with two fingers extended. The gesture is not an obscure Latin insult or a salute to the Republic; it means that the ride will cost you two pesos, whether you only go a few blocks or stick with the cab all the way down to the end of the line. These taxis have well-defined routes along the main streets of town, and naturally they are jammed full; at two pesos per, the driver crams in as many passengers as he can. When the cab is full, he doesn't put his arm out. Simple, cheap, and fun.

Danny hailed one of the cabs and we crowded in, along with a lady in a mantilla and two beautiful little black-eyed children and a fat man with no hair on top and a teen-ager wearing a bright-blue shirt and his girlfriend in a bright-green blouse. I was sitting on somebody's lap. I think it was Danny's, but it might have been the fat man's. People got in and out, stepping on assorted feet and murmuring gracious Spanish apologies, and finally everybody else was gone and the driver agreed to take us on to the museum for a few pesos extra.

The guidebook didn't exaggerate, and neither did Ivan, when they described that museum. It really is fabulous. Outside the long, modern white facade there is a colossal statue. The stone is dark gray and badly worn. Tlaloc, the rain god, has lost part of his face. You can see the hollows where the big goggly owl eyes which distinguish that god were once to be found, but the eyes themselves are gone. Yet you have a disturbing impression that the vanished eyes are still looking at you. The stubby, squared-off legs under the squared-off skirt press down on the earth.

Danny gave Tlaloc a dubious look; his idea of beauty is the Venus of Cyrene. We went in, paying our pesos, and

Danny graciously consented to approve of the internal architecture. The museum is built around a courtyard and the exhibits are arranged in chronological order, starting with the prehistoric cultures and going on, counterclockwise around the court, till you end up with the Aztecs and their friends. The courtyard is something else. There's a pool, with feathery green water plants, and benches all around. Half of the space is roofed over; and the single large column which supports the roof is a fountain. From its top a dazzling spray of water spills down into the pool.

We didn't have time to go all around, so we just wandered into one of the closer rooms. It was the Aztec room. I didn't know that, then; I went back later, with a guidebook. At the time it was just a room with big sculptured figures.

I'm still not enraptured with Aztec sculpture. Maybe I'm prejudiced—all those vague impressions of human sacrifice and bloody hearts and flayed victims. But the sculpture is hard to understand. The gods don't even look like human beings, they are ghastly composites of various animal features, so massive they look square, without a trace of the compassion we expect of a god.

Danny, who had been cheerful in the taxi and moderately agreeable in the courtyard, lost his smile. He didn't comment, however, until we came upon Coatlicue.

A book I read later said that this colossal statue is regarded as a "masterpiece of sacerdotal art." Tastes differ. I don't understand how an earth goddess and a patroness of childbirth can be shown in such a hideous aspect. She had a head like that of a giant, flattened serpent, with protruding fangs. More snakes, entwined, formed her skirt, and human skulls dangled from her girdle. Her breastplate seemed to be made of severed human hands.

I gave the statue a brief, repelled glance and was about to move on when I realized that Danny had stopped. Under his dark glasses his cheeks were pale.

"My God," he said, in a loud voice. "That's hideous. Grotesque. Sick."

"Sssh," I said, taking his arm. "If you don't like it, let's look at something else."

"They're all the same." Danny pulled his arm away and spun around, gesturing at the collection of monsters. "Bestial. Products of sick, warped minds. No wonder the Spaniards burned the temples. They should have been ground into powder, the whole foul pantheon, the whole—"

"Danny! People are staring."

He let me take his arm again; his lips were trembling. We went out of the hall and sat down on a bench facing the pool and the great fountain.

"Even that," Danny mumbled. He raised a white, blind face toward the fountain. "Even the pillar—massive, threatening . . . There's no pity in it. The whole bloody race ought to be wiped off—"

"Danny, stop it! People understand English, you mustn't say such things. They aren't true, and they're very offensive. You don't have to like this kind of art, but you can't expect to understand it right away, it's in a different tradition from the art forms we're accustomed to, and—"

"Beauty is truth," Danny said loudly. "Plato was right."

"That was Keats," I said.

"Was it? Look at the water. That's beauty. See the shape it takes while falling, the infinite delicacy of each drop, iridescent in the sun. . . ."

"You sit and watch the iridescent drops of water," I said. "I've got to meet Ines. I'll be back in an hour."

"No, I'll meet you at Sanborn's later. Around five." Danny stood up. "I loathe this place. I don't want to see any more of it."

"But—"

"I'll see you there. At five o'clock."

He left, walking rather jerkily, without a backward glance.

I asked one of the guards where the restaurant was and followed his directions, down a flight of stairs on the far side of the court. I went slowly, because I needed time to think.

Danny and some of the other people who smoked grass claimed it increased their sensitivity to sensory impressions. He was very sensitive to art anyhow, especially classical art; he had two huge pictures, one of the Parthenon and one of a headless Greek Venus, stuck up on his wall between his peace posters and Paul McCartney with a beard. Grass could account for his neurotic reaction to the snake goddess. Admittedly, she was not in the classic tradition. But I'd never heard him express an aesthetic judgment with such violence or such a total absence of concern for other people's feelings. The outburst was totally out of character for Danny—for the old, pre-Mexico Danny, at any rate. And with that in mind, some of the other things that had happened that morning took on a new significance—the dark glasses, which he wouldn't take off, even indoors, the hilarity, the loquaciousness. If pot had that effect, maybe it wasn't as harmless as Danny claimed.

Or maybe it wasn't pot Danny was taking.

I stumbled on the bottom step, so absorbed in my thoughts that I didn't realize I had reached the bottom. The stairs ended near a stone-walled patio, with the tops of trees and transplanted Mayan monuments showing over the walls. Tables and chairs were scattered around the patio. There were more tables inside the restaurant, behind sliding glass doors which could be closed in bad weather.

I had no trouble spotting Ines. Her costume made her look like a mature lady spy, out of E. Philips Oppenheim instead of Ian Fleming. She wore large, very dark glasses and a wide-brimmed black hat that flopped down over one side of her face. She was smoking a cigarette, which looked out of character.

The pale, porcelain profile hit me with such a wave of dislike that I might have turned tail, then and there, if she hadn't turned her head and seen me.

I raised one hand in greeting and she acknowledged it with an inclination of her head. She didn't smile. My pink cotton shift, which had seemed so smart and sophisticated when Helen brought it home now looked like a pinafore next to Ines's simple black dress. I managed to trip over someone's feet, and arrived at the table flushed and breathless.

It wasn't an auspicious beginning and Ines did nothing to improve it. She hardly spoke while I studied the menu and we gave our orders. I had fresh fruit salad, remembering and defying all the warnings in the guidebook about stomach upsets. I suppose it was good; it had fresh pineapple and bananas and other things I didn't recognize. I was too keyed up to enjoy it.

Ines was so damned ladylike I could have smacked her, or yelled out loud. She asked me how I liked Teotihuacan and I told her how much I appreciated Ivan's courtesy in taking us there, and we discussed the antiquities of Mexico in carefully rounded, grammatically pure sentences. The formal conversation was deliberate on her part. She wasn't ready to talk about people yet. Every time I referred to Ivan she went back to pyramids. She knew her subject; but as the time went on I wondered why she had bothered to see me if that was all she wanted to discuss. She could just have sent me a book.

She interrupted her lecture when the waiter came with our iced coffee, and after he had left there was a pause. Ines lit another cigarette and then said,

"You must be wondering why I wanted to see you."

"Well, I assume it wasn't to instruct me about the Aztecs."

The corners of her mouth twitched. It was the first break I had seen in the controlled serenity of her face, and I found it rather attractive.

"You listen with admirable patience," she said. "It is easy to see that you have been well brought up. I thought perhaps that you deserved an apology."

"I'm the one who should apologize," I said, oddly relaxed now that the preliminaries were over. "It was rude of me to barge in the way I did, the other night."

"Yes," she said calmly. "But understandable. For all these years you must have wondered."

"Not at all," I said, trying to imitate her calm. "I stopped wondering years ago. But since I happened to be in the city I thought I ought to pay a polite social call."

"Happened to be here? Why did you come, then, if not to see him?"

The direct question was so unlike her that I told her the truth. There didn't seem to be any reason to hide it, and I was curious to see her reaction. I didn't think she was my anonymous correspondent; if I had needed further confirmation, the expression on her face would have been enough. There was no sudden pallor, no theatrical start; but I knew she was upset by what I told her. Upset—and yet not surprised.

"Curious," she said.

"More than curious. Do you know who could have sent me those letters?"

"Could have? Anyone could have. Your father has many acquaintances in Mexico."

That was where she made her first mistake. If she believed I would accept that noncommittal answer as a negative, she underestimated me. It was almost as good as an admission; and it annoyed me so much that a section of my self-control crumbled. I said something I had never meant to say, something really unforgivable.

"Are you and my father married?"

She turned pale under the thick layer of powder on her face. It might have been anger, it might have been shame.

"No."

"Why not?"

"By the laws of my faith, he is still a married man."

I used to think I was pretty sophisticated about religion. But that statement, in that voice of hers, left me speechless. It was as final as a death sentence. I sat there with my mouth open, like the inexperienced fool I felt like; and another thought came creeping into my mind. All these years, living in the same house . . . And I thought: Oh, no, it isn't possible, not in this day and age. . . . And I looked at the shape of Ines's mouth and the way her hands were locked together, and I knew that it was possible, and I felt queasy with an emotion which wasn't pity and wasn't, surely, contempt. . . .

"I am going to say what I came to say," she burst out.

"Then I must go."

"You want me to go away. To leave Mexico."

"Yes. It is not what you think—"

"How do you know what I think—"

"I know the cruelty of the young," she said, between tight lips. "I know how you think of us—that we have no emotions, no right to love or hate. . . . No, no, I am sorry, I did not mean to say that."

She put out her cigarette. I saw that her hand was shaking, but I wouldn't let myself feel sorry for her; I couldn't afford pity.

"Your father is not well," she said. "It is essential now that he have quiet, peace of mind. Later, he means to send for you. Believe me, that is true. If you will leave at once—then, in a few months, a few weeks . . ."

"I'll be in school in a few weeks. This is my final semester. I graduate in June."

"In June then, you will return. In the summer."

"I don't understand. You want me to leave now and come back later? What kind of illness can be cured in a few months, or maybe a few weeks? What ailment can be aggravated by my presence in the same city? There must be several million people in Mexico City. He doesn't have to see me. I won't go near him again."

"You don't understand? After what happened to him ten years ago?"

"What happened? He walked out on my mother, on me. Are you trying to tell me that he's having a nervous breakdown now because he deserted his family ten years ago? A little belated, isn't it?"

We were leaning forward across the table; our faces were close together. My voice was louder than it should have been; her voice was controlled, but her face was not.

"You don't know," she said oddly. "You really do not know. What a curious woman this mother of yours must be."

"Well, really!"

"I beg your pardon, that was extremely rude. Please believe me, that I am speaking for the good of everyone. I myself invite you, now, to return in June, to be our guest. Give me time, only a little time. . . . There must be a way out. . . ."

She was beginning to crack; if I had held out a little longer I might have learned some of the things I badly needed to know. Not the thing that really mattered, though; she couldn't have told me that, not if she died for not telling. And I couldn't bring myself to torment her any more. I couldn't watch the woman fall apart right in front of my eyes.

"Don't," I muttered. "Please don't, it's all right. I—I'll think about it."

"Thank you." It was a long breath, like a sigh.

She lifted her hand to call the waiter. Our silence had the exhausted quality of the hush after a storm. It was a prolonged silence; the waiter was busy, she couldn't catch his eye.

I looked at my watch. It was barely two o'clock. Three hours before I had to meet Danny. There was another happy subject. What was Danny planning to do in the next three hours?

Perhaps my sensitivities were numb, after the battering they had taken. But at that time there was no reason why I shouldn't have mentioned the subject.

"Can you tell me," I said, "what the laws are, in Mexico, about marijuana?"

She froze, as if she had been sprayed with an instant fixative.

"I'm not in the market myself," I said quickly, misunderstanding her expression. "I just wondered. You hear so much about it, and about peyote and morning-glory seeds —"

"You do know," she said, in a voice like a death rattle. "You know, and you pretended . . . You sly, cruel, little —"

The waiter came gliding up just then with the check, so I never did find out what she was going to call me. I wouldn't have cared. Her attack, violent and unexpected as it was, disturbed me less than the suspicion it had planted in my mind.

Ines slapped a handful of notes down on the table and got up. She didn't say good-bye. The waiter looked from the money to Ines's retreating back, shrugged, and withdrew.

But the drama wasn't over. I saw the final act quite clearly from where I sat.

My eyes were so intent on her that I didn't see him until they met, at the bottom of the stairs. Maybe her eyes were blinded by the sunlight—or something—because she didn't see him either. She ran into him. He took her by the arms as she staggered, and her head fell back, like a flower on a wilting stem. She was tall, for a woman, but he was taller; they made a handsome picture there in the sunlight, clinging together, his silvery head bent down toward her upturned face. But there was nothing fond about his grip on her arms. Her shoulders hunched together, and one hand came up as if to ward off a blow.

He turned his head and looked straight at me.

It was the first time I had seen him in daylight, and under my shock and bewilderment an incongruous touch of pride stirred. He was still a handsome man, my father. In the sunlight his hair might have been fair, not gray; it contrasted strikingly with his deep tan.

For a second or two we stared at one another across the width of the patio. Then his hands relaxed, and he steadied her as she swayed. He took her arm; they went up the stairs together.

I called the waiter and ordered another glass of iced coffee. I wanted to give them plenty of time to get away.

II

It's funny how a subject keeps cropping up once you start thinking about it. Like having a rare disease that you thought nobody ever heard of, and finding that every other person you meet has a friend who has the same disease.

We don't really think that much about drugs. We talk about the subject, the way we talk about a lot of things, and a good many of us agree, I think, on certain points. Whether we smoke pot or not, we think the laws are stupid and too harsh and ought to be repealed. Dex and bennies are okay in the line of duty—for exams, that is—but it's juvenile to pop pills just for kicks. Heroin is simply out. Stupid, dangerous.

There were extremists of both kinds, even at our square school. But it was a minor issue, really; there were too many other things to do and think about. And nobody really investigated the question, at least I didn't. It's the difference between doing a serious research job, reading and checking sources, and simply absorbing a miscellaneous stream of information and rumor that comes your way.

After that lunch with Ines it seemed to me that I kept hearing about drugs wherever I went. I was worrying about the subject now. A week before, my eyes would have passed over headlines and stories that now stood out from the surrounding print in letters of fire. A sob story in the *Readers Digest,* an article in the Mexico City *News* about a successful raid, under the joint authority of the U.S. Bureau of Narcotics and the Mexican police—that sort of thing.

I read the newspaper and the *Digest* at Sanborn's, while I was waiting for Danny. I got there an hour early. I didn't want to hang around the museum, for fear of running into Ines or George, so I wandered around the Niza district, the section they call the Pink Zone, where the fancy shops and restaurants are located. Usually I love to browse through shops. But that day the pottery and the elaborate paper flowers and even the stunning embroidered dresses didn't interest me. So I went back to Sanborn's and drank one cup of coffee after another and tried to keep my teeth from grinding together.

I didn't want to face it, but I had to. There was something damnably peculiar about my father, about his past history and his present activities. I knew it when the letters started coming, though I tried to fight my instinctive knowledge; I postulated eccentric friends, well-meaning friends, even malicious friends, in order to explain something which surely had a more sinister meaning. I had been right all along; someone wanted me to come to Mexico City. And that someone was not Ines. She had tried her best to get me to leave, tried so hard that she lost her usual finesse and said things she hadn't meant to say.

It was at that point that I tried to distract myself by reading the newspaper, and the article about the marijuana raid hit me in the face.

I let the newspaper subside onto my untouched cup of coffee—I was already queasy in the stomach—and asked myself the question I had been trying to avoid. Was George involved in the drug business? All the time I had been imagining him as a romantic masked crusader for the FBI or the Pentagon—had he been a guy in a black sombrero instead? I had never admitted that possibility, and yet it was the most likely. The people who have the strongest reason to disappear, cutting all their former ties, are criminals.

The knight in shining armor had not passed away ten years before. He died again that afternoon, while I sat in Sanborn's drugstore and stared down into my cup of cold coffee like a scryrer trying to read the future in a pool of ink. Only it wasn't the future I wanted to read; it was the past.

If George had been involved in some illegal activity, that would explain so many things that had puzzled me. Helen's abnormal, long-lived hatred was understandable if George had committed some act she considered despicable, especially if it threatened her reputation and livelihood, by association. George wouldn't risk communicating with me if he had actually been in hiding for a time. Oh, yes, it made very good sense, and so did the corollary—that he was still involved in crime of some sort. The anonymous letters . . . his hostility toward me when I showed up . . . Ines's attempt to warn me off, and her terror when George found us together. . . . And her shock when I mentioned narcotics.

For a minute I thought I actually was going to be sick. I covered my face with my hands and swallowed, hard. Then somebody jogged my elbow, and I looked up.

Danny's eyes were as clear and blue as cornflowers.

Scrubbed and shaved and smiling, he radiated innocence.

His smile faded when he saw my face.

"What's the matter?"

"A touch of *turista*," I said. "Upset stomach. I'm all right."

It was the first break in our confidence, the first time I hadn't told him all my thoughts.

III

Ivan's friend, the one who was throwing the party, had a gorgeous new apartment out near the university, in San Angel. My first casual look at the furniture and decorations made me feel right at home. There were mats and cushions on the floor instead of chairs, and the walls were covered with posters and unframed sketches. Then I saw that the bookshelves were polished rosewood and realized that the collection of hi-fi equipment, some of it imported, must represent a sizable hunk of money. There was a grand piano, sitting out in the middle of the room all by itself. For a student pad, it was decidedly luxurious.

Our host's name was Ramón; the others were called Jorge and Anna, and also Betty and Kurt and Sven. It was one of those parties. International.

The place was vibrating with noise. The hi-fi was going full blast; I didn't recognize the tune, it was rock style with Latin overtones, a weird and wonderful combination. Some of the guests were dancing. Somebody was pounding on the piano—a different tune from the one the hi-fi was playing—and over in a corner a group of men were talking. The television set was going too; I felt as if I'd run into an old friend when I saw Tarzan, talking to Jane. I suppose they were speaking Spanish, but I couldn't hear, the hi-fi drowned them out.

Danny went wandering off to look at some bullfight posters. He was mad at me because I had refused to discuss my conversation with Ines. I told him she had tried to talk me into leaving town, but that was all; I hadn't mentioned George's appearance, nor my suspicions. Danny said naturally Ines didn't want me hanging around, but why all the fuss when I was going to be leaving soon anyway? It was a good question. I wished I knew the answer to it. But I didn't want to talk about it, and my evasive answers annoyed Danny. He knew I was holding something back. He could always tell.

The tune ended in a crash of calculated discords, and then a new piece started, something sweet and rhythmic, with lots of violins and guitars. The dancers melted together. Somebody turned off the overhead lights.

"Would you like to dance?" Ivan said.

I looked for Danny. He had joined the group in the corner. I think they were discussing bullfighting; one of the boys was on his feet, swaying his hips and moving his arms.

"Okay," I said.

If I had entertained any reservations about Ivan's kindness to Danny, that dance dispelled the last of them. Not that he was too free with his hands, or anything like that; it was a chemical thing. He was fun to dance with, he had a wonderful sense of rhythm and he moved like an athlete, with every muscle under control. By the time the dance was over, I decided I'd better not dance with him again. I was a little too conscious of those muscles, and of the hard curve of his cheek against my hair. It wasn't the first time I had been physically attracted to a man, but I'd never had the feeling quite so strongly, or so unequivocally, unmixed with sentiment or affection. I didn't dislike Ivan, but I wasn't sure I liked him, either; I didn't know how I felt. Which made it all the more important that I should keep it cool.

I danced with a man named Carl, who said he was an exchange student from Denmark, and with my host, Ramón, who offered me a drink and seemed to approve when I said I preferred Coke. There was plenty of the hard stuff around, tequila and gin and whiskey, but no one was drinking much.

"We get drunk on other things," Ramón explained seriously. "On music and love and politics."

He looked enough like Ivan to be his brother—a younger brother, not as handsome or as tall or as confident. Even his attitude was that of an admiring younger brother, but Ivan said they were the same age. They had known each other since infancy, and had gone to school together.

"What did you major in?" I asked, not really caring; I was too conscious of Danny, who was dancing with a pretty dark girl.

"I major in engineering," said Ramón. "But Ivan, he does not major in anything, he defeats subjects. History, languages, chemistry . . ."

We talked about the university, and Ivan promised to drive me around the campus. Of course I'd seen pictures of the different buildings, especially the library, with the mural which covers its entire facade. Ramón said no, it was only fair that he should show me the campus. After all, he was still a student, whereas Ivan had abandoned education for the filthy commercial world and the love of money.

"You talk too much," said Ivan, giving Ramón and his empty glass a disapproving look. "Come, Carol, and meet some who can carry on an intelligent conversation.

Most of the others were students, though there were some older men. Everybody spoke English, out of deference to me, and the accents ranged from American to Zulu. The talk ranged just as widely, from the work of a new young poet to American foreign policy.

Up to that point Danny really hadn't had much to drink. I don't know what made him decide to get loaded. Maybe he was still mad at me. Maybe it was a result of the discussion we all got into.

Danny was used to holding the floor in any discussion. He was a smooth, convincing debater—and one might say decided in his opinions. People disagreed with him, but no one had ever failed to take him seriously.

He was holding forth on campus dissent, and Vietnam, and oppressive laws, and American imperialism; he wasn't saying anything I hadn't heard, and agreed with, a hundred times. That night it bugged me. It's one thing to criticize your country when you're in it, and another to call it bad names among a bunch of strangers. These strangers weren't responding, either. They were very polite—too polite. I had the feeling that they found Danny's views rather naïve. I remembered that revolution—genuine, bloody revolution—was old stuff in Mexico. Maybe they weren't impressed with our sit-ins and love-ins.

The European students weren't as reticent as the Mexicans. One of the German guys referred casually to the tunnel he and some of his friends had dug, under the Wall in Berlin, and mentioned, in passing, the German student dissent back in 1848. But the man from Czechoslovakia was the finishing touch for Danny. He laughed when Danny started talking about the Kent State murders.

"Four?" he sputtered. "Four dead, in a stupid accident,

and you talk of fascism? You have never seen a firing squad, have you? You have never seen friends blown to bloody shreds at your side, or a university building shelled by army tanks. You poor little fools, with your rocks and your obscenities—you don't even do that well, you only know three dirty words—"

Somebody stamped heavily on his foot, and somebody else turned on the hi-fi and Ramón came rushing up to Danny with a drink. But the damage was done. Or maybe it had been done before, by me.

By midnight I couldn't stand it any longer. Somebody was playing the guitar, and Danny was out in the middle of the floor being a flamenco dancer. He had a tablecloth wrapped around his waist and he had found a pair of castanets. He was the life of the party. Everybody was laughing.

I looked for Ivan, but he was nowhere in sight. Ramón had disappeared too. The apartment wasn't very big, and the doors to the bathroom and bedroom were open, so I knew they must be in the kitchen. I heard them talking as I went down the hall. I wasn't paying much attention to what they said; but one phrase struck me because it sounded so weird. Something about rabbits. Then I went through the door, and they stopped talking.

"Excuse me," I said. "I'm sorry, but—could you take me home, Ivan?"

"Certainly," Ivan said, removing himself from the table where he had been sitting. "What about Danny, is he ready?"

"I don't know."

"Ah." There was comprehension in the word, and in the glance he exchanged with Ramón. "I will see, eh?"

I followed him along the hall, with Ramón close behind.

As we entered the room, Danny reached out and grabbed one of the girls, a plump brunette in a very short mini skirt. He tried to kiss her, but he was so drunk she held him off without any trouble. She was laughing; but one of the boys, who was sitting on the floor, began to unfold himself, slowly and deliberately.

"Ah-ah," said Ramón; and Ivan moved.

It was beautifully done. In two movements he had removed the girl and handed her over to her boyfriend, and punched Danny neatly in the stomach. Danny folded up, his mouth round with surprise. Ivan caught him under the shoulders and dragged him out.

"Thank you for a lovely evening," I said.

Ramón bowed. The guitar player went on playing.

The fresh air outside felt good against my flushed face. Danny was barely conscious. His head lolled on Ivan's shoulder and he was muttering querulously. I hadn't realized how strong Ivan was; he was lean, but it was all muscle. He maneuvered Danny's bulk over to the car and poured him into the back seat. Then he opened the door for me. The front door.

I thought maybe I ought to sit with Danny, to hold his head. And I thought maybe I shouldn't sit with Ivan because—just because. But I was too mad to be reasonable. I got into the front seat.

We drove for a long time in silence. The night air was cool, and soon Danny stopped crooning to himself and began to snore.

"There is no need to cry," Ivan said, in a matter-of-fact voice. "They will do it, sooner or later."

"Get drunk and make fools of themselves?"

"Employ whatever methods of rebellion the society affords them." Ivan laughed softly. "Stop thinking of him as an Unofficial Ambassador. He is just a boy. And it is such a little drunkenness—a two-hundred-rabbits drunkenness."

"That was what you said, in the kitchen! Were you talking about Danny?"

"I had noticed him earlier."

"What is all this about rabbits? I thought I had misunderstood the word."

"A little private joke some of us have," Ivan said. "A code, you might call it. It comes from our Aztec ancestors. The rabbit was the sacred animal of the sons of Mayauel, goddess of the maguey, the plant from which pulque is made. Her four hundred sons were the patrons of drunkenness. Thirty rabbits is merely, as you say, a slight buzz. Four hundred rabbits is the final stage—total inebriation, complete with pink elephants."

"Why rabbits, I wonder?" I forgot my embarrassment in amusement. Even the mention of such cute little furry animals in connection with Danny's performance seemed to reduce its importance.

"Perhaps because the Aztecs did not know about elephants. . . . He will have a bad head in the morning, poor Danny. It would be best if you would leave him to sleep it off in dignified privacy and come with me to Tula, where I take a couple from Minnesota."

"Oh, I don't think—"

"Believe me, he will not want to see you. In the afternoon, when you meet, he will be sober and sorry and very dignified, and you will not mention his indisposition."

"Are you giving me advice on how to deal with men?"

"Why not? I am a man. And you are not."

His eyes never left the road, his hands stayed firmly on

the wheel. A little shiver ran up my back.

"You will enjoy Tula," he went on, in a different voice. "It is the site of the ancient Toltec capital. I have only two passengers tomorrow, so there will be room in the car for you."

For the rest of the drive we talked about Tula and the Toltecs, the warlike invaders from the north who had conquered the splendid city of Teotihuacan before being themselves destroyed by a fresh wave of invaders, the relatives and predecessors of the Aztecs.

Fascinating.

When we reached the hotel, Ivan coped. He got Danny into his room with a minimum of fuss, and sent me off to bed. About ten minutes later I heard the door of the next room open and close. I thought of going in, to check on Danny, but I knew I didn't have to. I had a lot on my mind that night, what with Danny's performance and my new theories about George, but when I went to bed I found myself thinking about Ivan. He hadn't even tried to kiss me. Was it because he was too honorable to take advantage of a friend's indisposition; or was it because he didn't want to?

Naturally, I preferred the former reason.

CHAPTER 6

WHEN IVAN spoke of a couple, I thought he meant a husband and wife, but when I got down to the car the next morning I found two ladies. They were both elderly—in their fifties—but that was the only thing they had in common. One had iron-gray hair piled up in one of those short puffy hairdos. She was wearing a navy-blue suit with a white blouse, and gold-rimmed glasses. Ivan introduced her as Mrs. Gold. The other lady, Mrs. Faraday, had on a very short, full peasant skirt and an off-the-shoulder blouse. Her neck was wrinkled. She wore big round yellow sunglasses and her hair was the most gorgeous Titian shade. Her round pink face was Rubens at his most florid, and it didn't go very well with the hair.

I sat up in front with Ivan, thinking that the paying customers might not want to converse with the help. But we hadn't gone a block before I was turned around, leaning over the back of the seat. By the time we got to Tula, a drive of about an hour and a half, I knew more than I really wanted to know about the ladies. Both were widows, and it was clear that their late lamented husbands had left them well off. This was their first trip together. They had had a ball, Mrs. Faraday in the nightclubs and shops, Mrs. Gold in the cultural sites. They were so different I wondered how they could get along together, but they had an admirable tolerance for the other's enthusiasms; Mrs. Faraday drove her chubby legs through all the ruins, and Mrs. Gold sat grimly through the floor shows. I could picture her in her tailored suit and white blouse staring thoughtfully through her glasses at a row of wriggling chorus girls.

The country was sun-bleached, from the bare brown ribs of the mountains to the yellowed grass. But there were trees and big patches of the spreading green spikes of maguey cactus. When he could get a word in edgewise, Ivan lectured. He told us about the maguey, which has been a staple plant for centuries. The Aztecs made rope and a kind of paper from the fibers, and the fermented juice of the heart of the plant provided the alcoholic beverage known as pulque—the source of the rabbit count.

Even more educational was watching the way Ivan ingratiated himself with those two women. Ordinary, overt flattery wouldn't have succeeded with Mrs. Faraday; she was a lot shrewder than she looked and she didn't have a spark of personal vanity. She knew she looked awful in her bright, youthful clothes, and she didn't care. She wore them because she liked them. Ivan's compliments to her were so outrageous they were funny, and the more outrageous they became the more she enjoyed them. She laughed till all her chins were shaking.

With her friend, Ivan was more subtle. Mrs. Gold had done a lot of reading and fancied herself a cultured woman. Ivan discussed Aztecs with a grave deference that implied that she was the expert. When we reached the site she was practically purring. She looked a little like a cat, with her fluffy hair—a pug-nosed, aristocratic gray Persian cat.

I thought maybe I would be bored by pyramids after seeing the big ones, but Tula had an additional attraction: the famous Atlantean statues, monumental pillars shaped like giant warriors, which crowned the pyramid. Ivan said they had once supported the roof of the temple that stood on top of the pyramidal base.

Mrs. Gold and I climbed the pyramid; it was a cinch, after the Pyramid of the Sun. Mrs. Faraday took one look at the steep steps and declined. Ivan was relieved; one elderly female to support is enough. But Mrs. Gold didn't need his support. She plodded up, as stolid and erect as if she had been climbing the stairs in her house in Minneapolis. She wanted Ivan to pose by the pillars—to show comparative size, she explained solemnly—so I wandered off. There was room enough to wander, the flat top must have been over fifty feet on a side, and there was a wonderful view. It was a blowing kind of day, with thick puffs of white clouds that kept obscuring the sun just when Mrs. Gold was all set to take a picture. She had a surprising vocabulary for such a sedate-looking woman.

The site lay below like one of those aerial photographs, and I tried to locate the features Ivan had mentioned: the Palace of Quetzalcoatl, the Ball Court, the Burnt Palace. But my mind wandered.

This place didn't give me the same feeling as Teotihuacan had done. It was interesting, but it was alien. I had never belonged to it.

I recalled that the Toltecs, despite their skill in architecture and construction, had been ferocious fighters. They had invaded Teotihuacan, and some scholars thought they were the ones who introduced human sacrifice. No wonder

I felt no rapport with their dead capital.

Yet this same pyramid where I stood with the wind blowing in my hair was dedicated to one of the manifestations of the god Quetzalcoatl, and you'd have to be pretty dull not to be intrigued by him. The Feathered Serpent, Kukulcan, the Morning Star; the bearded, fair-skinned stranger who had introduced agriculture and the arts of civilization, and had then departed toward the rising sun, whence he had mysteriously come. For centuries people have been trying to figure out who Quetzalcoatl was, and where he came from. It has been suggested that he was a fugitive Egyptian, an enterprising Phoenician, a shipwrecked Viking—or maybe St. Thomas. Whoever he was, he stood for the good things: light and life and knowledge and growing things.

By then I had talked myself into the proper mood for private prowling, so I sneaked away, if you can call a slow backward descent sneaking. I left Ivan and Mrs. Gold flirting on top of the pyramid, waved to Mrs. Faraday, who made a bright collapsed splotch of color on a distant rock, and then went around the corner of the pyramid.

I was looking for the structure the guidebook described as the Serpent Wall. It runs parallel to the back face of the pyramid, and it has a sculptured frieze showing a sweet motif of a skeleton being eaten by a snake, or being resurrected out of a snake, depending on how you look at it. The skull sticks out of the serpent's mouth.

I didn't care much for the frieze, even though some of the red and blue paint was still there. That always fascinates me, that anything so thin as paint can endure all those years. Gradually, though, a vague uneasiness grew on me. The space between the Serpent Wall and the pyramid was rather narrow, and the wall was high; it was like being in a long, closed passageway, deserted and oddly silent. My sandaled feet made no sound on the dusty ground. I found myself starting to tiptoe.

The base of the pyramid, which formed the right-hand wall of my passageway, had once been covered with sculptured panels. Some of these had been restored. The sculptures were an improvement on the skeleton-snake design opposite; there were some little animals, like tigers or lions, stalking along in procession, and a human face between the fangs of a feathered serpent, which was probably a representation of Quetzalcoatl himself. I didn't have time to study it in detail. I thought the passageway was deserted, but I was wrong. Down at the far end there suddenly appeared the figure of a man. It was the man I had seen in the lobby of the hotel. I recognized him right away, by his shoulders—and his stare.

He came along the passage toward me, walking much more quickly than a casual tourist should have walked, almost like someone who is hurrying to greet a friend. But there was no smile on his face. His mouth was shut so tightly it looked like an illustration in a geometry book: the shortest distance between two points.

They say you can't tell from a person's expression what he is thinking. Maybe not, but you can get a general idea. I didn't like the man's looks and I didn't like the isolation of the passage. I turned and started walking back. I walked rather quickly.

I heard the rhythm of his footsteps speed up, and I increased my own pace. He didn't call out, and somehow that unnerved me; it was as if he were driving me, as a dog drives a straying sheep, into a prepared trap. When the other man came into view, at the end of the passage ahead of me, my breath caught in my throat. Then I recognized the slender body and shining black hair.

Ivan's eyebrows shot up as he glanced from me to the man behind me, and I felt like a fool. What had come over me, fleeing from one harmless tourist as if he were a pack of howling Aztec warriors waving spears? My pursuer didn't help matters any. He came strolling up, smiling affably. He had a nice enough smile, with lots of white teeth. If he had smiled instead of scowling, I might not have run.

"Hello, Ivan," he said. "Who's your friend?"

"Hello, Tom." Ivan wasn't wasting any charm on this one.

"You two know each other?" I asked, feeling even more foolish.

"Everybody knows me," said the man called Tom. "Except you. I've been doing my damnedest to change that, but I don't seem to be getting through to you. Whassa matter, honey, don't you like my type?"

Drunk, I thought incredulously. Drunk as a skunk, at this hour of the day. . . . It wasn't only the few slurred words, it was the slouched way he stood and the slovenliness of his appearance. He wasn't wearing a tie, and his suit, the same one he'd been wearing the first time I saw him, looked as if he hadn't had it off since.

Ivan said something in Spanish. His tone was even, and his face retained its half-smile, but I had a feeling that the words weren't as pleasant as they sounded.

The other man waved his hand and laughed.

"Don't gimme that *español,* Ivan, you speak English as good as I do. Maybe it's just as well I don't get it, huh? Introduce me to the pretty lady."

"I think not," Ivan said.

"Whassa matter? Nothing wrong with admiring a pretty girl. No offense."

He put one hand on his grimy shirt front and bowed.

"No offense," I said. "Now, if you'll excuse us—"

"Oooh." He screwed up his mouth and narrowed his eyes. "Thass mean, lady, talking that way. Freeze a poor guy to death. Listen, sweetheart, you don't have to put on all those airs with me. I've seen you around town with that baby-faced kid you brought down here with you. Fun and games in old Me-hi-co, huh? Well, I'm a lot more fun than Baby-Face and I know more games. More than old Ivan here, too."

I leaned heavily against Ivan, so that he fell back a step instead of moving forward as he had been about to do. "Don't bother with him, Ivan," I said. "He isn't worth the effort. Please, let's go."

"You are right," Ivan said, breathing through his nose. "I will not dirty my hands on such scum."

He took my arm and we walked off, leaving the Tom person standing there. He didn't follow us; but his attitude was probably the most maddening one he could have chosen. Legs wide apart, hands on his hips, he laughed out loud.

"Who is he?" I asked, as soon as we were out of earshot.

"His name is Andres. He claims to be a free-lance newspaper reporter, but since he has been here he has done nothing but drink and annoy women. I regret that it appears he has taken a fancy to you."

"I regret too," I said, feeling a shiver of revulsion run through me. "Has he ever—"

"Attacked a girl? No, but there have been some nasty incidents. I have warned him not to bother you. Emphatically. You must tell me if he tries to speak to you again."

"I will. But if your emphatic warning was in Spanish and he doesn't understand Spanish . . ."

"He understands it," Ivan said shortly. "Now let us forget him, he has darkened the day enough."

I agreed with the conclusion, but I couldn't follow the advice. There were a few things about Mr. Tom Andres that bothered me, in addition to his offensive manner. One of the things was his crack about my bringing Danny with me, for fun and games. His opinion of my morals didn't concern me; but how had he known that I was the instigator, and financier, of the trip? Most people would have assumed the opposite.

The other thing that bothered me was the suddenness of Mr. Andres's inebriation. When he first appeared and came after me, he showed no signs of being drunk.

We stopped for lunch on our way back to the city, in a town which had a famous cathedral of the lavish Baroque style called Churrigueresque. The ladies' examination of the cathedral was cursory. Even Mrs. Gold admitted that she had had enough culture for that day. Mrs. Faraday had a couple of tequila cocktails before lunch, and got pretty giggly. She didn't say anything distressing; but I got to thinking of some of the other women whom Ivan had guided. You read about things like that—bored middle-aged women and handsome young men. And Ivan had to be polite, he couldn't discourage his admirers the way a girl can when somebody tries to pick her up. I felt sorry for him, and I admired him. I guess that's why I accepted when he invited me out to the house for a drink.

We had just dropped the ladies off at their hotel, a tall, modern place on the Reforma. By that time we were all on first-name terms, and Ivan had agreed to take them to Teotihuacan, and all around the city, and drive them to the airport when they were ready to go home. But as Ivan waved back at the two waving figures on the sidewalk, the breath came whistling out through his fixed smile in a long sigh.

"Tired?" I asked tactfully.

"Sick and tired. Isn't that what you say? Oh, it is not such a strain as all that; I am very good at this, I do it automatically. You despise me, don't you?"

"Quite the contrary. You handle people beautifully. You didn't lead them on, you just made them feel good. That's all most women want, a little flattery, a touch of kindness."

Ivan didn't say anything; he just shot me a quick glance, unsmiling and wholly cynical. I laughed.

"Oh, all right, I said most women. I suppose now and then you must run into the other kind. That's why I admire you. I'm sure you handle them with the same skill and kindness you used on those old dears today."

"Those old dears are my living," Ivan said drily. "Ah, well, you are gracious, and I have no right to be so cynical. As you say, most of them are pleasant enough. Usually I regard what I do as a kindness: harmless at worst, and at best a help to the morale. But today I felt . . . Perhaps it was because you were watching me."

"Ivan, honestly—"

"We won't talk of it anymore. But you must do me a kindness. Come back to the house with me now, for tea, or a cocktail, or whatever it is you take at this hour. I need more of your company to take the taste of today out of my mouth."

After all, I told myself, it was his house. He had as much right to bring a guest as anyone else; more right than . . . some people.

I muttered something about Danny, and Ivan stopped the car by a telephone kiosk and went in it to call. Danny wasn't at the hotel. That cleared my conscience, so I agreed.

The big wooden gate wasn't barred; I learned later that it never was during the daytime. Ivan opened the gate and drove the car through.

It was the first time I had seen the place in daylight. I hadn't realized how far out of the city it was. There were other houses on the street, at least I assume there were; you couldn't see anything but the high inhospitable walls. Behind and around, the suburb petered out into fields and open country. At the end of the street there were clumps of the ubiquitous maguey cactus, like emerald octopi against the dullness of the coarse grass. In the distance the sharp-ribbed shapes of mountains framed the horizon.

I hadn't realized, either, how big the grounds were. The house was enormous. It was partially hidden by trees, but I could see bits of roof and isolated chimneys all over the place.

The open space just inside the wall, where Ivan parked the car, was reserved for the uglier necessities of living. Once again I received an impression of poverty and decay; a family who could afford servants, maintenance, wouldn't tolerate an area like this one. The unpaved, weedy ground was stained with oil drippings and covered with miscellaneous objects—rusting pails and tools, empty cartons, rags. The crude, tin-roofed shed in one corner was too small to serve as a garage for anything except a motorbike.

Ivan gave these objects an expressive look, his lip curling, but he said nothing, only took my arm and led me along a path that went into the trees beyond the parking area.

The leafy branches cast a cool shade over the path. Even here there were signs of neglect; the forested expanse on either side might have been left to run wild deliberately, but the path was beaten earth, unweeded except by the constant passing of shod feet.

It had its beauty, though, a neglected jungly loveliness, and so did the patio, where the path ended. I remembered this area from my first visit; but now the glare of sunlight mercilessly exposed the flaking plaster on the walls, and the weeds that had thrust tenacious strands between the stone paving blocks. The gate through which we entered the patio sagged on its hinges; it must have stood open for a long time, because vines had wound through the open metalwork. The fountain in the center of the patio was dry. The shape which had looked like a truncated column in the darkness was a statue—a squat, stubby-legged block with the big owly eyes that identified it as the rain god, Tlaloc. Very appropriate for a fountain. But the pipe that ran up Tlaloc's back was rusty and bone dry.

Two of the four enclosing walls were plain, except for the vines that curtained large sections. On the other two sides were roofed arcades supported by thick pillars. They had tiled floors and a number of doors that led into the house. The foliage was lushly green; two tall trees shaded the patio, and between the columns of the arcades stood pots of soft brown earthenware filled with tall, leafy plants.

I realized that the gate onto the street from which we

had entered must be a back door. The main entrance to a place this size wouldn't look so shabby. Perhaps the front door was on a street where a car could not be parked. At any rate, this was obviously the means of entry preferred by the family. One of the doors beyond the pillars stood open. It was the door through which we had passed that first night.

I had gotten this far with only mild qualms, but the yawning rectangle of the doorway reminded me of too many unpleasant truths. Ines didn't want me here, and neither did George. Ivan had the right to invite anyone he chose; but for me to accept took a certain amount of gall. The courtyard didn't seem quite so flagrant an intrusion as did the house.

"Oh, this is charming," I squealed girlishly. "Can't we sit out here?"

Ivan gave me an odd look.

"Certainly, if you like. Excuse me while I hunt for María; she is very deaf."

I sat down on a bench under one of the trees. The place was very peaceful; only the hum of insects and the musical comments of birds interrupted the silence, and the sunlight fell in dappled patterns across the stones. But I was ill at ease. I sat bolt upright, my hands stiff in my lap, wondering whether Ivan would tell his mother I was here—wondering precisely what I would say if she emerged from the house and discovered me without being warned. I worried about Ines because I didn't dare think of George. She was a source of embarrassment; George was potential disaster.

Something moved in a corner, and I twisted around with a gasp. One of the worn wicker chairs was half turned toward the wall; I had been vaguely aware of something in it, something unmoving which I had taken for a pile of rags.

The face that peered around the high back of the chair was familiar, but it was not one of the faces I dreaded seeing. I relaxed, with a deep sigh, and the old man whom I had met that first night got up out of his chair and came toward me. I wished to goodness I could remember his name.

"A thousand apologies, my dear. I have an old man's habit of napping in the sun, and I did not hear you come. You are waiting for one of my household? How I would like to think that it was for me!"

I don't know why that speech surprised me so; Ines and Ivan both spoke excellent English, there was no reason why the old gentleman shouldn't. He was younger than I had thought, or better preserved; he moved with a young man's agility, and the hand he extended was steady.

He kissed my hand. It was the first time anyone had ever kissed my hand, and I realized why people used to think so highly of the custom. He was an old man, and his lips barely brushed my fingers; but I saw possibilities there.

He sat down beside me, retaining my hand, and beamed at me. In daylight his skin had the color and texture of soft leather, delicately lined; his expression was as affable as Santa Claus's is reputed to be. I didn't pull my hand away. He kept patting it, in an avuncular sort of way—but not completely avuncular. I had the feeling he liked holding hands with a girl, not in anticipation of the future, but in fond memory of the past.

"I came back with Ivan, from a tour," I explained. "He went in to get us something to drink."

"Ah, good. You are enjoying your visit here? It is a poor country, this, compared with yours, but we who love it feel that its future will be great."

I rushed into polite disclaimers, praising the glorious past of Mexico and its gracious present; I meant what I said, so maybe the phrases didn't sound as trite as I feared they did. After a while I had the feeling that the old man wasn't listening. He kept nodding and smiling and patting, but his odd, expressive little eyes looked abstracted.

"Does your father know that you are here?" he asked suddenly.

"I don't know," I said, in some confusion. "If Ivan has told him . . ."

I stopped, seeing Ivan come out the door. He was scowling. I thought he was annoyed with me, or with his uncle, or with the combination; but he broke out into a diatribe on María's laziness, and apologized for being so long.

"At least you have found someone to compensate for my rudeness," he ended. *"Gracias,* Tío Jaime, for entertaining my guest."

"It is I who thank you, for giving me this pleasure." The old man released my hand, but he did not rise. "Yet I must scold you, Ivan, for leaving her, as you thought, alone. A guest—especially a lady—always should have the utmost courtesy from our house."

Ivan bowed his head—possibly to conceal the spark of resentment in his eyes. I couldn't see what else he could have done and I certainly had no fault to find with his behavior, but I thought I'd better keep out of the discussion.

The old man rose.

"If you will forgive me, I will go to hurry María. She is old and slow and deaf, but she is a dependent of our family and we must tolerate her infirmities." He moved slowly toward the doorway as he spoke. Then he turned. "I will find your father," he said, "and tell him that his daughter has come."

The darkness of the doorway swallowed him up.

Ivan made a convulsive movement, and caught himself.

"I am sorry," he muttered. "María is not the only old fool dependent on the family."

The words offended me. I've heard plenty of people knock their parents and relatives, but it was out of character for Ivan.

"He's your uncle," I said. "You shouldn't talk about him that way."

"My mother's uncle, not mine. No, I should not call him a fool, he is not that. But his notions of gentility are dead, mummified. I did not mean to subject you to the older members of the family—yours or mine."

"It doesn't matter." I shrugged, with an indifference I was far from feeling. "Maybe George won't come out. He probably doesn't want to see me any more than I want to see him."

"May be." Ivan sat down beside me. He looked at me searchingly. "What did he say to you?"

"Uncle Jaime? Nothing, we just talked about Mexico. He's charming, Ivan."

"Oh, he is charming. In his day he was the despair of the respectable mammas of the city. Now he is good for nothing but to sleep in the sun and smoke marijuana."

I suppose I'd be the world's worst poker player. The sight of my gaping face sent Ivan into paroxysms of mirth.

"How young you are," he said, choking. "Do you think it is a habit of the youthful rebels only? My uncle regards your 'potheads,' as you call them, in the same way that a connoiseur of vintage wines regards an alcoholic. He indulges with the discrimination of an elderly gentleman savoring his after-dinner port. His judgment is based on long experience; he even cultivates his own special vintages."

My incredulous stare transferred itself to the red pots and their leafy crop.

"Right here?" I said idiotically. "Right there?"

"Here, there, and all around the courtyard. Why not?"

"Oh, well . . . No reason. I mean, if that's his thing . . ."

"You are thinking about the police? But there is no problem; the Commissioner dined here last week and commended Tío Jaime on a new crop. No, you see, with us, it is a private matter. Now, to be sure, our police must cooperate with your authorities to prevent the wholesale export of drugs into the United States. It is politic to conform to the requests of a more powerful neighbor. But to interfere with a gentleman's private amusement . . ."

"Especially when he's a friend of the chief fuzz," I said.

For no good reason, I was annoyed with Ivan. Maybe it was his rude remark about his nice old uncle. Or maybe it was his suave cynicism, with a not so subtle dig at the U.S. Nobody can kick my country but me.

"One little old man and his herb garden is one thing," I said stiffly. "Peddling narcotics to high school kids and those poor hopeless dropouts in the ghettoes is something else. If you think it's funny—"

It was just as well I never got to finish that speech; I'm not an experienced debater. Ivan's eyebrows were rising and an amused smile was spreading across his face, when a queer little procession advanced out of the house.

The squat black figure of María led the parade. She was carrying a heavy tray. This time I didn't try to relieve her of it. Behind her, Ines's slim height towered over the old woman's bent body. Behind Ines was George.

I hate to admit it, but Ines was really something. She greeted me and apologized for not coming at once; from her bland smile and smooth words no one would ever have suspected that we had shared that dramatic luncheon party. George wasn't so well trained. He muttered something, but he didn't look at me. His studious avoidance of my face made me feel—more than rejected. As if I were some hideous, distasteful object he couldn't bear to see.

María dropped the tray on a tiled table with a thud that rattled cups. Hands on her ample hips, head cocked, she contemplated me in wooden silence. In broad daylight her face was hideous. Uncle Jaime's wrinkles were those of good nature; hers were the product of hard work and suffering, deeply incised.

I braced myself for another speech. It was obvious that the old lady was about to cut loose, like a little squat Cassandra. Just as well, I thought, that I didn't understand Spanish.

Nobody interrupted her. The rusty rattle of syllables, delivered in a voice wheezy with old age and overweight, went on and on. Ines's face remained calm, but her mouth tightened, and Ivan made no attempt to mask his impatience. George sat staring at the ground. I wondered why they didn't tell the old lady to shut up, if her tirades annoyed them that much. She might be old and faithful, but she was still a servant, and I had the impression that aristocratic families didn't put up with commentary from the lower classes.

This family did. When María ran down, she shook herself —the dust rose in clouds from her skirts—and turned to go.

"Well," I said brightly, "I'm sorry I annoy the poor old thing so much. I do seem to set her off, don't I?"

María had not yet reached the door. She turned and snapped out a question. Ines answered her. I got the idea, this time, if not the exact words; María wanted to know what I had said. As soon as Ines had translated María became agitated. Sputtering and mouthing, she started toward me. Involuntarily I recoiled a little. Her voice probably would have sounded menacing even if she had been crooning love songs, it was that sort of a voice; but I sensed a threat in what she said.

This time Ines cut her short with a brusque command. María divided an enigmatic stare between me and her mistress, and went into the house.

"I am so sorry," Ines said, with a silvery tinkle of laughter. "You must excuse her, she is so old."

"Of course. I just can't understand why she should take such a dislike to me."

"You misunderstand," Ivan said. "She does not dislike you. She sees in you a portent, a warning."

"Ivan . . ." his mother began.

"No, Madre, por qué? It hurts Carol's feelings to think that people do not like her; she will not be hurt if she knows that it is only a superstitious peasant who regards her as a warning of danger."

"Danger," I said. So that was the meaning of that word that had kept recurring, over and over. *Peligro—periculo*—perilous . . . I recognized the cognates, now that Ivan had clued me.

"Danger to whom?"

"To everyone, of course," Ivan said with a laugh. "To me, to this house, to you—to all of Mexico, probably, and to the world. Self-appointed prophets have a fertility of imagination."

"That is enough," Ines said suddenly. "Let us have tea."

She bent over the cups and the teapot, and when she straightened up the normal color had come back to her face. Or was it only my own fertile imagination that had fancied her sudden pallor? Ivan took the cup and brought it to me, and I reminded myself that, for all her breeding and sophistication, Ines had spent her childhood in that same atmosphere of peasant superstition, with nurses and servants who believed in witchcraft. Was that why she wanted me to leave? Though her rational mind might reject María's warning, the deep, unconscious levels often retain the beliefs of childhood.

Ivan didn't refer to María's prophecy again, but he insisted on discussing witchcraft, and if I had paid attention, I might have picked up some information that would have had more than academic interest to me later. He talked about magic among the Aztecs, and explained how Christian theology, with its fear of the Devil, had changed the original tradition. It was right about then that he lost me. I watched my father, who sat like a frozen image—unspeaking, almost unmoving—his eyes looking everywhere except at me.

For all Ivan's cheery chatter, the atmosphere was as thick as mud, and I gulped my tea as quickly as I could. This visit was turning out to be just as bad as the first.

I refused a second cup, and then, before I could begin my farewell speech, Ines rose. With a murmured apology, she went into the house.

Ivan babbled on. Then something stirred in the shadow of the open doorway, and I recognized the fat face of Uncle

Jaime, peering out like a mouse from its hole.

I smiled at him, and he smiled back; but when he spoke, it was Ivan he addressed.

"There is a telephone call for you. It is the *Agencia*, I believe."

Ivan glanced at George, and then at me.

"Tell them, please, that I am occupied."

"No, no," I said. "You mustn't be rude to your employer. Go ahead. But, when you've finished talking, I really ought to be getting back."

"Very well."

I thought perhaps Uncle Jaime was going to take over the chaperon post, but he didn't reappear. There we were, my father and I. Alone at last.

It was a moment I had dreaded and looked forward to; I must have composed fifty opening speeches. I didn't need them. George looked up, and the expression in his eyes struck me silent.

"How much longer are you planning to stay?"

"I don't know. A week, ten days . . . School starts on the—"

"Ten days." His voice was harsh with an emotion I couldn't identify. It might have been amusement; or it might have been anger. "I'm glad to know that your mother is so well off. A trip like this isn't cheap, especially if you insist on staying at the most expensive hotel in town."

There were several contradictory motives which shaped my reply. The loyalty I owed to Helen's pride demanded that I made it clear to him that she could get along without him very well. On the other hand, I could see one of his motives. It would relieve him of some of his guilt if he thought we were in good shape financially. But I didn't see why I should relieve him of any guilt.

"She inherited some money."

"Inherited? From whom?"

"I don't know. Some elderly relative."

"She didn't—"

His mouth closed on the words as if he wanted to bite them off. When he spoke again, I knew that the completion of the sentence was not the one he had originally intended.

"She didn't send you down here?"

"No."

And I will be damned, I thought to myself, if I will tell you why I did come.

"How is she?"

"Fine."

"Yes, I'm sure she is. She never liked being married."

He glanced at me and saw the blood come up into my face. He laughed, sharply and unpleasantly.

"You emancipated young things give me a pain. You have the gall to criticize my generation for being neurotic about sex, but you can't think of your parents as human beings, can you?"

"Was that why you left?"

"It had some bearing on my decision, certainly. . . ." My eyes were cowards now; I didn't see his face, but I heard the change in his voice. "Do you mean that Helen never told you why I left?"

"She never mentions your name."

"That's in character. . . . No, damn it, I'll have to give her credit. If she didn't blacken my name with you, she deserves a lot of credit."

"She didn't have to," I said.

"No. I did that myself, didn't I?"

"Did you ever—once—write to me?"

"No."

That single, unadorned monosyllable was almost the last chop of the ax. But he wasn't finished.

"Carol," he said, "it's all over, can't you see that? Don't be fooled by the old myths of the blood; the things that bind human beings together are not accidental physical relationships. A man is a father when he acts like a father, not when he contributes a casual cell to creation. Clinging to the past is futile." He paused, as if trying to choose his words; and, with a dreadful gentleness that was more final than a shout, he said, "I don't want to see you again."

I was standing up, though I don't remember moving.

"That makes it mutual," I said. My tongue felt the way it did after I got Novocain to have a tooth filled—thick and rubbery and disconnected.

"Why don't you spend the rest of your vacation in California? Palm Springs . . . Disneyland . . ."

I think he asked if I needed any more money. Somehow Disneyland was the final insult, it made my hearing cut out. I didn't hear Ivan come, but I felt his hand on my arm. I could see all right; it was just that I seemed to be seeing through a thick sheet of plastic, that distorted faces and shut out sound. I said to Ivan, "Let's go," and he led me away, down the path into the trees.

I got about halfway before my knees buckled. He felt me stagger; his arms went around me and I hung on to him the way you hold on to a branch or a rock when you're drowning. The trees shook and the sky faded in and out. After a while I heard the sound of my breathing. It was so fast and hoarse it scared me.

"I'm sorry," I mumbled, pushing the hair out of my eyes.

"Shock," Ivan said, through his teeth. "What did the—what did he say to you?"

"He told me he didn't want to see me again."

Ivan didn't answer.

"I can walk now," I said. "Please, let's get out of here."

"Wait a minute."

I looked up at him, about to reassure him as to my ability to go on. He wasn't looking at me. His face was taut with concentration, as if he were trying to reach a decision.

"I want you to come back. Slowly, quietly. No, don't pull away, I don't expect you to talk to him again. He won't see you. I only want you to see him."

I was too tired to fight. So long as I didn't have to face George again, I didn't care what happened. So I let Ivan lead me, along the shadowy path, until we reached a point from which we could see through veiling branches into the patio.

George was still there. He was leaning forward in his chair, elbows on his knees, his hands covering his face. A lock of gray hair had fallen forward over his clenched fingers.

At my side Ivan let out a small, controlled breath. His hand tugged at me, and I followed, like a well-trained doll, back along the path.

By the time Ivan had turned the car expertly in the small space, and closed the gate, I was able to talk.

"What was that for?" I asked.

"Just to show you that it was not easy for him to send you away."

"Thanks. Why should I care about his feelings? He hasn't been easy on mine."

"He has his reasons."

The long slow evening had come. The sun was setting in brilliant colors behind the mountains; the shadows were cool and dark.

"Ivan, I appreciate what you're doing. You're trying to leave me with a small shred of self-respect. And you've been very kind. But I've had it, I can't stand having my feelings ripped up every time I meet him. I'm leaving."

"You let him drive you away? There is much in Mexico besides one confused man."

"I know, and I love the country. I want to see it again, someday. But it's spoiled now, I couldn't enjoy anything."

The car edged onto the superhighway which surrounds the city, and Ivan, concentrating on bluffing the other drivers, did not speak for a time. Finally he said,

"You will return home?"

"No, I've still got some vacation left and my mother isn't home, she's off on a cruise. I'll go someplace else. Los Angeles, or . . . Disneyland . . ."

"What about Danny?"

The question hit me like a physical blow. I had forgotten about Danny. How could I have forgotten him?

"Oh, Danny . . . He'll go wherever I want to go."

"How nice that he is so submissive."

"I didn't mean that, I meant—"

"I know, I know." Ivan drove for a while in silence, his forehead wrinkled in a frown as he fought his way through the thickening traffic. Suddenly he swerved into a side street that led off the highway.

"We must talk," he said. "There is something you must know before you make your decision."

We were on a suburban street, tree-lined, with handsome modern houses and a few shops. Ivan found a café, with tables on the sidewalk, and after he had ordered for us he excused himself and went inside.

I opened my purse and got out a handkerchief. There was a sheaf of red-and-buff peso notes in the side compartment. I took them out and counted them. A little over a hundred pesos—eight dollars. I wondered how much money we had left. We hadn't spent much, outside of the hotel, but that bill would be fairly steep. Not that it mattered; we had our tickets home, and if worse came to worst we could camp out in some cheap place. Berkeley, maybe. Danny had friends at Berkeley. . . .

Danny. Before, when I thought his name, I got a single piercing emotional jolt. Now the impression was kaleidoscopic—bright shards and dark shards and shiny bits like mirrors, and a feeling of confusion.

Maybe I was falling in love with Ivan.

I had enough to think about, so that I didn't notice how long Ivan was gone; but he apologized when he came back, saying that he'd met someone he knew. The waiter came with tall glasses. I tasted mine and made a face, and Ivan shook his head.

"I know you don't drink, but you need something now. You have had a shock, and I fear you will have another. Carol, I have a confession to make. I heard part of your conversation with George. Returning to the patio I realized that you would not want to be interrupted, so I waited. Perhaps I should have gone away and not listened. But I thought you might need me."

"I did. Thank you."

"You may not thank me for this. I must be more impertinent. To interfere, that I do not as a rule approve. But I cannot see you so hurt without trying to make it easier.

Perhaps I make a mistake. Remember, that if I do make a mistake it is because I want to help."

"There's no need to be tactful. My private family affairs aren't all that private. You're involved in them anyhow, through no choice of your own."

He didn't much like that reminder, I could tell by his face. I had speculated before about his reaction to my father's permanent, unexplained presence in his mother's house. From my reading I had the impression that Latin males were particularly sensitive about the reputations of mothers, sisters, and wives. The problem I had with my father was a little different, it didn't involve that delicate question of honor. So he could intrude, as he called it, into my affairs without giving me the right to refer to his mother's situation.

I didn't press it; and, except for the brief, ugly twist of his mouth, he didn't volunteer anything. He went straight to the point.

"Is it true that you know nothing of the event in your father's past which made him leave home? When I referred to it, the day we went to Teotihuacan, you seemed not to know; but I thought possibly, with Danny there—"

"I don't know what you're talking about. I thought George just got fed up—with Helen, with family life and responsibility. Men do."

"Do you know that he has a picture of you in his room, still? A picture of a little blond child with braids tied in bows, and long thin legs."

"That's enough of that," I said, and shoved my glass away. "Why are you so determined to make him seem pathetic? He's not. He left home of his own free will."

"Not precisely."

"My mother told me—"

"He left because he had committed a crime."

Everything stopped. Breathing, movement, time.

"What crime?" I asked.

"Murder."

CHAPTER 7

"WELL," I said. "Well, well."

It was too much. I felt like laughing. Not because I didn't believe it—because it was the last bloody straw in a generally bad day. My brain couldn't take any more shocks, it was blown out.

"Not in the legal sense," Ivan said, looking relieved that I was taking it so calmly. "But morally he was responsible; and, what is more important, he feels he is responsible."

"Morally," I repeated, like a ventriloquist's dummy.

Ivan took a drink, and leaned back in his chair.

"You have heard, of course, of Timothy Leary?"

"Sure."

"The Pied Piper of LSD," Ivan murmured; he was smiling slightly. " 'Tune in, turn on, and drop out.' It was in the early nineteen sixties that Professor Leary and certain of his colleagues at Harvard became enthusiastic about the so-called mind-expanding qualities of the hallucinogens. Professor Leary is no longer a professor at Harvard, but he is still enthusiastic. He is still searching for the quick and easy way to wisdom.

"You must know that, like the Harvard experimenters,

your father was a psychologist? Naturally it would not have occurred to you to connect his aberrations with the LSD cult. Yet he was one of the first to be led astray by the fascination of the hallucinogens. Like his more publicity-conscious colleagues at a more famous institution, he felt that his students should share in the great experience."

I knew then what was coming.

"Poor George had bad luck," Ivan went on, meditatively shifting his glass to form a series of wet, interlocking rings on the top of the table. "The incidence of bad trips among users of LSD is not really terribly high. Statistics vary, of course, but I believe that only a mere ten percent are seriously traumatic. But percentages are so unfair—like the law of averages, which does not prevent a coin from turning up heads nine times in a row. Out of the ten students to whom George gave the drug, two died. One cut her wrists in her room and bled to death. She left a note. It was barely decipherable, but there was something about looking in a mirror, and seeing her face begin to melt.

"They kept that story quiet, the school authorities. The girl had a history of mental instability. To do George justice, he did not know of her history, nor did he realize at that early stage of experimentation that unstable people are particularly susceptible to the bad effects of the drug. It shook him badly though, this death, and he stopped giving out LSD, meaning to study it more carefully. Two weeks later one of his other students walked into his private office, which was on the fourteenth floor—and walked out of an open window, announcing that he had decided to fly to England. It happened in front of George's own eyes; trapped behind his desk, he was unable to reach the boy in time to stop him. The worst of it was that he knew the boy had not taken any recent doses of the drug. It is now known that such spontaneous trips can occur months after the last ingestion of the drug."

We were now the only people sitting at the tables. It was very quiet. Ivan's voice was hardly more than a whisper.

"You are such curious people, you Americans. When something bad happens you do not wish to discuss it, or find out how it happened; you sweep it all into a hole in the ground and hastily cover up the bad smell. Your local newspapers, controlled by trustees of the university, did not mention George's role in this second tragedy. Of course he was asked to leave his position. But it was not this which made him run away. Horror and grief and shame brought him close to a breakdown. Too many people knew the truth, including your mother. You know, better than I, what her behavior in this situation must have been."

"You know the truth too," I said, in a voice that did not sound like my own. "About George—all about LSD—how did you find out?"

"I listened. I spied, and I eavesdropped. I read, I asked questions of anyone who would answer. You are very young, and a woman, and therefore a fool; but surely you must suspect how I feel about your father. I was fourteen when he came to my mother's house, twelve years ago. That is not a good age to see your mother betray her honor and that of your dead father."

All along I had suspected that his exquisite manners must be a facade. I had wondered about the real man underneath. Now I saw the reality, and it turned me cold. The worst of it was that I couldn't blame him.

"Yet they never married," I said. "I find it hard to believe that anyone as sophisticated and intelligent as your mother—"

I stopped right there, and grabbed for my glass to hide my face. Ivan didn't know about my luncheon debate with Ines, and I guessed that she wouldn't want him to know. It wasn't tenderness for her that kept me quiet. I had no wish to admit any greater involvement than that which he already knew about.

He didn't notice my confusion; he was too upset to think of anything except his own misery.

"Madre de Dios," he exploded, "do you know nothing at all about human beings? Yes, she is intelligent, sophisticated, an aristocrat—whose faith is the most important thing in her life. She prefers to commit adultery rather than marry a divorced man. Stupid? Illogical? Of course! That is what human beings are!"

"Look," I said, "it's none of our business what they do. Besides . . . I think you're wrong. I don't think they are living together."

Ivan stared at me. He was so surprised he stopped yelling.

"You are mad."

"No. I may be mistaken, but I'm not that naïve. Call it feminine intuition." I remembered Ines's face, and her twisting hands; and an unwilling pity softened my voice. "If she wouldn't do one thing, she wouldn't do the other."

"You think that?" Ivan was still staring, but my conviction was affecting him. Slowly a smile spread across his face. "But how perfect that would be. He ran to her for comfort. And he found a kindly nun. Ah, that would be amusing!"

"I don't think it's at all amusing," I said sharply; and then, because I couldn't stand the subject, or his smile, any longer, I asked, "Why did he come to her when he left home? I can understand why he ran away, why he never tried to communicate with me. He must have felt like a leper. But why Ines? You said he met her twelve years ago. That was before the scandal broke."

"That, too, is ironically just," Ivan said, with a grisly satisfaction. "He met the family while he was here doing research on hallucinogenic drugs. They are very old in our culture: peyote, morning-glory seeds, the sacred mushroom. Like LSD, which is chemically produced, they are hallucinatory in nature. So is marijuana, though it is much milder than the others. It was natural that a mutual friend should introduce George to Tío Jaime."

"Natural," I muttered. "Dear God. I hate to think so."

"I share your feeling. There is something terrible in the web of causality, as its pattern manifests itself; something like a madman's humor. From Tío Jaime to my mother; the hallucinogens, marijuana to mescaline to LSD; the scandal, the flight; back again to my mother . . . and now, you and I, sitting across a table in the twilight. I wonder how we fit into the pattern of the web."

In the deepening dusk his face was hidden; but his pose, the taut hands and bowed head, suggested a somber fatalism that frightened me even more than his words.

"Well, I'm not going to be a fly in the web," I said, starting to my feet. "Ivan, please get me home. I can't take any more today."

In the car, on the final lap of the bizarrely interrupted drive, Ivan regained his composure.

"Now I regret that I have told you these things," he said.

"You needn't. Unless you regret being so candid about your feelings."

"Of course I regret that." He had recovered his self-possession; the corners of his mouth curved up in the now familiar, half mocking smile. But his mask of indifference would never fool me again, now that I had seen the sick, hating child under the man's facade. Compared to his, my hang-ups weren't so bad. At least I was willing to admit they were neurotic hang-ups.

"No man likes to indulge in self-pity before a woman he wants to impress," he went on. "I ask your forgiveness for that. As for your father—there, too, I deceive myself. I told myself I wanted you to understand his dilemma and pity him. But it was only a way of striking at him, of baring the secret he does not want you to know."

"I certainly won't mention it to him. Please don't—don't flagellate yourself this way. I appreciate what you've done. It's funny," I said, genuinely surprised. "This should have been an additional shock. But it seems to have nullified the first one. I feel much better. Though I'll be darned if I know why."

"If it has done that, then I will stop apologizing."

"Ivan, have dinner with us. You've been such a gracious host; it's our turn now."

"Thank you. But what about Danny?"

"He'd love to have you. He likes you."

"If he does, he is more tolerant than I would be in his place. . . . To be truthful, I would enjoy it very much. I will accept if I may spend the time trying to persuade you to stay on in Mexico."

"You can try."

He hadn't done badly, so far. I don't think I was overcome with tender compassion for George. I felt a lot sorrier for his victims. But I could understand why he had reacted as he did. And most important—we're all egoists, after all—this explanation took the blame off me. Kids feel guilty when they're rejected. Under the screams of rage a little insidious voice keeps asking, "What did you do to make them hate you so much? How did you fail?"

Now I could tell that small voice to be still. It wasn't my fault. I could even afford to feel a little—just a little—sorry for George.

But all the way up in the elevator, with the soft lights and elegant decor surrounding me, I kept thinking about that girl, the one who had cut her wrists. I kept seeing what she must have seen in the mirror—her features melting, sagging, running, like wax left too long by the fire.

II

They were talking about bullfighting. I thought that if Danny mentioned Ernest Hemingway one more time I would scream.

We decided to have dinner at the hotel; Ivan said the food was pretty good, and I guess it was. Helen is a TV-dinner and hot-dog type, so I'm no authority on gourmet cooking.

It was all very posh. The restaurant was at the front of the hotel, with big windows overlooking the Reforma and the shining column of the Angel. The *maître d'* murmured over the menu and the waiters tiptoed. There were candles on the table.

The candlelight made Danny's eyes shine like star sapphires. He was in a marvelous mood; I had expected him to be mad at my prolonged absence, but I guess he decided that our mutual sins canceled each other. He asked me if I'd had a nice time and welcomed Ivan enthusiastically. He didn't even complain when I told him he'd have to put on a tie and coat.

I had a new dress, one of Helen's Christmas presents. She must have gotten a tremendous discount on it; it was pale-blue chiffon in a Grecian tunic style, the pleated drapery caught in at the waist with a gold cord. It was very becoming—it would have been becoming to a sack of potatoes—and I should have felt gay and pretty and admired. I had the prettiest dress in the room and the two best-looking men. I sat with my elbows on the table, disregarding both manners and wrinkles, and listened to my two gallants talk about slaughtering beef.

"The Moment of Truth," Danny said, in capitals. "In *Death in the Afternoon* Hemingway says—"

I screamed.

It was a little scream, inaudible beyond our table, but it stopped the conversation.

"Are we boring you?" Ivan asked politely.

"Yes."

"But you've never even seen a bullfight," Danny said. "How can you condemn something you've never seen?"

"I've never seen a concentration camp, either."

I expected that to annoy him, but he loved to argue.

"The comparison is hardly valid," he said, his eyes gleaming. "No one has ever pretended to find mystical or aesthetic values in a concentration camp. But there is an enormous literature on the mystique of the bull ring."

He had me there, so I backed up and turned around and came at him from another direction. Unfair, but effective.

"I don't know why you think you're such an authority. You've never seen a bullfight. Or—oh, dear. Have you?"

"Spain."

"Humph," I said. I kept forgetting about that weird

childhood of his, when his mother, loaded with alimony, had dragged him through the hot spots of Europe. He seldom referred to it.

"That was a long time ago and I was too young to understand," Danny continued. "But at least I have an open mind. I'm willing to wait and see."

"So tomorrow we see," Ivan said with a smile. "Tickets are not easy to get, but I have, as you say in the States, connections through the *Agencia*."

"I thought you were taking the girls to Teotihuacan," I said.

"Girls?" Ivan looked so outraged that I couldn't help laughing. "Oh, a joke," he said gloomily. "Very funny. No, the 'girls' wish to go at night, to see the 'Sound and Light' performance."

"Horrible things," Danny said. "I saw one in Rome, in the Forum. Red and purple lights glaring on those magnificent columns, and some jackass bellowing 'I am Romulus!' over a loudspeaker."

"Oh, no," I said. "Not at my pyramids."

"It'll be 'I am Montezuma!' " Danny predicted.

"The 'girls' will love it," Ivan said, smiling. "It is given six nights a week, so I can take them at any time. The bullfights tomorrow?"

"You'll go without me," I warned.

Danny started to expostulate, but Ivan shook his head.

"No, if she begins with such prejudice it is better that she not go. Some of our people find it offensive when visitors loudly criticize our customs."

"I'm sorry," I said, in confusion.

"Why do you always apologize? I speak only of the less educated, who do not understand that customs differ. You will visit the museum, or the park, and we will return to take you to dinner."

So that was all settled. It didn't occur to me until that moment that something else was settled. We were staying in Mexico. At least until after tomorrow.

With his usual tact, Ivan changed the subject, and he and Danny argued about Aztec art for a while. The argument was good-humored; Danny expressed himself with less vigor than he had done at the museum, and, while Ivan defended his ancestors' taste, he did it dispassionately.

"I agree with you about Coatlicue," he said. "But taste is a subjective thing. Even you would find some of the animal sculpture attractive, I think."

"Like the dancing dogs," I said. "They're darling."

"They are probably fighting dogs," Ivan said, grinning.

"I don't care what they're doing, they're cute. I want to take them back with me."

"Great," Danny said. "For some cute dogs I'm expected to rob the museum? I bet they have a better security system than the Bank of Mexico."

"Copies, copies," I said. "They're very popular, I've seen them in shops all over town. Your friend Carlos, at Teotihuacan, has the nicest ones."

"And for you they will be less expensive," Ivan promised. "We will go back there, one day next week."

The table was a table for four, and we had taken the chairs that faced the window. None of us saw the man approaching; he must have been standing there for some time before Ivan noticed him.

"Hi," he said, grinning boyishly.

His hair was tousled. He didn't look boyish, though, he looked unkempt. He had on a tie, but the knot was halfway up under his ear. Already I was watching that tie as if it were a barometer: Tie here, thirty rabbits. Tie up there, two hundred rabbits. . . .

"Hello," Ivan said. "And good night."

"Now, don't be that way." He held out his hand to Danny, who took it, automatically. "Tom Andres. Fellow traveler. Get it?"

"Uh-huh," Danny said, viewing him with fascinated distaste.

Andres pulled out the empty chair and sat down.

"Buy you a couple of drinks," he said. "Waiter! Brandy all around. None of your local junk, either. French."

"No thanks," Danny said. "I don't drink."

The comment was unnecessary, untrue, and poor tactics. Andres whooped with laughter.

"You're missing a lot of fun, pal. Or do you turn on some other way? Buy you a couple of joints, then."

Danny got out of his chair so fast it almost overturned. Ivan caught it; he had moved just as quickly and more smoothly.

"We were just leaving," he said quietly, and gestured.

The waiter came hurrying up. Ivan spoke softly to him in Spanish, and the man's hostile stare focused on Andres, who was struggling to get out of his chair. All at once there were two other waiters closing gently in on us. Andres finally got to his feet, rocking back and forth, but he wasn't as drunk as he pretended to be. He began to retreat. Two of the waiters fell in behind him and I heard him muttering to himself,

". . . fella tries to be friendly. . . . Helluva note, all Americans in some damn foreign country . . ."

When he had left the room, Ivan relaxed.

"Sit down and have more coffee," he said. "We don't want to follow him out."

He pulled out Danny's chair and Danny subsided into it. He was looking queer.

"Fuzz," he said.

"What?" I stared at him.

"Fuzz. That guy Andres."

"You're crazy."

"Crazy, hell, I can spot 'em. Didn't you catch that crack about turning on?"

Ivan, chin in his hand, studied Danny curiously.

"There is much talk of marijuana these days. It means nothing."

"You know the guy," Danny said stubbornly. "What makes you so sure he's not a cop?"

"He doesn't act like one," I said. "He's a drunken, skirt-chasing bum."

"So what's out of character about that?"

"Oh, forget it," I said wearily. "Forget him. You're paranoidal, Danny."

"Sure I am. People who are persecuted by storm troopers and fascist laws get paranoidal, hadn't you noticed?"

"Danny." I was getting angry. "Danny, were you planning to smuggle some grass back into the States when we go home?"

"Not anymore I'm not. That guy has his eye on me."

"It would be wiser not to," Ivan said, giving me a warning glance. "I still think that was a coincidental remark. But you would be taking a risk with your customs officials if you attempted amateur smuggling. These men know hiding places you have never thought of, and they are now much more suspicious of students."

Danny nodded thoughtfully. He was more susceptible to Ivan's reasoned arguments than to my anger—naturally. If I just kept my big mouth shut and didn't get him mad . . .

Ivan gestured for the waiter and Danny signed the check. We decided to go for a walk, and Danny went up to get my sweater while Ivan and I walked down to the lobby. Ivan said,

"May I give you more officious advice?"

"Sure."

"Don't be angry with Danny, I think he will follow my suggestions more readily than yours. But—"

"I know," I interrupted. "I was thinking the same thing."

"But," he went on steadily, "do not leave Mexico before searching your own luggage. Search it thoroughly."

I stumbled, and Ivan caught my arm.

"No," I said. "No, he wouldn't do that. Not Danny."

"I am concerned about him. Users of drugs claim that they become more loving of their fellowmen. But their behavior does not support that claim. For the drug they will do harm, betray trust, hurt those who love them. I think my warning impressed him. But he might think that a pretty girl would stand a better chance of passing through customs without being searched."

"But—drugs!" I said incredulously. "Danny doesn't take drugs. He just smokes pot now and then. It isn't addictive."

"Not physically, no. Have you never heard of psychological addiction? You know Danny better than I, you would know whether his home life, his childhood, was sufficiently disturbed to make him susceptible to that sort of addiction."

While I struggled with that indigestible thought, he added,

"Those who wish to see marijuana legalized often compare it with alcohol. They do not seem to realize that the very validity of the comparison negates their argument. Alcoholism is a dangerous disease, dangerous to the individual and to society. Overindulgence in marijuana produces similar dangers."

"I've got to get him away from here!"

"You cannot run away geographically from a psychological weakness. And how can you make him go? He is not your child. Will you have him arrested?"

I was silent. There was no answer to that one.

"I am being overly concerned," Ivan said, squeezing my arm gently. "Give me a few days, let me talk to him. There is no harm in an occasional cigarette, if that is all he takes."

"I don't know," I said miserably. "He's acting peculiarly. That business tonight, about Mr. Andres . . ."

"I know, that was one of the things that made me wonder. But it is normal for people who plan to break the law to be wary of policemen!"

"But Andres, of all people! He's such a shabby human being."

"Now it is you who are being illogical," Ivan said. "If a law-enforcement agent were trying to win the confidence of criminals, that is precisely the impression he would wish to create."

III

Danny was charming the rest of that evening. We spent it in a funny little café, something like a nightclub, something like a neighborhood bar, where Ivan seemed to know everybody and a boy with a beard recited poetry to the music of a guitar. I didn't understand a word, but it sounded beautiful.

We got back to the hotel fairly early. Ivan admitted he was a little tired, and I know I was. It had been a full day. I hardly had time to close the door of my room before the phone rang.

I couldn't imagine who could be calling, unless Ivan had something else he wanted to say about Danny. But the voice, though distorted by the poor quality of the connection, was a woman's voice.

"Señora Oblensky?" I repeated unbelievingly. "Oh. Yes, of course. How are you?"

"I am well. But he, your father, is not. He wishes to see you. You will come, at once?"

I knew, in that moment, that George was wrong. It was not the blood tie, nor the casual cell he had contributed to my creation that made my heart turn over. You can't throw out twelve years of love like a pair of worn-out shoes.

"Is he hurt?" I gasped. "Sick? What happened?"

"Sick, very sick. He must see you."

"But how can I—"

"The doctor is coming. He lives not far away from you and he will stop for you. It is an American car, a Pontiac, black. If he cannot wait before the hotel he will turn down the street to the right, opposite the Monument, and await you there. Dr. Mendoza. Please hurry."

She hung up.

Now this was one of the times when I could have used that course in how to survive. Maybe a person with common sense would have stayed right where she was. But even now, looking back on it, I don't see how I could have taken the risk. In the back of my mind was all the information that made illness so horribly plausible—the hints in the anonymous letters, the sight of him as he had looked that very afternoon, beaten and worn and old.

What is common sense, after all? The ability to see what you shouldn't have done, last time. You don't expect things to happen to you—not to *you*. Almost everyone has it—that illogical sense of personal invulnerability. If we really comprehended the perils that press in on us, every waking moment, we'd never get out of bed.

I keep making excuses like that.

I wasn't completely foolish, though. After I had grabbed my coat and purse, I knocked on Danny's door.

After a while I knocked again. Still no answer. I pounded on the door, hard, twice more before I was forced to admit defeat. He couldn't be that deeply asleep, not so soon. He must have gone out.

His failure to respond completed my demoralization. I ran toward the elevator. Maybe I could catch up with him. Maybe he had just gone downstairs for a cup of coffee, or across the street to Sanborn's, to get something to read. I couldn't waste any more time looking for him, the doctor might not wait, and if George—if I missed my last chance to talk to him because of a treacherous, lying rat who wasn't even around when I needed him. . .

It was unreasonable, what I was thinking; but I was in no mood to be reasonable. After a hundred years or so the elevator finally came, and I helped push it down, muttering under my breath every time it stopped. I glanced around the lobby as I passed through, but there was no sign of Danny; the only familiar face I saw was that of Tom Andres, who was slumped down in one of the chairs looking as if he were asleep.

There were two black cars among the minor traffic jam

in front of the hotel. One was a small foreign car, a Fiat or something, and the other contained a loud, hilarious party of tourists. I asked the doorman, but he shook his head; so many cars, so many people coming and going. . . .

I started off along the access road beside the Reforma. Sanborn's was closed. Where had Danny gone, at this hour? I shook my head angrily—I didn't have any anxiety left over to waste on him—and went faster. I found a side street going off to the right; it had to be the one Ines had mentioned. Cars lined it in solid rows. Farther down the block there seemed to be a car double-parked. It was long and black, which fit the general description.

I turned into the street. Even then I had no sense of alarm. The street was deserted, and fairly dark; but I was still close to the gaudy lights and traffic of the boulevard.

The sound of the traffic was actually a disservice; it drowned out lesser sounds. I didn't notice the footsteps until I had gone some distance. Then—too late—my inefficient sixth sense sounded the alarm. I turned.

There wasn't much light, but I didn't need to see his face to know him. I recognized the shoulders. He came at me in a rush, but not quite fast enough; I had time for a loud yell before his hands found my face. They fumbled. Perhaps my scream surprised him. Anyhow, I had time for a second scream, and this one made the echoes roll.

The next time the hand reached for my mouth I bit it. I wasn't afraid; all my anger and worry and frustration boiled over into an exhilarating paroxysm of sheer fury. I didn't have breath enough to scream anymore, but it was almost a pleasure having something I could hit, with my fists, as hard as I could. I kicked him in the shins, which was a mistake, because I forgot I was wearing sandals. He grabbed my wrists, and I pulled my head back and brought it forward. It hit him on the nose.

That was where I made my second mistake. A blow on the nose is not incapacitating, it hurts just enough to make the victim good and mad. An arm that felt like a large python coiled around my shoulders and squeezed. His other hand still held my left wrist; it twisted sharply, and I shrieked again, this time with pain.

But this time there was a response. A light hit me full in the face, and a voice yelled something in Spanish. Andres let out a single, heartfelt expletive, and dropped me. Things got a little blurry after that. I thought I heard a car engine start up, but it might have been the ringing in my ears.

I sat on the sidewalk with my legs doubled up under me until the policemen arrived—beautiful tanned policemen in beautiful tan uniforms. They had a flashlight.

One of them didn't speak any English. He heaved me to my feet and crooned at me solicitously. The other man had a few words. He sounded like a list of useful phrases for tourists.

"Who? Where? What? You are hurt?"

"No," I said, answering the question that required only one word.

"Who?" my rescuer began again. "What . . . ?"

I did hurt, in fact. There was a cut on my lip, where it had got mashed against my teeth, and my shoulders and wrists were sore.

"Tom Andres," I said. "That's who. Damn his eyes!"

The monolingual cop said something, and the other one shrugged. I could see we weren't getting anywhere, so I tried again.

"Hotel," I said, wishing to God I had taken Spanish instead of World Philosophy in my junior year. "Hotel—that one, I live there. Take me home. . . ."

And then I did what I probably should have done in the first place, since nobody could understand me anyhow. I burst into tears.

IV

I created a sensation in the lobby when I limped in, surrounded by cops—and believe me, two policemen can surround you pretty thoroughly. I thought for a minute that the clerk behind the desk, a very prim young man with a British accent, was going to faint. One fat woman shook her head and said in an audible voice, "See, Frank, they can't keep out of trouble, these kids, even here."

One thing, though. Ivan's friend the guide was right about people. Most of them are pretty nice. Half a dozen total strangers asked if they could do anything. They weren't even all Americans. A German doctor and a Bolivian lawyer offered their services, and I had to fight off an international brigade of middle-aged ladies who wanted to bandage me, baby-sit me for the night, and feed me everything from sleeping pills to Grandma's special toddy for jangled nerves.

The desk clerk, who told me to call him Al, turned out to be another testimonial to the human race. After he had translated, explained, tactfully disposed of unwanted Samaritans, and chaperoned the hotel doctor while he checked me for broken bones, he shooed everybody out of the room; and then he said, addressing the thin air above my head,

"Your friend, Mr. Linton—don't you think he'd want to be let in on this? I'll call him, if you like."

"Never mind," I said. "He isn't there. He's out."

"His key isn't in the box."

"Then he must have taken it with him, he's always doing that."

"I didn't see him leave. Of course I might not have noticed. . . ."

"I'm sure he's out."

"Well, then, I'll watch out for him when he does come in."

"Please don't say anything to him. He isn't—I mean, we aren't—I mean, there isn't anything he can do about it. It can wait till morning."

Al looked dubious, but he left, after telling me to pick up the phone and yell if I got nervous, he would be on duty all night.

As soon as he was gone I picked up the phone, but I didn't call him. It rang and rang on the other end before someone answered. The whole household must have been asleep. I finally got Ines. They had to wake her up, her voice was blurred with sleep. It wasn't sleepy by the time I got through. She started asking me questions. I didn't answer them. I just hung up. I had found out what I wanted to know.

My father was perfectly well. She hadn't called me. No one at the house had called me that night.

CHAPTER 8

I WAS sitting on the edge of the bed, watching the bruises on my wrist turn purple, when I heard the sound at the door. It wasn't a knock. It was more like some big dog scratching at the panel with his paws.

"Who's there?" I called out.

After a long interval there was an answer—or rather, a response. Someone spoke my name. I knew the voice. I got up and opened the door.

"Where have you been?" I asked.

Danny was so pale he looked frozen. The fair stubble along his jaw might have been ice crystals.

"Oh, blast," I said. "I told Al not to say anything. What wild tale did he tell you?"

Danny began to laugh.

"It couldn't have been that funny," I said, backing away from the door. "It wasn't funny, if you want to know. It was damned unpleasant."

He went on laughing. The sound wasn't loud, but it didn't stop.

"Come in and close the door," I said. "I've made enough of a spectacle of myself today without you getting hysterical. . . . Danny! For God's sake!"

He stopped laughing. I think I'd have slapped him if he hadn't; it was that bad. But he didn't move. I had to take him by the arm and pull him into the room. The truth had begun to dawn on me by then. It was an effort for me to touch him. Nor was it easy to move him. He didn't resist, but he didn't help. It was like pulling a big, inert mass of something dead. I closed the door and got Danny to a chair. As I tried to get him to sit down he started, epileptically, and struck at my hand.

"Ouch! Hurts. Sharp—you've got needles on your hands, needles and fire, red-hot electric wire fingers, plugged in. . . ."

The burst of insane energy left as abruptly as it had come. He fell into the chair and stared anxiously at me. I don't know what he saw; judging from his expression, it wasn't pretty.

"You hurt," he said querulously. "Don't touch me. Don't move me; I can't move. If I do, it will all fall apart, the whole damned thing. Crack right down the middle and crumble away, the pieces falling out into black empty space, spinning. . . . Don't you see, I've got to hold it together, it all depends on me, all the people falling out into space, screaming, and dogs. . . ."

I stood paralyzed, hearing his voice rise, watching his eyes widen till I could see the white all around the dark irises. The last word was a scream; he covered his face with his hands, and when he took them away his skin was gray and slimy with perspiration. He leaped up. I don't think he meant to hit me, but I couldn't move, and his outflung arm was pushing away terrible things. It struck me across the breast, hard enough to make me fall back onto the bed.

Danny staggered into the bathroom. After a minute I heard him vomiting.

I lay there on the bed and listened for a while, and then I got up and went after him. My legs felt like sticks, without joints at the knees. Danny was sitting on the floor. He kept gagging and choking, but nothing else came up.

I flushed the john and then I sat down on the floor beside him and turned his face toward me. My heart had moved up into my throat and was thudding away in there, blocking my breath.

His eyes were blind with sickness. No longer blue, they were so dilated they looked black.

"What was it, Danny? What did you take?"

"Oh, God," he groaned. "I feel terrible. . . ."

"What did you take?"

I tried to shake him.

"Buttons."

"Peyote?"

He started to cry.

II

There are worse kinds of hangovers than the ones you get from too much booze. When I woke up the next day, I felt sick before I remembered why I should. Then it came back to me, and I felt sicker.

I hadn't drawn the draperies the night before, and the sunlight pouring into the room had wakened me. I squinted at the clock and saw that it was after noon. I hadn't got into my bed until 4 A.M.

Danny's tears had not been tears of repentance or regret; they were just one of the symptoms of the mescaline. One of the guys at school used to brag about eating buttons. He was a theology student; at least that's what he called himself, his professors weren't so sure. Peyote, the little green button of a Mexican cactus, has been taken for generations by certain obscure religious sects. The active ingredient is mescaline, which is supposed to induce religious visions. I guess that's what Keith wanted—visions. He said he had them, but his descriptions weren't very lucid. He also mentioned that the buttons sometimes made him sick.

Danny was sick to his stomach for quite a while, but if he lay perfectly still he didn't throw up. He told me all about his symptoms after I got him back to his room. He told me all about everything. He talked as if he were being paid by the word. At first I tried to answer him, but it didn't take me long to realize that he wasn't interested in what anyone else said.

I was afraid to leave him, and afraid to call a doctor. The things he said weren't frightening, they were just incoherent and senseless. They must have made sense to him, because he kept insisting that I write everything down, every word he said. Once he called me Mother. I was scared, then; but that was the worst moment, after that he quieted down and I figured the stuff was wearing off. I wished to God I knew more about it. It was a hallucinogen, like acid, Ivan had said, but not so strong. How strong? And how much like LSD? I kept remembering the boy who had walked out of the window on his way to London. I didn't dare leave until Danny had fallen into what seemed to be natural slumber, and before I left I locked the window and searched the room. He used an electric shaver, so that was all right, but I took the glasses out of the bathroom, and even his bottle of after-shave. The precautions probably weren't good enough; but I was out on my feet by that time. Tired as I was, I didn't find it easy to get to sleep.

The memories came flooding into my mind the way the sunshine poured in the window, but dark, not light—cold and dark. I had so many things to worry about I couldn't concentrate on one. My mind kept jumping from Danny to my father to Tom Andres. I hated all of them. I could have watched them step under the guillotine, one after the other, and counted heads like Madame Defarge, without dropping a stitch of my knitting.

I felt a little more human, and humane, after I'd showered and dressed. When I opened my door, there was Danny.

He was propped against the wall, and I knew he'd been standing there for a long time.

"Hi," he said.

His eyes were clear and blue, and uncertain.

"Hi," I said.

I walked down the hall and he trailed me, like a big dog.

"I'm sorry about last night."

"Me, too."

"Oh, come on. Don't be like that."

"Like what?" I punched the button for the elevator as if it had been somebody's eyeball. "Is that all you can say, I'm sorry?"

The elevator arrived, so he didn't answer. We went down together like strangers, staring straight ahead. He was pretty subdued; he waited until I got some coffee inside me before he tried again.

"I freaked out," he said.

"You sure did."

"What did I say? Did you write it down?"

"No. You said that the universe was a vast cesspool of love."

"What?"

"That was your best effort. You said it seventy-nine times. I counted. While I was cleaning up the rug where you threw up."

His eyes fell.

"I said I was sorry."

"You took that stuff as soon as you got into your room," I said, trying to harden my heart. "You ignored me when I knocked."

"I swear I didn't hear you! I must have been in the shower."

"I could have used your assistance. Or do you remember anything about last night except your happy hallucinations?"

"I know about your adventures, if that's what you mean. In fact, I talked to the fuzz this morning. They haven't found Andres yet. . . . Are you going to press charges, or whatever they do down here?"

"My immediate impulse is to skip town and forget the whole thing," I admitted.

"Leave Mexico? Hell, Carol, that would make me feel guilty."

"Oh, dearie me, I wouldn't want that to happen."

He gave me a reproachful look, and I said wearily,

"Okay, forget it. Why should you feel guilty? You aren't the only worm in the apple."

"I know, but I haven't helped. Look, honey, we've got another week. Let's make it the greatest, huh? Wipe out all the bad trips. I promise, I won't take any more peyote. I'll even kick the grass if that will make you happy."

"You really mean it?"

"I was curious, that's all. I wanted to see what it was like. Now I know. I'll be honest," Danny said, giving me another of those candid, blue stares. "If I'd had a good trip I might be tempted to take off again. It was interesting. But it isn't worth heaving my guts out."

That was believable. It came closer to convincing me than any solemn oath would have done.

"Well . . ."

"I love you," Danny said softly.

A week earlier I would have returned the compliment. Now I just smiled. Even that was an effort.

"Hey," Danny said suddenly. "I've got to hurry. Ivan's picking me up in ten minutes."

"Oh, yes. The bullfight."

"Yeah. You'll be sorry you didn't come."

He vibrated with health and anticipation. It wasn't fair; the drug fiend was cheery and hearty and I, the virtuous Florence Nightingale type, could hardly stand up. I yawned violently.

"Poor baby," Danny said. "You're beat. No wonder. Look, you go up and rest. Take a nap, read. Keep your door locked and by the time Ivan and I get back you'll be all rested up and the fuzz will have your boyfriend Andres in the clink, and—"

"All for the best in the best of all possible worlds."

Danny escorted me upstairs, supplied me with literature, and kissed me good-bye. I heard him whistling as he went off down the hall.

I gave him fifteen minutes. Then I threw the book he had given me across the room, got my purse, and went out.

The Reforma was crowded with Sunday strollers, middle-aged tourists in summer suits and local couples, gay in their best finery. I joined the promenade, under the shade of the tall trees in the center of the boulevard. I walked slowly, because I had a lot of thinking to do.

This was the first time I had come up against one of the hardest facts of life: that there are few blacks and few whites, only shades of gray. When people make a decision they think they are basing it on facts. But facts are hard to come by. You have to decide which statements to accept and which to reject, and usually you take the word of the people you think you can trust.

There was no one I could trust.

It wasn't Danny's copping out the night before that made me doubt him, it was his copping out when I needed him. Coincidence? Maybe. But the one undeniable fact in the whole confused situation was the fact that someone wanted to get me out of the hotel.

It might have been Ines, acting for herself or for someone else. Once she knew the attempt had failed, she would certainly deny having made the call.

The obvious villain was Mr. Andres. But the longer I thought about it, the less obvious he seemed. Surely the plot was unnecessarily complex, if all Andres wanted was to drag me off to his lair and ravish me. For one thing, he had to have an accomplice; the voice on the phone had been a woman's voice. And what woman is going to help a man attack another female? His mother? His wife?

It was ridiculous. Either Andres had interfered with someone else's kidnap scheme, or he wanted me for reasons which had nothing to do with my sex appeal.

Drugs. They were no longer a casual background motif,

they had become the dominant theme, overshadowing my father's past and Danny's present. Even Uncle Jaime's pots of marijuana were part of the pattern. I could visualize that pattern Ivan had talked about, like a great tapestry, with the figures of the people who were involved interwoven with the overall design of narcotics—leafy stems of the cannabis plant, squat green shapes of cacti, wound around with the twining stems of the morning-glory plant, whose shining black seeds are also passports into the kingdom of psychedelic insight. That kingdom of the mind which William James described so well: "There snake and seraph abide side by side." Madness and mysticism, terror and rapture. . .

For the first time I had seen someone when he was turned on, and I didn't like it. I didn't like watching Danny vomit and groan and babble. I didn't like the feeling that he was gradually but inexorably drawing back from me, from contact and warmth and communication. He kept talking about love. But his chief concern was for his own feelings, his own satisfaction.

Maybe he had been in the shower the night before. Maybe he had just swallowed down his dose of chopped up green buttons and didn't bother to answer the door. Or maybe—maybe someone had told him not to answer it.

I never realized how much I counted on Danny until he wasn't there. It was like having a stepping stone in the middle of a swamp suddenly sink down into the muck when you put your weight on it. There was nobody else. Helen had done all the right things—bought me pretty clothes, made me eat and sleep and wash at the proper times, given me her antiseptic lectures on "The Facts of Life." But she had never taught me trust. If I had trusted her I would never have come on this trip, searching for a man who didn't exist. George? My confidence in him was the first thing to be destroyed. I stood on a crowded boulevard, with the sun shining and a soft breeze lifting my hair, and it was like standing naked in the middle of a desert.

I turned suddenly and ran to the curb, my arm lifted to hail the green-and-white taxi I had seen coming up. It stopped. A carful of brown faces stared at me, some smiling, some blank; a fat lady in a black dress and black mantilla lifted her little boy onto her lap and shifted over.

"Gracias," I said. She smiled at me and the child stared solemnly out of big black eyes.

As the cab swerved out into the traffic I looked back. The man who had been following me from the hotel was waving at another cab. He didn't look like a businessman today, he wore the rough cotton clothing of a laborer. But the gray hair and the face were familiar. His was the same face I had seen twice before: in the hotel, the first day we arrived, and in the booth next to mine at Sanborn's, when I waited for Danny.

When I got out of the taxi, at the end of its route, I didn't bother looking to see whether he was still on my trail. I assumed he was—my attempt at evasion had been spontaneous and unskillful. Chapultepec Park was up ahead, so I decided to take a ladylike Sunday stroll in the park. A lot of other people had the same idea. I wanted people around me, the more people, the better. Not that I thought there was safety in numbers. I was lonely.

Eventually I found myself in front of the Anthropological Museum, so I went in and climbed the stairs to the second floor, which is the ethnological section. There were models wearing local costumes from different areas, and groups of models demonstrating handicrafts, weaving, pottery making, and so on. Even models of people were better than hostile Aztec statues.

I had been there for about half an hour, I think, when I looked up from a display of masks and saw Tom Andres across the room.

I gave him a big friendly smile. I raised my hand and wriggled my fingers coquettishly. I made beckoning gestures.

The look on his face almost compensated for what he had done to me the previous night. He glanced over his shoulder, to make sure I wasn't hailing someone behind him, and then came toward me, treading warily.

"Still on the loose, I see," I greeted him.

"Now, look, Miss Farley, I don't know what you're up to, but before you do anything, let me apologize. I was drunk last night, I didn't mean anything by it. . . . Just kidding around, you know what I mean?"

He looked different. His hair stood on end and his shirt had a button off; his brown suit was even more wrinkled than the gray one had been. The difference was not in his appearance; it was in my mind.

"Just do me one favor," I said. "Quit lying to me. You don't have to tell me anything you don't want me to know, but for God's sake stop inventing unbelievable tales. You weren't drunk last night, you weren't drunk the other times, and you haven't the faintest interest in me personally."

"How do you know I wasn't drunk?"

"Look, friend, any girl my age has met up with a few dirty old drunks. They reek of the stuff, you can smell them a block away. You weren't rough enough, either. A man may be a perfect little gentleman when he's sober, but he loses his manners when he gets stoned."

"All right, drop it," he said angrily. "The tough act doesn't suit you."

"Sorry. I'll have to practice. Maybe a cigarette dangling from the corner of my mouth."

He didn't smile, but his mouth relaxed. It made him look younger.

"Who are you mad at?" he asked.

"Nobody. Everybody."

"So maybe I was just trying to escort you home. If you're dumb enough to go sightseeing in the middle of the night —"

"I got a telephone call," I said, watching him. "From a friend of yours?"

"What are you talking about?"

He might have been pretending. Words lie. But I caught the sudden unguarded flicker of his eyelids when I mentioned the phone call, and I was pretty sure that it came as a surprise to him. When you're friends with a pothead you learn to notice signs like that.

"Never mind," I said. "But I'd take it as a favor if you would either tell me what you're after, or get off my back."

I started walking toward the exit, and he walked with me.

"What's so unbelievable about a guy chasing a pretty girl?"

"We've already discarded that theory, remember? You know," I said, half to myself, "I'm beginning to think Danny's right about you."

"And what does Danny think?"

"He thinks you're fuzz. A policeman."

"I know the word," he said drily. "What a compliment."

"It isn't meant as a compliment."

"Is that right? What makes your friend Danny so nervous about cops?"

"You know the answer to that," I said. "Or, if you don't—forget it. But it can't be Danny you're after, he's small-fry. Is it George?"

I looked at him, hoping to catch him off guard again, but this time he was ready for me. I guess the buildup had warned him. There was not even an eyelash flicker to mar the perfect blankness of his face.

"George Farley. My father. You know who he is."

I stopped in front of an exhibit of woven palm ornaments. They were pretty things, shaped like stars or like snowflakes.

"So you're George's daughter."

"You knew that."

"I was pretty sure. Makes a nice little human-interest story, doesn't it? 'Now that she is a beautiful young woman, Miss Farley seeks a reconciliation with her father, who ten years ago caused the tragic death of another beautiful young woman. . . .' That's not very good. I'll do better when I write it up."

"Are you trying to tell me that's what you're after? Common-garden-variety scandal?"

"I'm a newspaperman."

"And I'm the jolly green giant. A newspaper wouldn't buy that story; it's dead."

"Not with narcotics such a hot angle these days. Oh, it won't stand by itself, but it will make an interesting chapter in my exposé."

I stared unseeingly at the straw stars. Offerings to the gods in magical ceremonies, that was what they were—good-luck charms. Maybe I'd better buy a dozen and stick them on my door. His story was just plausible enough to be possible. I could believe it, if only because it was such a dirty motive.

"I'm leaving," I said. "Go ahead and snoop. But if you use my name I'll sue you."

"I will employ only conditional sentences and put 'alleged' in front of every noun." He followed me out the door and shook his head when I motioned him away. "I'll see you safely into a cab. You're too accident-prone."

"I wouldn't take any cab you got for me."

"Very wise. You don't object to my standing on the corner and watching?"

"It wouldn't do me any good to object. Obviously the police don't interfere with any of your activities."

We went down the stairs and through the courtyard in silence. As we left the museum he said abruptly,

"Something's worrying you. What's the matter?"

"Not a thing. I don't mind being grabbed, slugged, squashed—"

"Oh, hell, it isn't that, it can't be. You said I wasn't rough enough. . . . I didn't really hurt you, did I?"

I couldn't resist. I pushed up the wide copper bracelet and exhibited my wrist. The doctor had assured me it wasn't sprained, but the bruises were a handsome color, almost black.

I walked down the steps, leaving him standing there. At the corner I got a taxi. I didn't turn back to look, but I knew he was watching me.

In the role of a ruthless scandalmonger and/or sex maniac, Mr. Andres was a lousy actor. A man who was genuinely ruthless wouldn't have looked so dismayed at the sight of a few bruises.

III

I got back to the hotel before Danny did, which was just as well; I was in no mood for arguments and recriminations, or even for explanations. When the Dynamic Duo arrived they said they had stopped at a café to discuss the ballet of the bulls, and get it out of their systems so they wouldn't bore me with it. We went out to dinner, and everybody had a fine time. When we got back to the hotel I found another of those notes in my box. This one was not from Ines. I recognized the handwriting, which was strange, because I hadn't seen it for a long time. It gave me a queer feeling.

I felt even queerer after I'd read the note. Ivan and Danny were standing there, pretending not to stare, but they weren't pretending very hard. I handed the note to Ivan.

He read it in a glance, and a quick smile of genuine pleasure spread over his face.

"I will not say I told you so," he said, and gave the note to Danny.

"He wants us to come and stay there," Danny said, as if we hadn't already read it. "At your place, Ivan. Your mother—"

"My mother adds her invitation." Ivan's smile stiffened; then he recovered himself. "Yes, I am surprised, not at the invitation, but at its arrival just now. I knew that you would be asked."

"That's nice," Danny said. "The more I think about it the better it sounds. The prices here are pretty steep."

"I'll come tomorrow and help you move," Ivan said.

"I don't know," I said.

They both looked at me in surprise.

"But why not?" Ivan said. "What could be more natural than such an invitation?"

I almost burst out laughing. It was the funniest question I'd heard for weeks.

CHAPTER 9

UNCLE JAIME'S pots of pot were doing splendidly. When I wandered out into the courtyard he was watering them, using one of those long-spouted tin watering cans. His cute, round figure was a bit feminine; from behind he looked like a mannish little old lady in slacks tending her roses.

I thought my sandaled feet made no sound, but he had ears like those of a wild animal; I had already noticed, in the few days we had been at the house, how alert he was. He looked up as I approached and beamed at me. He always beamed at me. Sometimes I had the feeling that his were the only genuine smiles in the house.

"Aphids?" I asked. "Black spot?"

He understood and, what's more, he got the joke. Instead of explaining solemnly that cannabis doesn't suffer from black spot, he burst into one of his fits of sputtering laughter—more laughter actually than the feeble witticism deserved.

"Sit down, sit down," he said when he had recovered himself. "Where is Danny today?"

"Looking at bulls. He and Ivan have looked at bulls

every day. Or, if Ivan has to work, he drops Danny off at some ranch where he can look at bulls by himself."

I sat down on one of the benches and Uncle Jaime sat down beside me.

"I regret," he said sadly. "It is dull for you, with the young men gone. But how nice for me. It is not so often now that I have the undivided attention of a young lady who is both beautiful and intelligent."

You could say that Uncle Jaime's compliments were not subtle. I loved them.

"We have had good talks," he went on. "Have we not?"

"Yes, we have, and I've enjoyed them more than I can tell you. You have made Mexico come alive for me."

"But how beautiful," he said softly; I was touched to see that his black eyes were luminous with tears. "How beautiful, and how kind that you should say that."

"I mean it."

"I know." Uncle Jaime reached into his pocket and unfolded a huge white handkerchief. He mopped his eyes, without embarrassment, and turned another beam full on me. "We are sentimental, we Latins," he explained. "We weep, we shout, we sing. It is much healthier than your northern repression. No wonder your men suffer from nervous disorders."

"You may have something there," I admitted.

"I do not wish to be parochial—perhaps I am prejudiced—but I think Latin men make better husbands."

It wasn't the first time he had dropped this particular hint—if you could call that unsubtle suggestion a hint—but I wasn't prepared to take it seriously.

"Sir, are you proposing marriage?" I asked.

He grinned broadly.

"If I were forty years younger—ah, no, if I were a mere twenty years younger!—I would now be on my knees."

"And if you were twenty years younger I might accept. But I'm afraid no one else interests me. I don't think I'll get married, not for a long time anyway."

Uncle Jaime relapsed into disappointed silence. I leaned back against the trunk of the tree. We had sat like this before, in the companionable silence which can be more genuinely friendly than conversation.

Poor Uncle Jaime. He was incurably romantic, and I knew I ought to be flattered at his desire to get me married off to his nephew. Fortunately, since I was not in love with Ivan, I was sure the idea was limited to Uncle Jaime. Ivan still made gallant speeches, but I knew they were meaningless. He had no more interest in me than I had in him. Which was just as well, because I couldn't imagine joining this menagerie in the capacity of Ivan's wife. It was complex enough now, what with George—

It was like ESP, the way he always appeared when I was thinking about him. He came across the patio, moving a little stiffly; he admitted to having a touch of rheumatism. He seemed to me to have aged just in the last few days. There was a kind of fretful anxiety about the way he always looked at me, the way he was looking now.

"Carol, where have you been? I thought we were going to get those notes finished this afternoon."

"I thought you were still taking your siesta." I stood up, brushing at my skirt, which was covered with little yellow flowerlets fallen from the tree. "I'll come right now."

"Always you make the poor child work," Uncle Jaime complained lazily. "Your foolish book can wait another week, can it not?"

"Carol doesn't mind." My father's anxious eyes were fixed on my face. "Do you, Carol?"

"No, of course not."

I followed him into the house. Perhaps I was overanxious myself, in my desire to please him; but the change in him was so remarkable I couldn't get used to it.

This was our third day at the villa. When we arrived that first afternoon, bag and baggage, under Ivan's supervision, George was waiting. He had come down to the gate to greet me.

It was a formal greeting, an awkward handclasp and a peck on the cheek; but I hadn't expected even that much, after our last meeting. And when we went in among the trees, leaving Ivan and Danny to deal with the luggage, he did something that shook me all the way down to my shoes. He stopped in the middle of the path and put his arms around me. His clasp was so tight it hurt, and his breathing sounded like that of a man in pain who is trying not to cry out.

The approach of the others ended the embrace, and since then he had been affectionate, in a stiff, self-conscious way; but nothing had come anywhere near the warmth of that moment on the path. Yet that one moment was enough. It didn't wipe out the past, nothing can ever do that; but it gave hope of a new beginning.

George's study was the room that had been the library of the villa. It was the best-kept room in the house, and I rather thought that Ines herself kept it tidy. The tiled floor gleamed with wax, the dark chairs and tables were dusted daily. The bookshelves lining three of the four walls were rich with leather-bound volumes. Whatever other antique treasures had been sold to buy tortillas and beans—and the empty spaces in the house suggested such a necessity—the books had been jealously preserved. Maybe they weren't worth much, but my respcet for Ines went up another notch when I noticed them.

George had set up an old typewriter on a table near his enormous carved desk. Typing is one of the few practical skills I possess; for a couple of summers I worked at the credit office at Helen's store. When George found out I could type, he was delighted.

"I'm writing a book," he explained. "On pre-Columbian art. But my notes are in terrible condition and my typing is pure hunt and peck. If you wouldn't mind . . ."

Naturally I said I wouldn't mind.

I sat down at the typewriter while he rummaged around the desk, muttering to himself.

Uncle Jaime's question—why can't the book wait—had a touch of malice. It was obvious that the book had been years in preparation. George had masses of notes, but nothing beyond that stage; it was rather pathetic, busy work, with no end in sight. Certainly it didn't pay anything. I learned later that he had a small income, from an annuity, just enough to provide for his personal expenses.

George finally found what he was looking for and gave it to me—a sheaf of dog-eared papers closely covered with his abominable handwriting. I squinted at the top page. It seemed to be notes on Zapotecan culture.

"I didn't have a pen that day," George explained diffidently. "I'm afraid it's pretty smudged. . . ."

"I think I can manage. You always said I was the only one who could read your handwriting."

Another mistake. I had done it before, and his reaction had made the unspoken law clear: no talking about the past. He had closed it off, the good memories along with the bad. I had never referred to Ivan's revelations, and I assumed George thought I was still ignorant of the incident he found unendurable. But his refusal to remember anything, even the harmless memories, made our new relationship farcical. He treated me like a stranger, one for whom he had considerable affection, but not the child who had read and talked and played with him.

"Well," he said, after a long pause. "Let's see what you can do with this."

I wanted to bang my fists down on the keyboard of the typewriter, but I feared the aged relic wouldn't survive rough handling. Neither would George. Our new relationship wasn't perfect, but it was much better than anything I had a right to expect. I didn't dare jar its untested bonds with more demands.

"Right," I said, and began to type.

II

That night after dinner Ivan suggested that we go into the city. The idea was not well received. Ines pointed out that he had been working the last two evenings and needed his rest. George said I had promised to play chess with him. Even Danny yawned and said he wouldn't mind an early night himself.

It was Danny who ended up across the chessboard from George. He was a good player, and I was not. Chess players are probably the least sociable companions imaginable. Even bridge players sometimes talk, but every chess game I've ever seen is a study in paralysis. The players sit like life-sized models in a museum of ethnology; when one of them puts out a hand and moves a piece the effect is startling. They never talk. I suppose they're thinking.

Even Uncle Jaime, who was loquacious during the day, relapsed into silence after dark. I wondered whether he was enjoying the effect of his after-dinner marijuana cigar. Anyhow, that left me with Ines, and we had very little to say to one another. She was absorbed with her embroidery. After my early efforts in that field—pink-and-blue cross-stitched pillowcases—I found her work awe-inspiring. Her material was cream-colored velvet; her thread flashed gold in the firelight, or shone with deep crimson, and her stitches were so fine that, from where I sat on the couch beside her, I couldn't separate one delicate strand from the next. They formed a continuous surface, like paint. She told me what it was going to be: some kind of ecclesiastical garment.

Sprawled in his usual relaxed pose on the hearthrug, Ivan was so silent I thought he might be sulking over his mother's insistence that he stay at home. But his face wasn't sulky; it had a sleek look, half smiling, as if he were contemplating a pleasurable secret.

There was a fire in the giant hearth that night. The red light shone on Ivan's smooth black hair and smoldered along the folds of his dark shirt. It was a pleasure to look at him, he was so beautiful—the graceful pose, the slim brown hands and perfect profile. . . . Beautiful as a painting by Murillo, and rousing the same kind of detached admiration.

Feeling my gaze on him he looked up, and his smile widened.

"We are bad hosts," he announced to the company at large. "We do not entertain our guests."

Danny's hand moved, sweeping a white knight from its square, substituting his red bishop.

"I'm having a great time," he said.

"You, yes—you and your bulls," Ivan said amiably. "It is Carol who is neglected. What would she say, I wonder, to a few days in Acapulco? I offer her the best guide in Mexico; I have no false modesty, all the ladies tell me I am the best."

Ines's needle flashed into the firelight, plunging the crimson silk into the heart of the pattern.

"It is full of tourists, Acapulco," she said evenly. "All those naked bodies, roasting in the sun. . . ."

"Taxco, then," Ivan said. "Guadalajara, Puerto Vallarta, San Miguel de Allende—the de luxe tour, with an English-speaking guide, tested and licensed by the government of Mexico! Four days and five nights of carefree travel! You have, I believe, five more days?"

"Yes."

"Well, then?"

All at once it came over me—the certainty that the offer wasn't genuine, that it was only a move in a game. Moving out a queen into enemy territory to distract the other player from the hidden menace of rook and knight. As I watched Ivan's smiling face, I knew he had no intention of going anywhere. My eyes moved on . . . to the silent bulk of Uncle Jaime, motionless in his chair . . . to Ines, her profile as pure and unresponsive as the face of the Madonna in the cathedral, her needle darting like an exotic tropical bird, trailing brilliant plumage . . . to Danny, confident and smiling as he studied his next move . . . to George.

Was George the opponent for whom the queen was being displayed? He was the only person in the room who had responded, the only one, except Ivan, who was looking at me. The anxiety which I had seen come and go in his eyes was all over him now; his face was lined with it, his hands were clenched to hold it back.

"It's very nice of you, Ivan," I said, feeling my way like someone picking his footing across a swamp. "But I don't think . . . Danny?"

"It's up to you," Danny said agreeably, his eyes still on the board, where the little armies of red and white men had been decimated by casualties. "I'm having a swell time."

"I really haven't seen that much of Mexico City," I said. "I know we're intruding here. . . ."

"No," Ines said. The needle was moving faster, so fast it was almost a blur. "You do not intrude."

"Then I think we'll skip the tour. Thanks just the same, Ivan."

It was the right answer. I didn't know why it was right, but it was; I could tell from the way they responded. Ivan nodded, smiling, and George sagged visibly, shoulders and hands relaxing.

"I'm glad," he said. "I'd hate to lose my secretary."

"Check," Danny said. "Sorry, sir I guess you were distracted."

George looked down at the board. Casually he slid his rook into position.

"Check and mate," he said. "I'm afraid you were the one who was distracted."

III

Later, after everyone had gone to bed, I came back downstairs to look for a book. I wasn't in the mood for the one I had been reading.

There was a light in the living room, a brighter light than the glow of the dying fire. From the doorway I saw her, sitting alone in the silent room.

She looked hieratic, like a priestess or a nun, bent over a dedicated task. The room was cold, now that the fire had died; she wore a dark veil over her head and her black-clad arms held the glowing square of ivory cloth like a shield. Her arms were moving. There was the flash of a needle, but no following trail of crimson. In and out the slim steel went, slowly, ritually. The light spotlighted her hands, but I didn't need to see to know what she was doing. Earlier that evening, as she folded the cloth back into its box, I had caught a glimpse of the botched, unseemly work—the final sections she had embroidered. The flashing needle had moved with its usual speed, but at random, leaving great gaps. Now she was picking it out—like Penelope waiting for Ulysses, unweaving the section of tapestry she had woven during the day.

I avoided *tête-à-têtes* with Ines as a matter of general principle. It was something other than principle that prompted my retreat then—backward, step by step, never taking my eyes off Ines's bent head.

There were reasons why she might have made a mess of her embroidery that night. I thought of some of them, after I had reached the safety of the upstairs hall without being heard. The relationship between mother and son was peculiarly formal; I could easily believe that his unspoken contempt and her guilty pride might cover any form of twisted love or jealousy. Mothers may view a son's wife as a rival. If Ivan was pretending interest in me in order to hurt his mother . . . But I knew that wasn't the reason why her stitches had gone awry. They were the visible sign of the warped pattern of human lives in the old house.

The house had been wired for electricity, but the halls

were sparsely lit—a matter of economy, I assumed. I felt my way down two corridors before I reached my part of the house, where a dim bulb had been left on, to light me to the bathroom. The modernization of the villa had included indoor plumbing, but not to excess. Ines and I shared a bath.

We shared the same corridor, and we were the only ones on it. The sleeping arrangements would have satisfied an eighteenth-century duenna; girls on one side of the house, boys on the other. The house was so large that we could each have had our own separate wing. It had once been a convent, and passed into private hands in 1860, when Juárez's famous Reform Laws abolished religious orders. Since that time it had been remodeled so thoroughly that few traces of its original function were left; only the chapel remained, stripped of its former gold and rich ornaments, but containing a crucifix and altar. Ines used it for her private devotions. She was the only one who did.

She took me on a tour the day after we arrived, but I could never have found my way about if most of the house had not been closed up. Only the main section was in use; it was the part of the house farthest from the present patio, which was why it took María so long to totter out with afternoon tea. Most Mexican houses have one or two patios; this one had four. The oldest, which had formed the center of the first convent building, had been transformed by an eccentric hidalgo into a roofed Moorish garden. It was now Uncle Jaime's private sanctum.

Like the chapel, the huge stone-framed front door opposite the stairs was only used by Ines; at least she was the only one I ever saw pass through it. Ivan kept his car in the back, so it was natural for him to go that way, and Danny and I followed the same habit. I would have felt peculiar going out the great portal; it seemed to demand ladies in black lace mantillas, who had their carriages waiting.

The whole house affected me that way, in fact. It had no use for the likes of me. I kept thinking there ought to be secret passages behind the walls, with wraithlike people moving through them, living a secret life the outside world never suspected. There was one secret room, a kind of priest's hole, which had sheltered members of the proscribed religious orders after the Reform. It wasn't all that secret now; Ines showed it to me, a windowless, forlorn little cell in the east wing. There was a ghost, too. Her name was Doña Luisa, and she appeared on moonlit nights, looking out of one of the barred windows on the main facade. I never went up those dark stairs without expecting to see Doña Luisa strolling down the hall. I suppose even ghosts need a little exercise.

My room was pretty, and not as forbidding as the rest of the house. It was decorated in Baroque style. The figured satin on the walls was faded, and the gilt mirror frames were tarnished, but the sheets had a fresh fragrance no dryer can produce, and the room was immaculately clean. The windows were barred with delicate grillwork.

I had opened them before I went downstairs. When I came back into the room, the filmy white curtains were fluttering in the night breeze. It was chilly; I was glad to get into bed and pull the blankets up over my knees. Then I reached for the book I had not wanted to read.

It was called *The Drug Culture*. I had found it at Sanborn's the day we left the hotel.

The book was a collection of articles by various authorities—doctors, law-enforcement types, and psychologists. In an effort to sound impartial, the editor had included a few articles by people like Leary and Huxley—enthusiastically pro—but the majority were anti, and the effect was worse than depressing, it was gruesome. You kept thinking that they must be exaggerating; then the cold scientific chromosome patterns and statistical charts would give you another jab of terror and belief. But the main reason why the book depressed me was because it confirmed my growing fear.

To all outward appearances Danny had kept his word. I never saw him high, never spotted any obvious signs of drug use. But when you knew what to look for, the other, more subtle, signs were there. None of them were conclusive, that was just the trouble. If he didn't always shave, if his clothes weren't as immaculate as they had been—well, we were on vacation, taking it easy, and poor old María had enough to do without pressing his pants. If he wore sunglasses most of the time—the sun was very bright. And if he lost the first game of chess he had lost in two years, to a man who claimed to be rusty and out of practice—maybe he was being tactful to his host.

But they were all there, in the book: carelessness about personal appearance, dilated pupils, decrease in capacity for complex reasoning. Connected, by some authorities, with the excessive use of marijuana. Denied by others. That was the trouble, nobody seemed to be sure. Least of all me. I thought probably Danny wouldn't try mescaline again, not after being so miserably sick with it. But there were other instant panaceas available that didn't have the same disadvantages as mescaline.

I turned to an article about heroin, just to cheer myself up. I felt like someone whose brother is suffering from all the symptoms of gout, tuberculosis, and chicken pox: at least he doesn't have cancer. Heroin was for jerks, Danny always said.

One thing that struck me, in that article, was the amount of money involved in the hard drugs. Talk about profits! Ten kilos of raw opium from Turkey, where the best stuff is grown, costs about $350. To convert the opium to heroin reduces it to about ten percent of the original weight. Figure a kilo of heroin for ten kilos of opium. By the time the heroin gets to New York, after being cut several times with a cheap substance like milk sugar, it is worth almost $100,000 in sales to addicts. No, not a bad profit.

It was such a fascinating story that I almost forgot the horribleness of the end result. The poor, hard-working Turkish farmers, with their pretty fields of poppies, were performing a necessary, useful job, with the approval of their government; the existence of the sick and dying would be hellish without the opium derivatives. The Turkish government knows how many acres each farmer cultivates, and buys his entire crop. But, as every gardener knows, it's impossible to calculate precisely how large a crop you can get from an acre. Weather, soil conditions, and so on make for yearly variations. So, if the underpaid farmer stashes away part of his crop and sells it to the persuasive city slicker for double the legal rate, who can catch him—or blame him? He's never seen a junkie.

Pretty things, the poppies—white, pink and purple tulip-shaped blossoms, waving in the breeze. They must be hard to hide; still, with a profit like that, I wondered why more people in more countries didn't grow them and put the opium through the necessary processing—eliminate the expensive middle men. It turns out that it isn't that easy.

The opium comes from the bluish-green pod under the flower petals, and you have to know not only when to cut, but how. If you cut too soon, the oozy juice will be too thin; if you wait too long, the morphine will turn to codeine. If you cut too deep, the inner juices will water down the opium, but if your cut is too shallow, you won't get all the good stuff.

Still, if a Turkish farmer can learn how to do it, other people could. Producing the morphine base, the next step, seems simple too. All you need is a pot over a fire and a few simple chemicals such as lime and ammonium chloride. You end up with a brown-gray powder, which is the morphine base, and which amounts to about one tenth the volume of the original raw opium.

Then I got to the next step and I realized why few people have gone in for illegal heroin production in a big way. The step from morphine base to heroine requires a chemist and complex laboratory equipment. It's dangerous, too. Not only is the chemist exposed to the poisonous fumes produced by the conversion process, but, if the temperature is not precisely controlled, he can blow up the whole laboratory.

Nice bedtime reading. I turned out the light and finally fell asleep; and I dreamed I was visiting the pyramids of Teotihuacan, only they weren't pyramids of stone, they were heaps of gray-brown powder topped by a temple built out of shining white crystals. Temple base—morphine base. I can't even dream in conventional Freudian symbols.

IV

I decided to take the dream as an omen, and go back to Teotihuacan. Danny and Ivan were going to have lunch at some ghastly restaurant that was built around a bullring, so that you could watch the performance while you ate. I can't imagine a more unattractive combination.

They offered me a ride out to the pyramids, though, and I accepted; it wasn't far out of their way. Ivan said I could probably get a ride back into town with one of his friends in the guide business. I had met most of them, and they would be glad to oblige.

"I'd better make sure I have money enough for a taxi, just in case," I said, and investigated my wallet. "Gosh, I didn't realize I was such a spendthrift. Five dollars gone in three days. Danny, I hope you brought the traveler's checks."

He produced the little black folder.

"How much do you want? Fifty do you for today? How about a hundred? This is great, you know. Makes me feel so generous, doling out your own money to you."

"It's Helen's money," I said.

"Even better. Makes me a gigolo once removed."

Laughing, he put his arm around my shoulders, and a wave of sheer happiness washed over me. It was like the time before we came to Mexico, before my selfish stubbornness pushed us into George's mixed-up life. If Danny had been moody and withdrawn—we all have our moods, don't we? He was wearing sunglasses; so was I, so was Ivan. The sunlight is bright in Mexico. I started singing, "Let the sunshine in." Danny joined in, in his famous falsetto, and Ivan contributed a mellow baritone. We went on to "Age of Aquarius," and to other songs, everything from the Beatles to Gilbert and Sullivan. Ivan knew them all. I wondered if there was any subject that man hadn't mastered.

After they dropped me off I watched the car roar off

down the road, veiled in dust, and I almost wished I'd gone with them. Then I remembered the bulls, and was glad I hadn't.

The usual crowd of cars and drivers was gathered under the shade of the trees. I recognized some of the men, but I didn't want to get involved in conversation just then. As I turned to face the man-made mountain that soared up toward the sun, I felt again the odd sensation of coming home.

I climbed the Pyramid of the Sun and sat on top of it. I could picture myself telling Sue how I spent my vacation. "What did you do in Mexico?" "I sat on top of a pyramid." She already thought I was a little weird. At any rate, I'd have a nice tan to show off around the snowy prairies.

The view was even better this time because now I knew what I was looking at. I'd been there. Like looking down on your home town from a helicopter and spotting all the familiar landmarks. The Citadel square outlined by its low walls, with the Pyramid of Quetzalcoatl; the Avenue of the Dead and the Pyramid of the Moon with its templed plaza. People were brightly colored blobs, decorative, without identity: white blobs and black, blazing fuchsia and bright primrose, crimson and gold and green. The men were generally drabber blobs than the women. One in particular, near the steps of the pyramid—white shirt, khaki pants, a head of hair as brown and sun-bleached as the ground on which he stood.

The sun was high overhead. That was why I decided to go down; it was hot, and I was getting thirsty. My decision had nothing to do with the man waiting by the stairs.

The stairs divide at the bottom. I took the left-hand branch, out of perversity; he was standing on the other side.

He was watching me, though, and by the time I reached the ground he was there.

"What brings you back to Teotihuacan?" he asked, before I could speak. "Second time, isn't it?"

"I like it here."

There were little stands near the parking lot where you could buy soft drinks. I headed that way, with Mr. Andres trailing me.

"That's why you keep coming out here?" he asked. "Because you like it?"

"Yes."

"Weird," said Mr. Andres.

I said nothing. It seemed the best way to handle his impertinence—to be calm and affable and more or less silent. It was only partly effective. He didn't get mad, which I had hoped he would.

After I had drunk my Coke I started back toward the pyramid.

"Where are you going now?"

"All over."

"Mind if I come along?"

"Yes."

"How are you going to stop me?"

I stood still and meditated.

"Well," I said. "I could try complaining to the handsome guard I see over there."

"Yes, I guess you could."

"What would happen?"

Mr. Andres looked thoughtful.

"It's only a guess, but I think he would politely attempt to dissuade me from going in your direction."

"Let's find out," I said.

"How about a compromise? I'll trail you at a respectful distance, far enough away so that I don't interfere with your rapt contemplation of antiquities. That," he added, with a touch of malice, "is why you want to be alone, isn't it? So you can meditate in peace? Not because you have any illegal activities in mind."

"It's a deal," I said coolly. "Ten paces, not an inch less."

I left precipitately; if I had stayed any longer, his mocking smile might have provoked me out of my calculated calm. I didn't feel as cool as I looked. One of his remarks had shaken me. I had concocted a number of far-out theories to explain Mr. Andres and his ubiquity, but the idea that he might be suspicious of me had never occurred to me.

You really are too stupid to go out without a keeper, I told myself bitterly; you and your Girl Scout inagination. Naturally, if Andres suspected George of anything illegal, I was potentially guilty by association. Especially now that George had welcomed the long-lost child back into his paternal affections.

The implications of that last thought were so ugly I refused to face them. I walked fast, not only to shake off my evil thoughts, but to inconvenience Mr. Andres. The latter aim failed; when I came to rest in the Plaza of the Moon I was chagrined to observe that he wasn't even breathing quickly.

I sat down on a low stone wall, trying not to perspire. Andres sat down on another wall and stared solemnly at me. The distance between us, as nearly as my inaccurate senses could measure it, was almost exactly ten paces.

Our eyes met across twenty feet of dusty air. I got up, sooner than I had meant to, and walked away. Something had flared up between us in that wordless exchange of glances—not love at first sight, or anything so corny, just a mutual acknowledgment of how absurd we looked with our ten-pace limit. Whatever it was, I didn't want it to develop any further.

He cheated a couple of times, closing up the gap with a smooth speed that was unnerving. It happened whenever I got out of his sight, even momentarily—behind a section of wall, inside an enclosed chamber. The awful thing was, I got used to him. Later in the day, when I had hiked out to a place called Tepantitla, he had reduced the distance between us considerably.

Tepantitla, in case anyone wants to know, isn't in the temple area proper; it was part of the surrounding town, maybe a priest's house. The house has been restored, and it contains some remarkable murals. As I studied the mural which according to my guidebook shows the earthly paradise presided over by Tlaloc, the rain god, I wished Danny could see it. It was such a cheerful painting; the little people who filled up the wall from top to bottom, with a complete disregard of perspective, were having fun—swimming and splashing each other with water, chasing butterflies, picking flowers, singing and dancing. It was such a contrast to the gruesome statues Danny hated. But, I remembered, the people who built Teotihuacan weren't the Aztecs.

I must have spoken aloud.

"Nobody knows who they were," Andres said, right at my left ear. "But they must have been a kindly, civilized people. I've always suspected that this is where Queztalcoatl came to."

"I wonder where he came from."

"It's one of the most provocative myths in the world,"

Andres said. "A lot of ancient civilizations had similar stories about a great culture hero who led them out of barbarism and taught them the arts of civilization. But this one is so blasted circumstantial that it stirs up my imagination."

It didn't occur to me that this was an incongruous conversation to be taking place between pursued and pursuer. My own imagination is easily stirred up.

"Thor Heyerdahl thinks maybe he was an Egyptian," I said eagerly. "You remember, he sailed that boat—"

"Bloody fool," Andres said rudely. "The Egyptians didn't use papyrus boats, except to paddle back and forth across the Nile. They were first-class shipbuilders: wooden hulls, sails with yards and a mast that could be stepped, a full bank of rowers. And they never wore beards. Quetzalcoatl was a fair-skinned, dark-bearded man, all the legends agree on that. And what about the time gap? Egyptian culture was moribund long before 300 B.C., when Alexander conquered the country; it was all Greeks and Romans after that. The Classic period in Central America doesn't start till about 100 B.C.—"

"What about the Olmecs?" I demanded. "They were earlier than 100 B.C., and they were a big deal as far as culture goes."

Andres winced.

"Your vocabulary is terrible and so is your information. Forget about the Egyptians. It's much more likely that Quetzalcoatl was—"

Somebody laughed. He wasn't laughing at us. I never saw him, before or after—he was just a boy, standing with his girlfriend in front of the mural. But for a minute it sounded like Ivan's laugh. I don't know whether it struck Andres the same way, but it interrupted his intellectual enthusiasm. He stared for a moment, and then relaxed when he saw who was laughing; but the invisible barrier between us slid back into place and I wondered how I could have forgotten it, even under the influence of Quetzalcoatl. I left the room, and when Andres followed he was back to the agreed distance.

Tepantitla is close to one of the parking lots, so I went that way. My feet were dragging. The sun had gone in and the sky was a solid gray.

The crowd was thinning out; there were only three drivers waiting, but I recognized one of them—the melancholy man whom the lady from Schenectady had taken for her long-lost son.

Andres closed in again as we approached the parking lot.

"Going home now?"

"Home?" I said; and saw his eyelids betray him again. The man was breaking down; if he went on this way, he might even smile. "Yes, I'm going home."

"Want a ride?"

"Not with you."

Ivan's colleague greeted me gallantly, not quite kissing my hand, but looking as if he wanted to. He didn't have room in his car, but one of the other men had a bus tour, an entire chapter of the DAR or the Eastern Star or the PTA, and he said he'd be delighted to take me home. Sure, he knew where it was, the DAR would never know the difference and if they did he would point out a church along the way and tell them he was giving them an additional attraction. They were supposed to leave in about an hour, if I didn't mind waiting; could he buy me a Coca Cola, or a lemonade, or—

I declined the drink with my best manners. There was

something else I wanted to do, since I had an hour. This might be my last trip to Teotihuacan, and my money was burning a hole in my pocket.

Andres kept at a discreet distance while I arranged for my transportation, but when I started off again he was right behind me, my not so symmetrical shadow. I had to pass a group of souvenir stands, but none of the pottery was as nice as the things I remembered from Carlos's shop. Since he was a friend of Ivan, he might give me a discount.

There were several other customers in the shop. I looked them over, with the suspicion that was becoming second nature, but they were all ordinary-looking tourists except for one man—the tall blond one who was one of Ivan's fellow guides. He recognized me and gave me a smile and a bow, but he was fully occupied with his tourists—a sallow little man with a moustache and a chattering woman wearing a cheap, brassy wig. The other family party was on its own. The two kids were dressed in those matching outfits you see advertised in expensive magazines—white sailor suit for the boy, white pleated skirt and red-trimmed top for the girl. They had done their best to spoil the effect, both were coated in yellow dust and the boy's pants were torn. They whooped around the shop like Comanches, and their mother kept yelling, "Don't break the pots! You break them, I have to pay for them!"

Carlos watched the two children, his brown bandit's face unperturbed. Their mother was right; if they broke anything, she'd pay for it, and if I knew Carlos she would pay plenty.

He came out from behind the counter when he saw me, bowing and grinning. I found him even less attractive than I had the first time, if possible; his charm at close quarters was too concentrated for comfort. As we stood talking I heard the bell over the door of the shop tinkle. Carlos glanced up. His expression didn't change, but an odd opacity clouded his eyes.

"How may I help you, señorita?" he asked formally.

"Silver, I think, to begin with." I added, unsubtly, "Ivan isn't with me today; I came by myself."

"Ivan? Ah, *sí, sí.* The friends of my friends, always I give them good price. Like these friends." He indicated the blond guide and his customers.

We moved to the counter where the jewelry was displayed, and I said casually,

"Did Ivan bring the two ladies from Minneapolis here? Mrs. Gold and Mrs. Faraday, their names were."

Carlos shrugged apologetically.

"I regret. There are many who come. . . . This necklace, it is beautiful for you."

I bought the necklace and a ring set with opals for Helen and a bracelet for my roommate. Then Carlos excused himself, to wait on another customer, and I went to browse among the figurines.

The statues were on shelves along one side of the shop. I started at one end and worked my way down. Andres was at the other end.

I was familiar with the statues now, I'd seen so many of them; there were only about a dozen types. The Smiling God had a happy, flat face, which reminded me of those Chinese statuettes, the ones whose stomach you are supposed to rub for good luck. The Old God was a squatting figure, a hideously accurate rendering of scrawny, sagging old age. My old acquaintance Tlaloc was there, complete with his big owly eyes. The most popular types were the dogs, in various poses—standing, sitting, or dancing. They were all of the same breed, a small, short-haired type with stubby legs and endearingly fat tummies. Danny had told me why they were so fat. I wished he hadn't.

There were a good many copies of each statue type, but they came in different sizes. I preferred the larger ones, since they were more detailed. The glaze was a soft brownish red, polished and cunningly antiqued.

Andres had planted himself solidly in front of the shelf of dancing dogs.

"Pardon me," I said.

He moved, about six inches. I reached past him and lifted one of the statues off the shelf. It was about a foot high, and surprisingly heavy.

"Cute," Andres said sarcastically.

It *was* cute. The dogs were up on their hind legs with their front paws wrapped around each other. Their teeth were bared. Maybe they were snarling, but I preferred to think of the expression as a friendly smile.

"You know why they're so fat, don't you?" Andres asked. He didn't bother to lower his voice.

"Yes, I know," I said coldly.

I put the dogs back on the shelf and selected another copy; the left-hand dog had a friendlier smile. Clutching it, I turned away to look at some bowls. Their inlaid design was one of the effective modern adaptations of Aztec patterns. The colors were lovely—clear, glowing greens and ambers, with touches of orange.

"How are you going to carry all that?" Andres asked.

"No trouble, no trouble," said Carlos, from behind me.

I started and almost dropped my dogs. Carlos's hand came out and steadied them, squeezing my fingers as it did so.

"I pack the dogs, pack very good," Carlos said, grinning till all his molars showed. "You buy them for this lady, señor?"

"I'll buy my own dogs," I said. "I don't know this gentleman. Could you pack them in one of those pretty straw bags, the way you did for that lady the other day?"

Carlos bowed.

"Which bag you like? The blue, the green?"

It was hard to decide. The bags were all pretty, embroidered with bright raffia flowers and leaves. The design covered the entire side of the bag, and it was done in different shades of a single color—every variation of green or blue, or all the hues of red, from pale pink to magenta.

I decided on the red. Carlos took the bag and the dogs and the bowls and retired to the storeroom behind the shop. My rudeness did not rid me of Mr. Andres. He was standing beside me, staring at the pile of straw bags with a blank expression, as if he were brooding over some profound problem.

"What are you going to use it for, when you get back home?" he asked. "It's too big for a purse, surely."

I shrugged, without bothering to answer; but the lady in the bright golden wig, who was also sorting through the bags, said casually, the way people do when they meet fellow countrymen in a foreign country,

"You could use it for a shopping bag, or a beach bag, or a knitting bag. . . . Gosh, it has a lot of uses, hasn't it, miss?"

"That's right."

"He's just trying to talk you out of buying things," she said, fluttering her eyelashes at Andres. "Harry always does that."

Harry, who had been following her like a worried nursemaid, sighed audibly.

"Women," he said, addressing Andres. "Think they've gotta buy a lot of junk or it isn't a trip. Aw, Gloria, you aren't gonna buy another one, are you? You got three of those bags awready."

"This is prettier," Gloria said, selecting a bag in shrieking shades of purple. "Look, Harry, this would go good with that pant suit I got."

"Aw, Gloria—"

"Aren't these the prettiest bags you ever saw?" Gloria asked me.

I don't go for this "we girls have got to stick together" routine, but I was feeling a trifle antimale at the moment. Besides, I agreed with her.

"Yes, they are," I said honestly. "I've seen these bags all over town, but Carlos's patterns are unique. Much more attractive than the ordinary ones."

Harry sighed again. Gloria giggled and gave me a conspiratorial wink. We were all getting so matey I was afraid they were going to suggest a foursome for cocktails, but just then Carlos came back with my bag, bulging with dogs and bowls and packing material, and I escaped as Gloria started reaching for Harry's wallet. Andres didn't follow me. Good old Harry had buttonholed him, and was holding forth on the iniquities of the female, while Andres stared in glazed boredom at the purple bag.

V

The bus driver dropped me off at a little plaza near the house. I only had to walk about a block, but my poor feet had swollen during the bus ride; I was limping when I reached the house, and my sandals felt as if they were filled with gravel. I took them off at the door and tried to wipe some of the dust from my feet before I walked on the dark polished floors. My shoes were swinging from my hand as I passed down the dark hall toward the stairs.

Then I heard the voices from the living room. They were speaking English—because of María, I suppose—and Ines's voice was louder than it should have been. I hardly recognized it.

"How can you do this? Don't you know what you are doing to me?"

"Yes, I know." It was George's voice, equally distorted by emotion. "I can't help it, Ines. It's too late now. I couldn't stop it if I wanted to."

"I tried to send her away."

"It's too late for that, too. At least, here, I can keep an eye on her."

"Ah, you are insane," she said angrily. "You cannot believe that she—"

"I hope I am crazy. But I can't take any chances—you of all people must see that!"

The silence lasted so long that I thought they had gone. I was about to put my poised foot down on the floor when she spoke again, in a voice from which all emotion had died.

"Yes, I see. Whatever happens—this, between us, it is over."

"It never began." There was no reproach in his voice,

only desolation.

She started to cry. Then I heard George again, his voice broken:

"*Querida,* don't cry. I'm sorry. I've never brought you anything but tears, but this . . . At least it will be ended soon. My love, don't . . ."

I didn't dare go on, past the open door; I couldn't stay where I was, one of them might come out. I backed up, slowly, cautiously. Then I put on my shoes and came back down the hall, thumping. When I passed the door, I glanced in. No one was there.

CHAPTER 10

THE household dined early, for a Latin family; by nine we were all gathered in the living room like any congenial group of friends. Beside me, on the long couch, Ines bent over her embroidery. Her face was as calm as ever, her stitches delicate and precise. There was no sign of the aberrant patterns of the previous night—and no sign, either, of the odd little scene I had overheard.

Danny, who had finally come nose to nose with a bull that afternoon, kept yawning violently. After an hour he excused himself and said he thought he'd go to bed. I was tired myself, after hiking all day; but I caught Ines's eye and decided I'd better not follow Danny up right away. She needn't have worried. Except for the single exhibition of mild affection that morning, he was as distant as a brother. I wondered whether he had found another girl.

He had plenty of time for it—gone most of the day, shut in his room—ostensibly—for ten hours each night. That in itself was indicative; usually he was up half the night and boasted of never needing more than six hours' sleep. He could easily sneak out of the house, with or without Ivan's assistance.

I looked at Ivan, who was stretched out full length, with his hands clasped under his head. He was wearing a black shirt and black slacks, and he was as sleek and lithe as a panther as he lay there. At the beginning, he had shown some interest in me. Now he no longer bothered to pretend. He was courteous and charming—and cold as a statue. The coldness wasn't physical; I suspected that, when he wanted to be, he was probably an accomplished lover. His frigidity was emotional. He observed others, but they never moved him.

Yes, Ivan was perfectly capable of introducing Danny to another girl, and encouraging an affair, without caring about my feelings.

I wasn't sure, any longer, what my feelings were. I thought I was falling out of love with Danny; it's a process just as distinct, and as hard to define, as falling *in* love. The thought of him with another girl still gave me a sick feeling. But, in a way, it would have been easier to face than some of the other possibilities that had occurred to me.

The more I thought about it, the more plausible it became. There had been a number of pretty girls at the party we attended; Ivan probably had a long waiting list of his own. And if Danny had fallen for someone else, he'd be too ashamed to let me know about it. You can't help falling in love, but it's a cheap trick to court one girl while you're living on another girl's money.

When Ines folded her work and went upstairs, I followed. But I had no intention of staying in my room.

If Danny did sneak out at night, he would have to go through the patio. The house was miles from town, and public transportation was limited even during the daytime, so he would have to use the car—which suggested Ivan's connivance. At any rate, I knew where to lie in wait—the patio, with its shadowing trees and vines.

I felt shabby and cheap as I got into the only dark outfit I had brought with me, and tied my hair back under a navy-blue scarf. The outfit happened to be my bathrobe. Of course I didn't intend to make a scene, or even admit that I had seen him. I just wanted to know. And if anyone saw me—well, it wouldn't be unnatural for me to sit in the garden if I couldn't sleep.

I had one of those little purse flashlights, whose beam is about as strong as that of a match, but I didn't dare use it much, and by the time I got out of the house half my toes felt mashed. Furniture and doorways kept popping up in places where I didn't expect them. I had brought the flashlight primarily to help me undo the bars on the door without fumbling. There was a bar, and a chain, and a lock; the heavy key hung on a nail beside the door.

I managed it all right, but the lock hadn't been oiled for a hundred years, and it gave off a squeal when I turned the key. I froze; then I realized that my nerves made the sound seem louder than it was, and that the miles of empty corridors between the door and the sleeping quarters would keep anyone from hearing me. I opened the door.

The darkness was uncanny, unnatural, much worse than the unlit interior of the house. You don't realize how dark night can be when you're used to streetlights, neon signs, and lighted windows. There was no moon; even the stars were veiled by clouds. And there were sounds—not the familiar sounds of settling floors and creaking windows, but little rustlings and breathy murmurs. Anything might have made those sounds.

I don't know how long I would have stood there, like a

baby scared of the dark, if a bird hadn't wakened and let out a sleepy chirp of complaint. The sound brought me back to my senses. At least there was something else alive out there. The other sounds became familiar—leaves rustling, insects creeping. As my eyes gradually adjusted I could make out the darker outlines of trees, and the lightness of stone benches.

I knew where I wanted to go, and I got there with a minimal amount of noise and damage to my bruised toes. There was a bench in a far corner, kitty-corner from the door, where a heavy fall of vines hung down over the wall. Against its dark curtain my own dark shape would be virtually invisible. I sat down on the bench and put my feet up, wrapping the skirt of my robe around my toes.

It was surprisingly comfortable, and after a while I began to enjoy myself. Several of the birds were wide awake; they were carrying on a throaty conversation, and practicing arpeggios for the next day. I almost forgot why I had come; it was humiliating to admit my real motive, much more pleasant to congratulate myself on my taste for adventure. The moist air against my face held a threat of rain. If it started raining I could reach the house in a hurry; my eyes had adjusted to a point where I could distinguish objects fairly well.

With my back up against one wall and my cheek pillowed against the vines, I dozed off.

I didn't fall asleep. The position wasn't that comfortable; every time I started to drop into deeper slumber one foot slipped or my chin banged onto my chest. I was beginning to think of my bed upstairs with nostalgia when I heard a sound.

I was accustomed to the normal night sounds now, and I

recognized this one immediately—the crunch of a shoe on stone. I stiffened. I had almost forgotten my suspicions.

Then I stared unbelievingly at the figure which came tiptoeing across the court—a pudgy, round figure. Not Danny after all. It was Uncle Jaime.

Relief relaxed my muscles. I almost called out to him. I don't know what stopped me—embarrassment, probably. When I saw what he was doing, I had another reason for keeping quiet.

Instead of sitting down to enjoy the night air, he crossed the patio toward what appeared to be a blank wall, and stood facing it. The wall was the one directly opposite my bench, so I could only see his back; but it seemed to me that his hands were raised. I wondered if he could be praying. But that was silly; there was no shrine or holy statue on the wall; it was blank except for the hanging vines.

I sat bolt upright. Uncle Jaime had disappeared.

Now you see him, now you don't—it was that sudden.

Of course only one thing could have happened. I think I'd have figured it out by myself, after the first shock of surprise had passed. I didn't have to. Someone else came out of the house, crossing the patio on quick, noiseless feet. He too faced the wall, and this time, because I was prepared, I saw the shielding cascade of vines shift. He went under it and vanished as Uncle Jaime had done; this time I heard the soft *click* as a door shut.

A door in the wall, hidden by the vines. Hidden by intent, or by the natural growth of untrimmed vegetation? It was not so strange that Uncle Jaime might decide to take a midnight stroll, along paths that might seem as prosaic to him as they were mysterious to me. For all I knew, the old gentleman might have a girlfriend in a nearby villa. But there was no prosaic reason as to why George should be following him.

It's impossible to measure time subjectively, especially when you have been half asleep. But I knew I must have been in my place for at least an hour, possibly longer. I could reasonably abandon my vigil. If Danny had had a date, he surely would have left by now.

But I knew I wasn't going to go back upstairs. I wouldn't be able to sleep until I found out where that oddly matched couple was going.

The door wasn't really a secret door. It had hinges and a handle, and it was made of ordinary wooden boards. But it had been painted the same dull buff color as the wall, and with the vines hanging thickly over it, it was no wonder I had never noticed it. I tugged on the heavy handle to no avail, and then realized that it probably opened the other way. When I pushed, the door gave way so abruptly that I almost fell through the opening.

I found myself in a miniature jungle. I couldn't see a thing. Branches thick with leaves cut off the sky, and the door behind me had closed. There was a dank, heavy smell of plants growing and rotting. Prickly things jabbed at my feet and clung to my skirts.

I had landed on something that felt like a cactus, so I got off it in a hurry. Like a fool, I moved away from the doorway instead of toward it, and by the time I had hopped, and pulled thorns out of my feet, and turned around a few times, I was lost. There wasn't a sign of any other human presence.

Eventually I found what seemed to be a path; at least it was free of thorns. The dust was soft under my bare toes. I struggled through that weird place for what seemed like hours, sliding my feet along and keeping my arms stretched out in front of me. The maddening thing was that I knew I must be within a few feet of the house, but I couldn't see, or feel, anything except vegetation. I remembered a picture I had seen once, an old engraving of the Mayan temples in Yucatán as they had appeared when they were rediscovered. Trees had grown out of cracks in the walls, vines wreathed the faces of the crumbling stone gods. I realized how quickly nature can efface the flimsy creations of men, and I began to feel as if the vines and branches that caught at my body were sentient and hostile, intent on obliterating me as they had the abandoned cities. Some day, when an archaeologist of the future excavated the ruins of the villa, he would find me in the garden, with vines clasping my bony legs and a rose bush growing out of my rib cage.

I was getting discouraged. I didn't care what game George and Uncle Jaime were playing; if I had overheard them plotting to blow up the White House I'd have said, "Fellows, I sure am glad to see you. Get me out of this."

Then I saw the light.

It was a smoky yellow light, feeble and small as a firefly's tail, but it was the prettiest thing I had seen for hours. I groped toward it. After I had bashed myself on a tree trunk or two, the going became easier. The trees began to thin out. Best of all, I knew where I was.

Ahead of me, between the trees, I could see a section of stone paving, and—beautiful, commonplace sight—a clothesline. I had seen this place during the house tour Ines led me on; it was the kitchen patio, behind the domestic offices and servants' rooms. Here the household activities were carried on: washing, drying, cooking. It looked humble enough the day I saw it, with the clothesline flapping with shirts and sheets and underwear, and María's old washtubs in a corner. This part of the house was her private domain. Like Uncle Jaime, she had pots filled with plants, but hers were herbs, which she used for cooking. Beyond the farther wall of the patio was a small kitchen garden, tended by María's toothless old gnome of a husband. I had seen him only once, that same afternoon; he never came to the front part of the house. I could understand why the gardens and grounds were in such a state, with only that poor old man to tend them.

The kitchen patio was a small island of life in the midst of decay. The house enclosed it on three sides, but only the rooms on one side were still in use. The arrangement reminded me of restored colonial plantations back home, which wasn't surprising, because the original establishment here was probably of the same period. Storerooms, pantries, and laundry rooms had once lined the sides of this patio, but they were abandoned now; the doors were nailed shut and the windows gaped empty. There was no need for them any longer. The vast household they had served was reduced to a few people, and the old servitude had ended. That was something to remember when I became sentimental about the collapse of the good old days. The cultured leisure of all colonial aristocracies is based on slavery, whether it is called that or not.

More to the point, the fourth side of the patio was the area where I was standing. Ines had indicated the formidable green wall of jungle, and explained that it had once been a garden with specimens of exotic trees, when the family employed a whole staff of gardeners. It covered a sizable area; I had gone along one whole side, and the corner, of the west wing.

And, I thought, I am not going back, not even if I have to sleep in María's washtub for the rest of the night. I remembered that the old lady's room wasn't too far away, but even if I'd had the nerve to waken her, I might not be able to make her hear. If she wasn't deaf, she was selectively hard of hearing.

I took two more steps; and then the fire, and the things beside it, came into sight. I stopped as suddenly as if I had run into an invisible wall.

The fire was small, but the flames were bright. María bent over it. The play of firelight on her withered features brought out the ancestral resemblance that had been obscured by age and modern surroundings. The reddish-brown skin looked like bronze; the hooked profile might have walked out of one of the murals at Teotihuacan.

On the ground beside the fire was a woven mat on which stood a collection of strange objects. A battered cardboard box that had once held shoes now formed a container for a doll-like shape cut out of black paper. Beside the box stood two bottles of wine, three eggs, and a bowl of fruit. There was also a pile of straw; it had a pattern of some sort, but I couldn't make it out. Propped up behind the offerings of food and wine was a framed picture of some saint; I could just make out the gilded halo. There were other objects on the farther side of the fire, where I couldn't see them distinctly.

María held a flat, square clay bowl over the fire; as she moved it slowly back and forth, the sweet smell of incense came wafting across the air to my nostrils. It seemed to blend with the mumbling chant which came from the crouching figure of the old woman.

I felt the hairs on the back of my neck prickle. I knew

what she was doing. Hadn't Ivan said that María was a witch? Witchcraft is an "in" activity these days, and I had read a couple of books about it, pressed on me by a wild-eyed junior in the dorm. All the ingredients were present: the incense, to attract the gods by its sweet smell; the offerings of food and wine and . . . María moved back to put her incense brazier on the ground and I saw the heap of limp white feathers beyond the fire.

It was only a chicken; but the hairs on my neck went higher. Another offering—or the source of the blood that gave life to the inanimate shape of the doll? The poor creature was dead, anyhow. If we had chicken tomorrow for lunch . . .

I wanted to leave, and yet I wanted to stay. The ceremony had an unholy fascination. Besides, I didn't think I could find my way back without making noise, and the last thing I wanted was to attract María's attention. I wasn't really afraid. She didn't look homicidal; in fact, there was a grave dignity in her face as she moved through the steps of the ritual. It would have been like interrupting someone at prayer.

She picked something up from the straw pile, and I saw what it was: one of the star symbols woven out of palm fronds that I had seen at the museum. Offerings to the gods . . . I leaned forward, trying to see better—and put my hand onto something that felt like a section of barbed wire.

I didn't yell, which took a lot of self-control; when you clutch a cactus you are entitled to yell. But the old woman heard the sharp intake of my breath. She came hurtling toward me like a big black basketball. The speed of her movement stunned me so that I couldn't move. She caught me by the wrist and dragged me out into the open.

“I’m terribly sorry,” I stuttered. It was a stupid thing to say, even if she could have understood me. “I didn’t mean to disturb you, I couldn’t sleep, so I went out and I got lost . . .”

She stood peering up into my face while I went through this imbecilic performance. She wasn’t trying to understand, she was thinking; finally she seemed to come to some decision, because she nodded vigorously and towed me into the middle of the patio, next to the fire. I went unresisting; I could hardly struggle with the old woman. Then she faced me. She took a deep breath. Her small black eyes stared into mine so intently that they might have been reading my thoughts. But the effort at communication which began, then, was a lot tougher than mental telepathy.

She pointed to the black paper doll in the box and then to me. Then she struck her hands together and shook her head frantically.

“Okay,” I said soothingly. “I’m not the doll. That wasn’t what you meant. Try again.”

The sound of my voice must have reassured her, or at least convinced her that I was trying. She gave me an odd grimace which might have been meant for a smile. She pointed to the black doll again.

“Malo,” she said, forming the word with exaggerated precision, the way you talk to a small child, or a deaf person. *“Sombra”*—the doll—*“malo. Comprende?”*

“Bad,” I said. *“Malo* means bad.” I shook my head and made a face that was supposed to express disgust.

“Sí, sí,” she said eagerly. *“Malo—la sombra. Usted . . .”* Now the bony finger pointed squarely at me. I recoiled. *“Bueno, bueno,”* she said apologetically. *“Usted—bueno. Pero hay peligro para usted.”*

There was that word again. Danger.

Danger to me, or from me? There was no use kidding myself, she meant the former. She was trying to warn me. But what about? In my eagerness I tried to ask, and succeeded only in confusing both of us. She got excited and began lecturing me in rapid Spanish.

Then a new and brilliant idea struck her, and her wrinkled old face lit up. I wondered how I could have mistaken her attitude for malevolence. Even her odd ritual need not be evil; if she was a *curandera,* as Ivan had called her, her specialty must be white magic. The holy picture was an encouraging sign, too.

She pulled at my sleeve, and squatted down on the ground. I squatted too. Taking up a stick, she swept a dusty patch of stone clean of footprints, hers and mine, and began to sketch. We were back to the primeval means of nonverbal communication: picture writing.

The symbols she drew left me absolutely bewildered. Not because I didn't recognize them; the round body, with a skillful suggestion of fur in the wavering line, the round head, and the long, pointed ears. . . .

"A rabbit," I said doubtfully. "It must be a rabbit. But what—"

She didn't know the word, and I didn't know the Spanish word she pronounced. I nodded, all the same. I really thought for a minute that she had flipped. Rabbits, of all things . . .

She made more rabbits, a whole row of them. Then she abandoned zoology and began to make strokes. One, two, three, four . . .

"Cuatro," she said, and raised four fingers.

I nodded.

"Cuatrocientos conejos," she said, and made the fingers vibrate—multiplying rabbits.

"Four hundred," I translated obediently. *"Cuatro,* four; *ciento,* hundred. Four hundred rabbits . . ."

The phrase was infuriatingly familiar. When I did succeed in placing it, my bewilderment increased. Four hundred rabbits was the old Aztec measure for drunkenness—dead drunk, stoned, smashed.

I feel sorry for the first interplanetary explorers who encounter intelligent life. I can't imagine how they are ever going to talk with the aliens. Communication isn't just words; it is concepts. María had succeeded in telling me about platoons of rabbits, but I hadn't the faintest idea of what she meant. Somebody was drunk? Somebody was an alcoholic? The ceremony she was performing might be a cure for illness; alcoholism is an illness. The black paper doll, the shadow—got it!—*sombra* must be shadow. That could represent the patient, the person she was trying to cure.

I was so pleased with this reasoning that I smiled enthusiastically at María and nodded my head. She scowled; and my elegant train of logic collapsed, as I realized that it did not apply. Nobody in this house could be an alcoholic. They were so abstemious they could have joined the WCTU.

María tried her best. She was like a teacher trying to explain the ABC's to a retarded child. Again she dragged me by the wrist, this time to her pots of herbs along the wall.

"Treinta," she said, and gave me all ten fingers, three times. *"Treinta conejos."*

Conejos were rabbits. I had accepted that.

"Thirty rabbits," I said, and stared, baffled, at the pots of thyme and rosemary, while María waved her arms around like a windmill and, I think, swore.

I doubt that we'd have got any further, but maybe I'm underestimating María. She had persistence, if nothing else. We didn't have the chance to proceed. A door slammed, and Ivan walked out into the patio and stared down at the piles of offerings.

Hands on his hips, he radiated disgust and disapproval. To me the incongruous collection no longer seemed abhorrent; it was pathetic, an old woman's feeble attempt to get control of a crazy, unstable universe.

Ivan put out his foot and swept it across the things on the mat. The bowl overturned and the bottles fell; one broke, spilling out a dark stain. María was a rock; she had pulled back into her shell like a turtle. She didn't stir, even when Ivan's foot jarred the dead chicken and the blood-dabbled cloth on which it lay.

Hands still on his hips, Ivan pivoted and spoke to the old woman. His voice was low. The words washed over María's stony impassivity. I admired her guts. I couldn't understand what he was saying, but the tone of his voice made me cringe.

Then he switched to English, and it was a different man talking.

"Poor Carol. I hope you weren't too frightened. Did you think you were next, after the white cock?"

"I wasn't frightened at all."

"What splendid scientific detachment." The corners of his mouth lifted, mocking me. "Perhaps you can write a paper, when you return to school, about the superstitions of the primitive Mexican people."

"She's no more superstitious than most of the people I know," I said defiantly. "My mother's friends are hooked on astrology, and one of the girls in my dormitory claims to have raised the devil."

"Do you know what your weakness is?" His smile vanished; he looked at me almost pityingly. "You have too soft a heart. Very well, I won't scold the old hag anymore. Though she has been told often enough that I won't tolerate this rubbish. . . ."

He spoke to María again. She made no response, only stared grimly back at him. With her lower lip outthrust, her resemblance to an Aztec statue was uncanny.

"All right, Carol, time for bed," Ivan said.

I said *"Buenas noches"* to Maria. She didn't answer. We left her there, like a dark, dusty garden ornament, and passed through the door into the house.

"Speaking of bed," Ivan said, "What are you doing out of yours, at this hour?"

I started on my prepared lie, and gulped to a stop as I realized I couldn't account for my presence in that blasted jungle without giving Uncle Jaime away. I might have stumbled on the semihidden door in daylight, but I'd have had to have owl's eyes to discover it by night. So I had to admit seeing Uncle Jaime. I didn't mention George.

Ivan chuckled.

"The old rascal," he said.

"I shouldn't have followed him. Not that I was really following him, if you know what I mean. . . . I was just so surprised to see that there was a door there, I couldn't resist finding out where it led to."

"Very natural."

We passed through the door that led into the main section of the house and Ivan stood back to let me precede him, now that we had entered territory familiar to me.

"I feared," he said, "that María had dragged you from bed in order to practice her spells on you. She is absolutely harmless, but she seems to have some strange notion about you—that you are in danger of attack from the confounded spirits of the air."

"Oh, is that what she meant? She kept talking about danger, but that was the only word I could understand."

"She is a crazy old woman. That ceremony was a healing rite. It is called *el costumbre* by the Tepehuas—that is the tribe from which María comes, in the mountains of Hidalgo. You saw the black figure cut out of paper? That is the *sombra,* the shadow of the person afflicted—his soul, you would say. The ritual is a mad mixture of Christianity and pagan beliefs; it endeavors to call the wandering soul back to the body, or, in your case, to bind it fast so that the evil spirits cannot steal it."

We reached the top of the stairs, where the corridor branched to left and right—boys' side and girls' side.

"Good night," Ivan said. "Sleep well, for what is left of the night. And don't forget to bandage your feet, thorns fester if they are left in the flesh."

He went off down the hall, humming softly to himself.

I took his advice, finding antiseptic, bandages, and tweezers in the well-stocked medicine chest. My feet hadn't hurt till I looked at them; then they started to ache. I wondered morbidly if I had left bloody footprints along the hall. That would make a nice omen for poor old María if she came upon them next morning.

Poor old María, who thought she was tying my soul to my body. There was nothing wrong with the theory, but there was something very wrong with Ivan's version of it. In most forms of magic the magician uses some thing which has been in contact with the person who is the object of the spell—a lock of hair, nail clippings, even an article of clothing that has been worn next to the skin. This confers identity on the little image, waxen or paper, which represents the person. Black is a magical color, in some systems; so perhaps the black doll was not necessarily meant to represent a person who often wore black, and who had black hair and black eyes. María could easily have borrowed a pair of socks or a slip from me. But the bundle of cloth on the far side of the fire—dabbled, sickeningly, with the blood of the murdered cock—hadn't been one of my garments. I was almost sure that it was a shirt—a man's shirt.

I was tired enough, after my misadventures, to get to sleep without counting sheep. What I counted was, of course, rabbits. Hundreds of them, one after another, in a long, furry line. And every one of them had beady black eyes, which stared into mine with a mute and terrible frustration.

CHAPTER 11

I WASN'T in the best of all possible moods when I came downstairs next morning and entered the dark little room where breakfast was, to use the term loosely, being served. Ines had explained, the first day, that María couldn't be expected to produce food all morning long. The lazy ones who didn't appear for eight-o'clock breakfast had to fend for themselves. The food was left out, in a room not far from the kitchen—bread and rolls, bowls of jam, and coffee in a big samovar affair which had its own warming unit.

Ivan was usually up and out before I came down, but this morning he was still at the table. Even more surprising, George was with him. Ordinarily they didn't seek out one another's company, but there they sat lingering over the dregs of their coffee together.

George looked warmed over, like some kind of casserole that gets soggy in the middle and burned around the edges when you reheat it. The only thing alive in his face were his eyes; when they turned toward me I seemed to see a reddish glow in them, like dying coals. I wondered whether he had

had any sleep at all, and how far he and Jaime had walked.

When I asked how he felt, he growled at me.

"Nothing wrong with me. Start treating me like a senile old man. . . ." Then his eyes flickered, and the look he gave me was one of terrified apology. "I'm sorry, Carol. Didn't mean to shout. . . . Sit down, you haven't had breakfast. I'll get your coffee."

"I'll get it." I put my hand on his shoulder and felt, not a shiver, but a kind of internal tremor, like some machine whirring out of phase. "Would you like another cup? Ivan, how about you?"

They both accepted, and I served them, like any well-trained female. Ivan pushed the other goodies across the table toward me and remarked,

"In three days a terrible thing will happen. Our Carol will return to school having seen no more of Mexico than two pyramids and a collection of ruined temples. Something must be done about this before it is too late."

"I've seen the museum," I protested.

"More ruins." Ivan waved a contemptuous hand. "You have missed five hundred years of history and art. Today, tomorrow, you may at least see more of the city. What should she see, do you think?"

He spoke to George. His tone and the deferential inclination of his head were superbly courteous, but I noticed, as I had done before, that he did not address George by name. He didn't call him George, or sir, or hey you. He didn't call him anything.

"I don't know," George said vaguely. "The Cathedral, I suppose; the Palace of Fine Arts, the various monuments. . . . That's your specialty, Ivan."

"True. Shall we make a tour of the city?"

This time he was talking to me, but George answered before I could.

"That sounds like a nice idea. I'll ask Ines if she'd like to come with us."

"You forget," Ivan said. "Today there is her novena at the convent."

Two pairs of eyes met, and locked like fists clenching. A shiver ran up my back. The hatred was mutual, and all the stronger for being so generally concealed under a coating of courtesy.

"So I did forget," George said.

"But perhaps Tío Jaime . . ." Ivan indicated that gentleman, who had just come in.

Tramping the terrain all night seemed to have done wonders for Uncle Jaime. Bright-eyed, humming, he poured himself a cup of coffee, spooned jam lavishly on a roll, and swept an all-inclusive beam around the table.

"No 'perhaps,' " he said breezily. "Certainly. Whatever it is that Tío Jaime must do, he will do."

Ivan explained. His uncle was, characteristically, delighted.

"Do not plan to lecture," he warned his nephew. "I will talk today. I know more than you of our history."

"But of course!" Ivan grinned and stood up. "I will go up, then, and hurry our other guest. Carol, you must speak to Danny, he adjusts to what he thinks is the Latin way of life. He sleeps too much."

"He'll wake up fast enough when he gets back to snow country," I said; and broke off with a cry of alarm. George, in the act of rising, stumbled and swayed. I threw my arms around his shoulders and he lifted his face toward me and tried to smile.

"It's all right," he mumbled. "Get these spells . . . now and then. . . . Nothing serious."

"Medicine," I said. "Is there medicine you're supposed to take?"

"No, no. Lie down . . . rest . . ."

Uncle Jaime's arms took part of my father's weight, and George, with a visible effort, straightened up.

"I'll go lie down," he said. "Carol . . . stay with me?"

"Of course." I took his arm. "Ivan, I'm sorry about your plans—"

"But, my dear, do not think of that; naturally you must stay."

As always, voice, pose, and expression were so absolutely correct that many people might not have noticed the false note. He had risen from his chair when George faltered, but he had left it to a woman and an old man to support the stricken man's weight. It wasn't lack of manners. He literally could not bear to touch George.

By the time we got upstairs, George was walking well, and he insisted that he was all right, only a little tired. I mentioned a doctor, but both George and Uncle Jaime said there was no need. Uncle Jaime tactfully withdrew, giving me a nod and a smile which reassured me. George said he couldn't sleep and asked if I would read to him. It appeared that he wanted a particular book, and I stifled a sigh when he said it was somewhere in the study. It might be on the desk—or maybe he had put it back in the bookcase—try the third shelf on the north wall, toward the right. . . .

I expected to be in the study for hours, but by a miracle I found the book right away, though it was not on the shelf where George had told me to look. Instead of going straight back upstairs, I went to the breakfast room to get some coffee. I hadn't finished even one cup, and I thought George might like something hot.

There was only one telephone in the house. It was in the hall, in a cubicle under the stairs—tucked away in obscurity like some idiot relative. The only advantage to the dark, cramped little nook was that it afforded a degree of privacy to anyone using the phone. The cubicle was on the side of the stairs away from the main hall that led to the living room, library, and the other main rooms. With the door into the hall closed, the only way it could be approached was from the kitchen—or the breakfast room.

Trying to balance a book and two cups of coffee, I walked delicately. I wasn't thinking about the telephone; the sound of any voice would have startled me. The voice I heard was more than startling, it was unbelievable. George was supposed to be upstairs, flat on his bed.

"I'm supposed to be resting," he said, like an uncanny echo of my thoughts. "I'll have to make this fast. You had better come out here. I've got the house under control, but he's a tricky devil. It could be tonight, and if it is . . ."

There was silence, while I stood frozen, with a wobbly cup in each hand.

"I don't know," he said, in answer to some question from the unknown on the other end of the line. "I just have a feeling. It might be tomorrow, but it has to be soon, you know why. I've got to go now, she'll be coming back. For God's sake don't fail me."

The receiver went down. Footsteps tiptoed down the hall, a door opened and closed. Then there was silence, except for the uneven pounding of my heart.

I forced my legs to move and steadied the wavering cups in their saucers. As I passed the telephone cubbyhole I saw why George had thought himself safe from eavesdroppers. He could see the door that led to the hall and the living area, but an angle of wall cut off his view of the kitchen region, where he did not expect me to be. María was the only one who would be in that part of the house at this time of day. María didn't understand English. And heaven knows his conversation had been oblique enough. He hadn't mentioned a name, nor referred specifically to the mysterious business he was engaged in. But now I knew for certain what I had only suspected before. George was involved in something illegal, or dangerous, or both—and it was due to reach a critical point soon.

Tonight.

I had to put one of the cups down on the floor in order to open the door, and as I bent over, an odd swirling grayness obscured my vision. When it cleared, I found myself sitting on the floor, with the two cups beside me. They looked absurd there, like two escapees from the Mad Tea Party. I felt all right—dizzy and rather as if my head were detached from the rest of me, but I was thinking, I believed, quite rationally.

My thoughts could be reduced to a single exclamatory sentence: Get out of here.

Exclamation point.

Since Sunday, when I had been on the verge of leaving for home, George's changed attitude had bemused me so much that I had been able to ignore my doubts. Now they were back, stronger than ever.

Coldly I considered ways and means of getting away. If I did decide to leave, I would have to forget about excuses and good manners. I would have to slip out of the house and run, like a thief. I couldn't tell anyone about my plans.

At best such a move would mean delay, and if I was going, I had to go at once. At worst, I might approach the wrong person, the unknown source of that "peligro" María kept trying to warn me about. I couldn't trust anyone.

I had my ticket for the plane. I didn't have a reservation, but that was no problem. I could sit at the airport until a seat was available, a seat on a plane to almost anywhere north of the border.

The trouble was, I didn't have any money. Danny had given me fifty dollars. I had spent almost all of it. I had about four dollars left. Maybe I could get a taxi to the airport for four dollars, but then I would be destitute. I had purchased a round-trip ticket, expecting to go back to college, but the college would be deserted now; I couldn't go to the dormitory, and without money I couldn't go to a hotel. If I went home instead of to school, I would need more money for the additional fare. No matter how you figured it, I needed more money. And Danny had the traveler's checks. He had them because I was a soft-hearted sucker. I hadn't wanted to hurt his masculine pride by paying bills in his presence.

Meditatively, still sitting on the floor, I picked up a cup and drank some coffee. The liquid cleared my head and I started to have second thoughts. In order to skip town, I had to get some of those traveler's checks from Danny, and I didn't trust Danny any more than I did the others. Not that I actually suspected him; but I knew he would kick up a fuss and want to know what was bugging me. And if I told him, he would send for the little men in the white coats.

Because—what did I have to go on, really? Mysterious phone calls, people creeping around in the night, an addled old lady's comments in a language that was Greek to me—and a peculiar character named Andres who kept following me for un-obvious reasons. All of this could be explained. Even if George was involved in some unsavory activity, I wasn't in danger so long as I kept out of his affairs.

I got up and picked up the coffee, tucking the book under my arm. I had been gone long enough; but not as long as it seemed to me.

That was one of the longest days I've ever lived through. Around noon Ines came up with a tray and sat with us while we ate—or rather, while we pushed the food around on our plates. George never ate much, and I didn't think my stomach was in good enough shape to digest anything—much less chicken.

Ines said very little. She was composed, almost too much so; she seemed abnormally withdrawn, like a mystic who has retreated into his inner world and abandoned the sordid details of everyday life. When she left, she made a graceful excuse about duties that called her. I suspected that the duties included scrubbing floors and waxing furniture. Ines's dignity did not prevent her from doing the work her elderly servant couldn't manage alone, but she didn't want anyone to know she did it.

Later on, while I was doggedly plowing through Vaillant's *The Aztecs of Mexico,* Ivan put his head in the door to say that he had gotten a rush call from the agency. Two rich tourists had suddenly decided that they wanted to be taken out to dinner and to the Sound and Light performance at the pyramids. Was everything all right? Did we need anything before he left?

I thanked him, and he left. The afternoon wore on.

Uncle Jaime came upstairs, looked in, and went into his room, which was next to George's. The doors were all open to catch the breeze; it was a warm day. As I read on, I heard Uncle Jaime puttering around in his room, then the creak of the bedsprings and, after a while, a series of bubbling snores.

The sound was contagious. I started yawning. George could hardly keep his eyes open, but he fought sleep; every time I stopped reading, thinking that he had drifted off, his heavy lids would lift and he would ask me to go on. Finally I let out a huge yawn that almost split my jaws, and George said fretfully,

"If you're sleepy you'd better lie down and take a nap."

"I'll take a nap if you will."

He agreed, but he was in a querulous mood. First he sent me down to look for Ivan, saying that there was something he wanted from town, if Ivan hadn't left yet. He wouldn't accept my statement that Ivan had been gone for an hour; I had to go look.

As I went back upstairs I saw Danny standing in the doorway of the living room. It gave me a start; I hadn't seen him or thought about him all day. The shades were drawn against the sun's heat, and in the shadows his face looked pale and elongated.

"What's the matter?" I asked.

"Sssh." He put his finger to his lips. "I've been trying to talk to you all day. Where've you been?"

"With George. He's not feeling too well."

"Oh."

"Danny, something is wrong. Are you sick? Worried about something?"

"No. I'm afraid."

His voice had the sharp, unmistakable ring of truth. I was shocked, but I was also relieved. Perhaps I had found an ally after all, someone with whom I could discuss my worries.

"What are you afraid of?"

"I'll tell you. But not here." He made a wild, uncontrolled gesture with his hands. "I keep thinking people are listening."

I kept thinking that too.

"I've got to go back to George," I said. "But I want to talk to you. If he goes to sleep, I'll come back."

"Come out to the patio."

"All right. As soon as I can get away."

Getting away took some time. I told George that the car was gone and Ivan nowhere to be seen; and I asked if he would like me to go into town to get whatever it was he wanted. The suggestion seemed to annoy him.

"No, no," he said angrily. "It doesn't matter; it can wait. I want you here."

"All right."

Suddenly he caught at my hand. "I'm being very selfish," he said. "But I feel—I feel better when you're with me. I know I don't deserve anything—I haven't any right to expect you to—"

I had been waiting, for days, to hear him admit the past. Now, seeing his drawn, twitching face, I couldn't endure watching him abase himself.

"It's all right," I said quickly. "Of course I'll stay, if you want me to."

I leaned over and kissed his cheek. He didn't respond; he just lay there staring at me with the queerest look on his face.

"Go and rest," he said, after a long moment. "You must be tired. Just promise—promise me you won't leave the house; you'll be here when I wake up."

I gave him my promise. The patio was part of the house, really; I would be close by if he needed me. The sound of Uncle Jaime's peaceful snores followed me as I walked down the hall, my emotions more confused than ever. If George was pretending illness, he was a superb actor. Surely his concern, and his affection, must be genuine. If they were . . . and I ran away . . . and something happened to him . . .

I went down the stairs and out of the house—leaving one problem only to face another.

The shadows of the trees lay long across the paving stones, but the patio was hot, after broiling in the sun all afternoon. Danny was bending over the table. As I walked toward him he started convulsively, spilling some of the liquid from the glass he held.

"Don't sneak up on me like that!"

"You *are* nervous," I said. "What's that—lemonade?"

"Yes. I brought you some."

"Thanks." My throat was dry after reading for hours. I gulped down half the glassful before I noticed the taste. "Good gosh, what did you do, empty the sugar bowl into it?"

"The old woman made it," Danny said. "I just carried it out."

I sat down on a bench in the shade.

"All right," I said. "Start talking."

Danny started pacing instead. He kept looking uneasily at the house.

"Where is everybody? I don't want to be interrupted."

"Ivan is working, and George is asleep. I don't know where Ines is."

"I saw her go out a while ago. To church, I suppose. What about Uncle Jaime? He's usually out here at this time of day."

"He was still asleep when I left George." I finished the overly sweet drink, and debated as to whether I should tell Danny why Uncle Jaime was sleeping late today. I decided I wouldn't. I wanted to hear his story before I gave away any information.

"We can go someplace else if you're afraid of being overheard," I said. "My room?"

"No, not inside. That house gives me the creeps."

"All right," I said impatiently. "Get on with it. The longer you stall, the greater the chance that someone will come."

Danny paced up and down, nibbling on his lower lip.

"It's about your father," he said finally.

"What about him?"

He started telling me about George's experiments with acid. After a while I tried to interrupt him.

"Danny, I know all that."

"I don't think you know the whole story."

That grim hint kept me quiet for a while longer, as he recapitulated the story in wearisome detail. I waited for some new revelation, but there was none, only the things I knew too well already.

"You haven't told me anything I didn't already know," I said finally.

"You never told me about it."

"How could I? It was George's affair, not mine."

"Or mine?"

"All right, it wasn't your affair, either. Let's not fight, Danny, there's no percentage in that. If you don't want to tell me what you're afraid of—"

"All right, I will tell you. He's still at it."

"At what?"

"Drugs, narcotics."

"Danny, make sense. You mean George is taking narcotics?"

"No, dammit, I mean he's dealing in them. He's smuggling drugs into the States."

I sat there like a block of wood while he went on talking. It was a long, rambling story, and it seemed to me that he went into every aspect of the narcotics problem except what George had to do with it. I didn't interrupt. I felt numb.

Finally he got specific. Uncle Jaime was the patsy of the story, the innocent victim. His harmless pots of marijuana had provided George with an inspiration and a source of income. He had forced Uncle Jaime to help him buy land, hire workers, and raise a crop.

"There are isolated areas, in the mountains, where the stuff is grown openly," Danny said. "A few bribes to the local fuzz and nobody bothers you. The country is too big to patrol; the narcotics agents concentrate on the distribution end, and on the transportation of the product across the border. But George is smart. He wasn't even suspected—till recently.

"I was right about Andres, he is fuzz. An agent from the U.S. Bureau of Narcotics. Not their local man in Mexico City. Andres is a special agent, he was sent down here so that Ivan wouldn't be compromised by dealing with the regular man. Everybody knows who he is."

"Ivan," I repeated stupidly.

I looked at the glass in my hands and thought about putting it down on a table. I could if I wanted to. I could move my legs—there they were down there—hi, legs—and stand up and walk over to the table and put the glass down. If I wanted to. But I didn't.

"Yes, Ivan's the hero. He got wind of what George was doing and notified the fuzz. Not the Mexican police, he wants to keep Uncle Jaime out of it, and he was able to make a deal with the U.S. people. It's George they want. But they have to catch him in the act before they can land on him."

There were gaps in the story. I saw them, as clearly as I saw the cracks in the wall beside me, and I thought of the questions I might have asked. The story didn't explain my anonymous letters. It didn't explain why Ines had tried to get me to leave Mexico, or why George wanted me here, at the house. It didn't explain other things. I knew what they were. I was thinking more clearly, more logically, than I had ever thought in my life. But I didn't say anything. I didn't want to.

The glass slipped from my hands and shattered on the stone paving. There was nothing left to spill; only a few drops of liquid darkened the dust.

Danny stopped pacing.

"It's time," he said. "Let's go."

He walked toward me. As he came he shrank, till he was only about a foot tall. I could have picked him up like a baby. But when he put out his hand it was enormous, a giant's paw that clasped my whole arm. He pulled, and I came up off the bench, all in one piece.

"Walk," he said.

I looked down at my feet. Hi, feet. But now I couldn't

move them. I tried. They just sat there on the ground and wouldn't talk to me, even. I started to cry, because my feet wouldn't move, or talk to me, and nothing would ever talk again, and people were all shut up in little boxes and couldn't get through to each other. The tears ran down into my mouth. I was crying champagne; the stinging, sparkling taste was delicious.

The patio disappeared. We were in the middle of a jungle and the trees reached down long, green arms. I knew they wanted to wrap themselves around my throat and tighten. They wanted to kill me. I was still crying. Danny's arm was around me. I hid my face against him. Now I couldn't see the trees. But I knew they were there, bending, threatening.

After hours, Danny pushed me away and I had to open my eyes. The trees were gone, but I could see them trying to drag their roots out and follow me. I opened my mouth to scream, but no sound came out, though I felt my vocal cords straining till they seemed to cut through my skin. I saw Ivan. He wanted to hurt me. I was terribly afraid of him. The wall was leaning; it was going to fall, fall on me and crush me.

People talked, and I knew the words and their meanings, but it was like talking to María about the rabbits; there was a gap between understanding and comprehension. They were telling me to go to the gate and open the door and let him see me. I didn't move. I couldn't move. I was afraid of the gate, and of them—and of "him," whoever he was. A vast impalpable menace pervaded the universe and every object in it.

They pushed me to the door, eventually, and Ivan opened it, standing well back out of sight, and I stood there till he closed it again. Someone screamed. It might have been me. The door burst open and then I saw him, Tom Andres. Ivan hit him from behind, with a piece of pipe, and he fell. I stood watching, as detached as a spectator at the theater, only more so, because a good play moves me, and I wasn't at all moved except by the formless panic.

I watched while they lifted Andres's limp body and jammed it into the back seat of the car and I watched myself being put into the car too. They made me lie down. My face was so close to his that I could feel his breath against my cheek, and see the red thread that trickled from under his hair down the side of his face. I saw these things and I knew what they meant, but then the process of awareness stopped, as if someone had walled off the part of my brain that felt and reacted. There was no room in me for any emotion except terror, and the very irrationality of the fear made it worse. I dreaded the unconscious man beside me as much as I feared the man who had struck him down; the car was an object of terror, and so was the fly that sat on Andres's forehead. If someone had showed me a kitten, I'd have cringed and cried out.

After a time the panic faded somewhat and I began to see things. The hallucinatory drugs are unpredictable, not only in the way in which they affect different people, but in the varying symptoms a single user may experience in the course of one dose. Of course I wasn't thinking that. I was simply limp with relief that the terror was going away. The hallucinations were a pleasure compared to that.

I was sitting up by then, but I might as well have been blindfolded because my senses were so twisted that I didn't recognize anything I saw. Colors had sound and sounds were palpable. Green was a deep baritone hum; the tone rose to a shriller note when the sun-bleached grass of the open fields appeared. The hiss of the car's tires on the road surface hurt, like ground glass grating against my skin.

The visions went on and on, while people talked to me and moved me, and did things. Toward the end the old panic came back, ebbing and flowing, alternating with wilder hallucinations. I don't remember them too clearly. I don't want to.

II

The room was almost dark. A feeble, oily light cast a faint glow over bare walls and a beaten earth floor. There was a strong stench of animal refuse, blended with other powerful smells: perspiration and oil lamps and cooking. My left sandal strap was twisted, cutting into my foot. I could see both feet, and the legs to which they were attached, stretched out on the dirt floor. Someone was holding me against his shoulder. My cheek lay against his chest.

"You're all right now," he said. "It's wearing off. How do you feel?"

"Okay," I said dubiously, and then, as another section of memory slipped into place, "How about you? They hit you."

"I'm fine."

His arm steadied me as I tried to sit up. I did it slowly, expecting the thudding headache of a hangover, but I felt okay, except for a passing dizziness.

I could see more of the room now. It wasn't big; about the size of my bedroom back home. The walls were adobe, unpainted and dirty. There was a single door of heavy wooden planks. No windows. The furniture consisted of a battered table and two packing cases. Originally the place might have been a storage shed or an animal pen. Now it was a prison.

I looked at my fellow prisoner and he returned my look with an unconvincing attempt at a smile. The dried blood on his cheek looked black in the poor light. He was in his shirt sleeves; his coat, rolled and wadded, was on the floor behind me, where it had served as a pillow for my head.

"What time is it?" I asked.

"I don't know." He held out his arm, and I saw that his watch was smashed. "It's night. Late."

"Where are we?"

"I was hoping you could tell me that."

"I'm afraid I wasn't paying attention to where we were going."

"I'm not surprised." His arm tightened reflexively; it wasn't an embrace or a gesture of reassurance, it was as if he were squashing something. "They gave you a heavy dose."

"Dose of what?"

"Psilocybin, maybe. Derived from a local mushroom. It's considerably more potent than mescaline, and less apt to produce nausea. Possibly ololiuqui—morning-glory seeds. Ivan seems to have access to a lot of things."

"Ivan," I said.

"He's our boy. I don't know what they told you—"

"A pack of lies. Except—you are fuzz, aren't you?"

"I guess my cover is wearing pretty thin," he said drily. "I'm from the Bureau of Narcotics."

"What are you doing down here?"

"Making a complete ass of myself. Don't get any ideas, Carol. I don't carry bombs in my shoes, and my karate belt isn't black. It's pale gray."

"I could have picked a better person to get kidnapped

with. . . . I'm sorry. I didn't mean that."

"You are only too right." His mouth relaxed in an unamused smile. "But you haven't heard my excuses. I have some great excuses. I underestimated Ivan. I thought he was a two-bit punk like most of the lower-echelon narcotics types. He isn't. He's paranoidal and dangerous. And this is not a two-bit operation. If he brings this deal off, he'll be in the big money. And it looks as if he'll succeed. Tonight's the night. The night of the four hundred rabbits."

He wasn't making a lot of sense, but I knew he wasn't trying to explain; he was talking, out loud, to himself. But for me all the whirling clues of the past week suddenly snapped together, like a jigsaw puzzle when the one strategic piece has been found.

"That's what she meant," I gasped. "Not her pots; his . . . Uncle Jaime's pots of marijuana, that's what she meant when she talked about thirty rabbits. They use the rabbit scale to describe drugs. Ivan and Ramón, at the party . . . And if thirty rabbits refers to marijuana, then four hundred rabbits . . ."

"Heroin. I think we're on the same track; why don't we carry on a conversation instead of having two separate monologues?"

"I don't know where to start. Heroin? Is Ivan growing poppies? I remember thinking that it was surprising more people didn't cultivate them."

"No, you're off the track again. Ivan is enough of a megalomaniac to think of something like that eventually; his interest in chemistry may have been stimulated by some such notion. But that isn't how the narcotics business works, it's too complex for one man to control all the stages. You know something about heroin?"

"I read an article once. From the poppy fields of Turkey to Marseilles by way of Beirut or Damascus . . ."

"Then I don't have to give you the complete lecture. The point is that after the morphine base has been turned into heroin, the problem of smuggling it into the States still remains. The poor, hard-working smuggler has it rough these days, we've caught on to his best tricks."

"I never even heard of your little group," I said repressively.

"We work in the dark, unseen and unsung; our only reward the—"

"Tears of the grateful mothers of the boys you save," I suggested.

He grinned. It was a much better effort than the first smile.

"We do get a little help from the Customs boys."

"And the FBI, and Interpol, and the police forces in various countries and states and—"

"You know too much," he said resignedly. "Now can I get back to the lecture?"

"Never mind the lecture. Tell me why you're looking for heroin here, instead of back home."

"Because a lot of the heroin that reaches the States today comes in via Canada and Mexico."

"Doesn't that double the risk for the smuggler? Why not take it in directly, through New York or San Francisco?"

"Because we have the major international ports and airports pretty well covered. It's much more difficult to patrol a long land border. Canada and Mexico don't have as great a problem with narcotics. We're everybody's favorite customer; most of the stuff is aimed at us. We got cooperation from the Canadian and Mexican police, but they have problems of their own; they don't always initiate action unless we prod them. That's what I and my associates do, mostly—prod and bribe and argue. We don't often run into the big shots, the ones with substantial holdings in New Jersey and Palm Springs. Most of the crooks we catch are small time. Like Uncle Jaime."

"Uncle Jaime? I thought Ivan—"

"It started with Uncle Jaime. And George. Do you know about George's LSD experiments?"

I nodded, and he went on.

"Jaime has been smuggling pot for years. He doesn't see anything immoral about it; the only pothead he's ever seen was some lousy peon who, by Jaime's aristocratic standards, would never have amounted to a damn anyhow. The old man uses the stuff discreetly himself, he enjoys it, and he likes to share the fun. Okay. Everything was comparatively peaceful until Ivan got into the act. When he found out what his uncle had been doing, he was disgusted. He felt the way I would if I saw somebody who owned an oil well pumping up just enough oil to keep his car running.

"There is a narcotics underworld. That's one of the strongest arguments against marijuana, which isn't even a narcotic, medically."

"If it were legalized—"

"Carol," Andres said wearily, "I know all the arguments. I even agree with a few of them—in my private capacity. But my job is to enforce the law, and the cases I see are the bad ones, the tragedies. The progression from marijuana to acid or snow isn't inevitable; but it does happen. How many tragedies prove a point? One was enough for me; one kid, seventeen years old, lying dead in the garbage of a slum alley. I don't worry about the casual experimenter either. But how do you restrict the stuff to him? How do you keep it out of the hands of those who are going to be destroyed by it? The kids who get hooked on marijuana are the same types who are going to want stronger, more effective methods of escape."

He stopped, breathing hard, and I sat looking down at my folded hands. We were both thinking the same thing.

"I'm sorry about your friend Danny," Andres said, in a voice that was surprisingly gentle, after his outburst.

"Friend?" I said. "Never mind Danny. Tell me more about Ivan. He fascinates me."

"Ivan decided to expand his uncle's business operations. Through contacts in the narcotics underworld I mentioned, he learned that a big European syndicate was on the lookout for a man in Mexico who could get their snow across the border. Ivan set up the deal, but the big boys wouldn't take him by himself; his uncle has a reputation for running a good operation, and this is too expensive a proposition to be handed over to an inexperienced kid. One of the big wheels is now in Mexico. We know who he is; we know who a lot of these bastards are, but we can never pin anything on them. If we can catch Mr. X and Uncle Jaime in the act of closing the deal, we can nail them both on conspiracy to sell narcotics and we may get a line to Mr. X's associates."

"And the meeting is taking place tonight?"

"That's right."

"I can see why Ivan wants you out from underfoot. But why kidnap me?"

"Use your head."

"It's got to be George," I said. "If Ivan wants me for a hostage . . . Then George isn't one of the smugglers."

"George," said Andres sardonically, "is one of the good

guys. He's the one who tipped us off. George has always known about Jaime's pot smuggling. After his experiments he wasn't too keen on marijuana, but he couldn't see too much harm in it. Then he found out about the heroin deal. He says Jaime told him about it, and maybe he did; the old coot is the weirdest mixture of cunning and naïveté. George couldn't take it. After weeks of soul searching he contacted Jack—our man in Mexico City. We decided it wasn't smart to have George continue dealing with Jack, he's too well known. So they sent for me."

I stood up in a surge of joy and relief that made me forget the lingering discomforts of the drug. The romantic twelve-year-old had been right all along. So maybe George's shining armor was a little tarnished. I was willing to settle for that.

"Mr. Andres . . ."

Andres, unaffected by my private euphoria, was squatting morosely on the floor. He glanced up.

"Such formality is a little bit silly, isn't it? And what are you looking so damned cheerful about? I suppose it's nice to find out that your old man is not a crook, and I'm happy to have been the one to tell you. But I'm such a selfish louse, I keep thinking about what Ivan's going to do to us."

"He's already done it! He wants his precious meeting to go off without interruption. Once it's over . . ."

I didn't need Tom's somber, unblinking stare to tell me what a fool I was. The conclusion was inevitable.

Tom stood up. I caught at him as he swayed, and he grabbed my shoulders for support. After the first second or two, I wasn't holding him up, he was holding me. I was shaking all over, like someone with a chill.

"Honey, I'm not trying to frighten you; God knows

you're scared enough already. But you can't fight a danger unless you admit it's there."

"He'll kill you," I stuttered. "He'll have to kill you."

"That doesn't matter. I mean, that's not the—"

"It matters," I said.

I've been told that kissing a girl with braces can be tricky. Kissing a girl whose teeth are chattering like castanets isn't easy either. It isn't just the teeth that move, it's the whole lower part of the face. But after Tom found my mouth my teeth stopped chattering.

When his face came back into focus, he looked gloomier than ever.

"That's all we need," he said.

"Well, I'm sorry—"

"You should be. This whole thing is your fault, you know. If you hadn't gone bumbling around like a kitten trying to cross a superhighway at rush hour, I might have been able to control what few brains I have."

He kissed me again, more efficiently, and then moved away.

"If I were a nice guy I might let you dream on until the ax actually fell—spare you the pains of anticipation. But I can't adopt pacifism at this late date, and I'll be damned if I'm going to sit here on my hands till Ivan gets ready to polish us off. I think you're too smart to kid yourself anyway."

"Yes, I wasn't thinking straight. Of course he'll have to dispose of us. The meeting is just the first step, once the smuggling is actually underway, we'll be just as great a threat to him."

"It's not as simple as that."

"The old fate worse than death?" I suggested, with a

lightness I did not feel.

"There are several fates worse than death. How would you like to be in the shape you were in this afternoon—permanently?"

"Oh, no. He wouldn't."

"He didn't have to give you the drug. He could have slipped you knock-out drops, or just slugged you."

"I'd prefer to be slugged," I admitted.

"It was pure sadism." Tom's face was strained. "The chances of a bad trip with the hallucinogens are much increased if the person doesn't know he's taken something. I don't like the way Ivan's mind works. And he has a complicated problem on his hands. George also knows about him. But George is not exactly persona grata around the Bureau; my immediate boss, for one, is very skeptical about his story. Remember we don't have a damned thing on Ivan or Jaime without George's evidence."

"I thought you said Uncle Jaime had been smuggling pot."

"He's never been caught at it, and he's certainly been as innocent as a baby since George alerted us. Either he has temporarily retired, waiting for the heroin to arrive, or he's got some new method of getting the stuff through, one we don't know about. No, the whole thing rests on George. I can see what you're thinking, but don't get excited; George is the safest man in town right now. His death would give his story a verisimilitude which it presently lacks. So long as Ivan holds you he can keep George quiet; but he can't lock you up indefinitely, and he can't kill you without destroying his hold over George. Does that make sense so far?"

"Yes, but it doesn't relieve my mind. Sooner or later

Ivan will have to do something. And what about you?"

"Having me turn up dead would have the same effect as George's death, unless he can arrange it to look like an accident. And it would have to be a damned convincing accident. . . ."

His voice died away. Watching his face, I felt a responsive chill run down my back.

"Don't tell me," I said. "You've thought of a convincing accident."

"I hope Ivan hasn't thought of it. But knowing him . . . We've got to think of some way to get out of here. Fast."

"It won't be fast enough," I said. All at once I was very calm. "Don't you hear? There's someone at the door."

CHAPTER 12

IVAN WAS wearing his favorite black shirt and slacks. I'm sure that his fondness for that color was deliberate, and theatrical; he looked like a mod, up-to-date version of Mephistopheles. Even his expression of smug triumph reflected the way in which an actor might have elected to play the part—portraying not the majesty of evil, but a sick malice. There ought to have been a smell of brimstone about him.

The smell that came in with him was that of fresh night air, and I sniffed it appreciatively. The air in that foul little room was pretty thick.

The door didn't stay open long enough to do much for the atmosphere. I caught a glimpse of darkness, unrelieved except for a few stars, and I thought, we're out in the country. But I couldn't see what good that information was going to do me.

Ivan wasn't alone. Two of his companions were nondescript, shifty-looking strangers, but I recognized the third; he had the gall to grin and bow, just as he had done the last time I left his shop. Carlos and Teotihuacan . . . The recognition set up a train of thought, but I didn't have time to pursue it. Ivan said,

"I dropped by to see how my patient was. Feeling better, Carol?"

"I loved it," I said. "I can see now what I've been missing."

It was cheap defiance. I regretted the remark as soon as I'd made it, especially when I saw Ivan's smile widen. He was such a ham himself that he brought out the ham in other people.

"On your way to the meeting?" Tom asked.

Ivan closed his eyes and looked pained.

"Please don't be clever, Mr. Andres. It does not suit you. You know where I am going, and I know that you know, so don't let us fence. You are not a skillful antagonist. And don't tell me that I cannot get away with this, or that your friends have been following me. I know the precise state of affairs and I have matters under control. My respected uncle has already left, through his private exit from the house; and George is sitting quietly in the parlor pondering various matters over his chessboard."

"With Danny?"

I didn't like giving Ivan the satisfaction of being curious, but I couldn't help it. I had no hate to spare for Danny. I wouldn't have traded places with him and his poor twisted conscience for anything in the world.

"No, no. Do you think I would be so foolish as to send Danny back to the house? The loyalty of an addict can be bought by anyone who has the price. I could not risk my Judas goat. He is happy now. It takes so little to make him happy."

"One small handful of buttons," I said. "The carrot for the Judas goat. He doesn't charge much for betrayal."

"We must be fair," Ivan said judiciously. "He does not believe that you will come to harm. Why should he not win paradise for himself, at the cost of a few hours' inconvenience to you? It is selfish, I admit; but altruism is not one of the characteristics of the addict."

"He's been useful to you, though," I said. "Wasn't it nice of me to bring him along?"

Ivan shrugged.

"I use the materials which are at hand. If you had come alone, I would have managed just as well. If Danny had not been so . . . flexible . . . I would have dealt otherwise with him."

"Then you were the one who sent me the letters."

"And arranged for that convenient inheritance. Perhaps Mrs. Farley did not mention that the terms of the 'will' gave you half? A less clever man might have dealt more directly with George. But I knew that such methods would actually defeat my purpose. George's reputation with his compatriots is not of the best. In fact—let us be honest, my friend—his veracity is still in doubt, is it not?"

Tom didn't answer, but his face must have been expressive, for Ivan laughed aloud.

"Yes, it is. He has no proof of his wild accusations. If George fails to alert the police tonight, they will dismiss his story as a pathetic attempt to curry favor with his government. That would be success enough for me. However, my plan is more clever. George will not give the signal tonight; he will give it tomorrow night. And when the police creep into the darkened house in San Angel, they will find a harmless old gentleman enjoying the society of a married lady. There will be blushes and apologies; and I do not think that George will be popular in his adopted country after that."

"That is clever," I said. I had to say something, and

quickly; Tom's face was red, and he was beginning to bounce up and down on his toes.

"A trifle," Ivan said modestly. "I wish I had time to tell you of my other plans. But, alas . . ."

He glanced at his watch. It must have been a signal; his three little helpers moved. One produced a gun, and Carlos pulled out a knife. I didn't see what the third man was doing, I was otherwise occupied. Grinning from ear to ear, Carlos walked toward me.

"Wait a minute," I said, retreating. "You don't want to kill anybody, you're too smart for that."

"Don't be a fool," Ivan said sharply; he was addressing Tom, not me. "The woman is right, I shall not harm her—unless you fail to obey orders."

Tom didn't move. He was between me and Carlos, and his shoulders were drawn up like those of a bull about to charge. Ivan gave an irritated hiss and spoke emphatically in Spanish. The man with the gun moved to one side, and Carlos, looking glum, handed Ivan the knife. Then I saw the third man, and the object he held in his hand.

A glass of orange juice.

Ivan moved, with his catlike swiftness. His left arm pinned my arms to my sides and pulled me against him. His right hand balanced the knife delicately on my earlobe.

"Mr. Andres," he said. "Take the glass and drink."

Under the blood and the bruises and the tan, Tom's face turned white. He shook his head.

"If you do not," Ivan said calmly, "I will be forced to hurt Carol. Not fatally, of course; but perhaps a small portion of her anatomy might be a convincing gift to her father."

The knife twisted. It was surprisingly painful; I kept telling myself that girls had their ears pierced all the time. But they used a nice sharp, antiseptic needle.

Blood began to trickle down my neck, under the collar of my blouse. Tom snatched the glass and drained it.

"Good," Ivan said approvingly, and removed the knife.

I put my hand to my ear, and he tut-tutted, and handed me a handkerchief.

"What was in it?" I asked sickly. "One of the rabbit family, or just plain arsenic?"

The smile left Ivan's face.

"So she did tell you," he said. "The treacherous old bitch did tell you."

I saw death in his eyes. The round blackness of his pupils seemed to shift and shimmer and change shape; I saw a huddled, black-clothed body, the body of an old woman.

"Tom told me," I said. "What old bitch are you talking about?"

"I see."

His arm relaxed. He had been holding me so tightly that my ribs hurt, but I hadn't felt the pain. I thought I had won a reprieve for María, but I wasn't sure; if he thought she could not be trusted she was as good as dead. Sentiment had no place in Ivan's scheme of things.

"So you know the rabbit code," he said. "Amusing, I thought."

"Very. How many rabbits were in that glass?"

He laughed.

"Not four hundred, no. I do not have that substance, not yet. This would be—oh, let us say approximately three hundred and fifty. On the conventional scale, that is. Personally I believe it should be rated higher than heroin. The effects, permanent and temporary, are so much more drastic."

Tom had been trying to look unconcerned, but this was

too much for him.

"Acid," he said, and it wasn't a question. "How did you get hold of it?"

"I made it," Ivan said calmly. "For experimental purposes; there is not enough profit in that trade now. But it is so very simple to make—acid. That is what it is, lysergic acid diethylamide, to be precise. It is related to psilocybin, the active alkaloid of the mushroom, but it is many times more powerful."

He went on talking—bragging, showing off; maybe he even gave the recipe, I don't know. I wasn't listening. I remembered the boy who had walked out of a fourteen-story window, on his way to London, and the girl who had seen her face start to melt. . . .

"She's going to faint," someone said, from a long way off.

I came struggling up out of a gray fog to find myself on the floor, with Ivan slapping my face. It was like the time I had my appendix out; I heard myself calling him names I had never expected to say out loud. He laughed, and gave me a final slap, for luck, that made my head rock.

"I must be on my way now," he said, with another glance at his watch. "I need not remind you, Andres, that LSD is quickly absorbed into the system. Don't waste your time trying to rid yourself of it now."

He sauntered toward the door, but something about him —the tilt of his head, the swagger with which he walked— told me he wasn't quite through. Sure enough, he turned. Carelessly, he tossed the knife onto the table.

"A present for Carol. I strongly advise you to take it, my child. Acid is unpredictable. Mr. Andres may come to believe that you are the enemy he hates most. After all, I did promise George that you would come to no harm."

The humor of it made him break up; he was laughing so hard he couldn't talk. After the door closed, I could still hear him laughing.

It was very quiet, after the laughter died. I looked at the knife; and then I gasped and started, as Tom made a sudden movement.

He dropped onto his knees in the corner and stuck his finger down his throat.

When he got to his feet his face was greenish gray and there were beads of perspiration on his upper lip. I handed him Ivan's handkerchief.

"Sorry it isn't clean. I thought he said it was too late for that."

"Rule one," Tom said, mopping his forehead. "Never believe the other guy. He'll say anything."

"Then it's all right."

"No, he was right about that. Acid is fast-acting. But—rule number two—you don't neglect even the slightest chance. Get the knife, Carol."

"Tom, I will not—"

"Let's not argue. I don't have much time."

"Couldn't I—tie you up, or something, till the effects wear off?"

"The first four or five hours are the worst. That was when a guy in Brooklyn murdered his mother-in-law. The letdown starts after about twelve hours; it was during that stage that a kid in L.A. tried to offer up his girlfriend as a sacrifice. One man became psychotic twenty-four hours after ingestion, others had psychotic episodes for months. How long do you want to wait? Take the knife."

"I won't!"

"God damn it, I'm trying to get us out of here! I want to get away from you, a long way away, and fast. I'm scared, and that's making it worse; some of the people who have had the worst trips were doctors, professionals, who knew what was coming. . . ."

I took the knife.

Tom threw himself at the table with a manic energy. He moved it to a spot beside the door, and got into position on the other side, where the door would hide him when it opened.

"Look at the table, as if there were something under it, something frightful. Now scream. Keep on screaming."

It was no trouble at all. I just opened my mouth and let it out.

The plan was desperate and makeshift, and it worked the way such plans often do—much better than the elaborate ones. It was reasonable to assume that Ivan would have left a man on guard, but I didn't understand the rest of Tom's reasoning till later, when I had time to think. Then I realized that he was correct in assuming that the guard would interfere if he thought I was in imminent danger. That was Ivan's convincing accident—not that Tom should injure me, but that I should kill him while both of us were drugged. Ivan didn't really expect me to use the knife. The "real accident" would be staged later, this episode was just Ivan's idea of fun. But if a narcotics agent was murdered by a freaked-out girl, the daughter of a man whose past experiments with acid were well known—George and the Narcotics Bureau would be effectively distracted from the original suspects for some time to come.

Tom miscalculated on only one thing. There were two

men on guard.

Luckily for us, it was the first one who had the gun. He was still peering stupidly at the shadows under the table when Tom's fist came down on the back of his head. He fell like a log.

The other man's behavior was predictable, even though we had not considered him. Instead of retreating, as he should have done, he rushed forward to help his buddy, and tripped over the body. I stamped on his hand, which was groping like a big brown spider toward the gun. Tom took care of the rest.

He staggered to his feet and bolted out the open door. I went after him. Somewhere along the line I had dropped the knife, and I decided I wouldn't go back for it. When Tom stopped running I almost ran into him. He leaped back away from me as if I were contagious.

Behind us the open door of the shed spilled yellow light out onto a stretch of weed-covered ground. There were other buildings around, low and dark and undefined. They were not houses; we were in the open country. Except for the single light, a vast, star-sprinkled darkness covered the world. There was a dim half-circle of moon. In its light Tom's face was bleached of color. His lips were parted as he panted for breath; his mouth was an opaque black hole in his face. This is the way a dead man looks, I thought. This is the way he'll look if they catch us.

"Your hair is burning," he said, in a remote voice. "Cold fire, silver flame . . . Why don't you stop following me? Go back to Ellis. He wants you, I don't."

"Tom," I gasped.

I meant the word as an incantation; and, magically, it worked. He shook himself like a dog coming out of the water, and his eyes narrowed.

"Oh, God," he said. "Carol. It's Carol. Run. Go that way. I'm going the other way. You take the high road and I'll take the low road. Low is right. . . . I don't know where the hell I am."

There was blood on his chin; his teeth were sunk into his lower lip. I reached out for him, and again he moved away, with the same horrible jerking movement, like an animal reacting galvanically to electric shock.

"Call George," he said. He spoke in a series of isolated gasps, as if each word were a separate effort. "Can't remember . . . number. . . . Find a phone . . . telephone . . . road. . . ."

The words didn't fade out, they broke, like a piece of dry stick snapped straight across. He flung himself around and began to run, frantically, like something pursued by dragons. I watched till the stumbling, swaying figure disappeared into a patch of shadow. Then I ran—the other way.

I was taking a desperate chance, weighing one catastrophe against another. In his condition he might kill himself, by design or carelessness. But he was too strong for me, I couldn't have stopped him even if I were with him, and I certainly couldn't keep him from killing me if he decided to do so. I had to get help, and quickly.

Then I came out of the belt of trees that surrounded the buildings and I stopped short, with a gasp of recognition.

Straight ahead, a silver ghost of structure in the moonlight, was a vast pyramidal shape. It was so lovely in the soft healing light, which covered the scars of time, that for a second I forgot the urgency of my purpose. The Pyramid of the Sun, at Teotihuacan. Now I knew where I was.

I knew more than that; I knew everything. Fatigue and

horror and surprise blended with the blinding flash of understanding to give me a feeling that must have been like the insight an acidhead claims to get from a good trip. Everything made sense. There was a vast pattern, a Master Plan, and I saw it plain; saw how even the weirdest, most unrelated acts fitted into the intent of the Planner.

Two full days I had spent at this site. I knew it. I could tell from the contours of the pyramid, even at this distance, where on that vast archaeological area I was now standing. Off to my right, its lower heights hidden by the level of the ground, was the so-called Citadel area, with the ruins of the Quetzalcoatl pyramid. From it, straight as a ruler, the Avenue of the Dead led past the Pyramid of the Sun, to the other pyramid and the Plaza of the Moon.

And this was important knowledge. Because far off to my right, between me and the houses there, I could see a light. It wasn't the light of a window; it flickered and moved—the light of a flashlight in someone's hand, moving as he walked, searching. They would expect me to go that way, where the houses were, where there were people.

I started running toward the pyramid.

I guess I wasn't reasoning as brilliantly as I thought I was, but there is some excuse for me. Two conflicting desires tore at me—the need to stop and think, using all the knowledge I had; and the need for haste.

The famous meeting was not an object of concern to me, though I knew it would be driving Tom wild, if he had been in any condition to worry about ordinary things. The meeting was going to take place, and there wasn't a thing I could do to stop it. I didn't intend to try. I only wanted to get help and locate Tom before he walked off the edge of a cliff.

Telephones are so common back home that we don't realize how rare they may be in another country, especially away from the cities. I might have to wake up a dozen people before I found one, and by then the fat would be in the fire, because I didn't know who was on my side and who was against me. If Carlos was involved in the smuggling business, his friends and relatives might be crooks too.

There were two places where I knew I would find a telephone. The Cultural Area near the Citadel, which included the museum and one of the restaurants; and the other restaurant near the parking lot that served the Pyramid of the Sun. They would be closed at this hour, but I was quite prepared to do the necessary breaking and entering. If I roused an indignant guard or night watchman, so much the better.

Even now, looking back on it, I think that was fairly good reasoning. There were only two minor details I failed to take into account. One was a piece of information I didn't have, though I probably could have figured it out if I'd been as clever as I thought I was. The other detail I should have realized. It was a question of time.

So many things had happened that I didn't realize how little time they had taken up. Tom had started moving the moment Ivan left the shack, and after that the action had been rapid. I don't suppose Ivan had been gone more than five minutes when we erupted from our jail over the prostrate forms of our guards.

I assumed, naturally, that he had gone by car.

I wasn't even thinking about Ivan as I stumbled across the rough ground. I was beginning to realize the difference between broad theoretical knowledge of a place, and foot-by-foot familarity. I couldn't get lost, the vast moonlit shape up ahead kept me pointed in the right direction. But the ground under my feet was not familiar, I had never been in this area before, and even if I had traversed it once, I would not have remembered details. Details are important when they are holes in the ground and clumps of cacti. I must have fallen six or seven times, taking another chunk of skin off my knees on each occasion. I went under a fence once; I never did find out whose fence it was or why it was there, but it was a barbed-wire fence and the lowest strand took my blouse half off my back as I squirmed under.

The fence did things to my morale, too. I couldn't remember any fences, and I began to wonder if I was wandering around in some innocent farmer's field, with the pyramid twenty miles away instead of two hundred yards. Then I came to the top of a little rise in the ground, and I knew where I was again.

The terrain near the pyramids looks flat from up above, except for the neat geometric shapes of the ruined buildings. Close up, it isn't at all flat, as my scraped knees could testify; I had fallen over, or into, a good many of the convexities and concavities.

Now, on my little hill, I realized that I had miscalculated, but not as badly as I might have done. Ahead of me, only a few yards away, was the dark, indistinct line of the Avenue of the Dead. Off to the right was the Citadel, with its platforms and staircases and pyramid. The Pyramid of the Sun was on my left. I was about halfway between the two areas where I hoped to find a telephone.

I looked back, in the direction from which I had come. I thought I caught a brief flicker of light, but I couldn't be sure. It didn't matter. I knew they were there, whether I could see them or not—behind, and to my right. If they anticipated my reasoning, one of them might already have reached the Citadel, hoping to head me off. The safest course for me was to go on, toward the restaurant near the pyramid.

I had had enough of holes and cacti and rocks, so I went straight toward the ruined buildings that lined the Avenue. I could run when I reached its paved surface.

He tripped me. It was pure meanness, he could have reached out and grabbed, I passed so close to the terraced wall in whose shadow he was concealed. I landed flat and hard. It was like falling onto a vegetable grater, the harsh weeds and stones lacerated my whole front from forehead to toes, and the impact left me without breath for a moment. I thought I had tripped over a stone or a tree root, until his hands grabbed my wrists.

He had them behind my back and tied together before I could catch my breath; and the inhalation that was intended to come out in a loud scream was choked back into my throat as a strip of cloth was whipped over my mouth.

I tried to struggle, but his knee was planted in the small of my back, and it stayed there until he had the gag firmly anchored. Then he took me by the shoulders and yanked me up. I hung from his hands like a big stuffed doll.

"What a busy night you are having," he said, grinning. "How did you manage it? Don't try to talk; you will only choke yourself. I will answer the questions which I know must be worrying you. How do I come to be here? But I saw the lights, and observed activity near the hut, before I had gone far. I sent my man back to assist his stupid associates while I continued on my way, to head you off if you came in this direction. I suspected you would be drawn by your beloved pyramid. Now I think I had better keep you under my own eye. Come along, I shall be late."

My first impulse was to kick him. But he was holding me at arm's length, alert as a watchdog, and my legs had all the strength of watery paste. Even if he let go of me I wouldn't get far, bound and gagged, and when he caught me again . . .

"You can walk, like a lady," he said, reading my mind, "or I can leave you tucked into a crevice, with your feet tied. I would come back to get you later; but there are snakes, and a few poisonous insects. Since you have demonstrated your inability to accept the inevitable, I would also consider it necessary to give you a sample of the same substance I gave Mr. Andres. Do not deceive yourself, I can force you to take it. I have dosed other reluctant animals. Make up your mind; I have not much time."

There wasn't any choice. I tried to look limp and cooperative. The first part wasn't hard. He gave another of his infuriating little chuckles.

"A wise decision. Let us go."

It was a nightmare walk, something out of a pothead's wilder visions. The man who named the place "The Avenue of the Dead" must have seen it by moonlight. Gray and silver and still, the long stretch of stone reached out into the distance; and there were ghosts thronging every paving block; pale painted faces peered out of every empty doorway. The figure beside me was from a nightmare too, slim and black and strong. His hand lifted me along, and after a while I lost all sense of reality and seemed to float a few inches above the ground.

This is it, I thought. This is how it ends. I'm as good as dead, and I'm walking down the Avenue of the Dead arm in arm with a killer, toward the spot where two murderers of another kind are waiting—men who dispense death in kilo weights to thousands of walking corpses.

For that was the second vital piece of information I had not considered, during my wild dash across country, and the reason why Ivan was on the spot, waiting for me, instead of being ten miles along the road to Mexico City. The meeting, the Four Hundred Rabbit meeting, was taking place at Teotihuacan.

It made sense because of its very unorthodoxy. The places the police would expect were the usual ones—bars, restaurants, hotels, Uncle Jaime must know Teotihuacan as well as he knew the rest of his beloved Mexico. If the other man was followed to the meeting, Uncle Jaime could slip away—and there would be Mr. X, a visiting tourist who had taken it into his head to examine the ruins by moonlight. The evening Sound and Light performance would be a perfect excuse. A man could conceal himself among the crowds, in the darkness, and let the police follow his conspicuous car back to the city. If he was seen returning to his hotel later, it wouldn't matter; the damage would have been done by then.

But these were only extra precautions. The visitor would not be under close surveillance. Why should the police waste manpower on that job when they had an informer watching the other suspect? They would wait for George to call. And he would not. I had no more doubts about George. All his aberrant behavior was explained by one overriding truth. He still cared about me.

No wonder George hadn't seemed surprised to see me that first night. The authorities must have known of my trip even before I arrived. But my arrival had really upset the apple cart. Poor George had tried to get me to leave, and so had Ines, independently. Ivan had counteracted their clumsy attempts easily. The telephone call that lured me out of the hotel was a final demonstration; it was never meant to succeed even if Tom had not interfered. It was only another warning to George: that I was vulnerable wherever I happened to be, in Mexico or out of it. But George couldn't get me off the hook by telling me the truth; that would have given Ivan another reason to want me out of the way. There was only one thing George could do, and he had done it—got me into the house where he could watch me himself. And he might have succeeded, except for Danny.

So now the game was played out. I didn't even care. I just wished we would get to our destination, so I could stop dragging my aching bones around. We passed the Pyramid of the Sun. Its bulk loomed up like that of a primeval monster, obscuring the stars. Ahead was a matching shadow, the Pyramid of the Moon. I wasn't floating any longer, I was stumbling, and I weighed about two hundred pounds, and I couldn't breathe through the gag; and my feet ached clear up to my calves, where they met another set of aches from my skinned knees. The pyramids fell in on me. It was wonderful, not having to walk any longer.

II

When I came to, I was completely disoriented. Maybe it was the lingering effects of the drug; but I thought at first I was in a straitjacket, lying on the floor of a cell. A streak of moonlight showed a stretch of gritty stone floor, but everything else was dark, and I couldn't move my hands or my feet.

Then I heard voices, and the rising wave of panic subsided as memory returned. I knew the voices: Ivan and Uncle Jaime.

They were speaking Spanish. I couldn't make out the words, only the characteristic cadence. I knew I couldn't have been unconscious very long. I wondered where in blazes I was.

I rolled over. That isn't as easy as it sounds when you're tied up like a clumsy parcel. When my position was reversed, I still couldn't see much, but again I blessed the instinct that had led me to explore Teotihuacan. Directly in front of me was a square black object, too shadowed to be distinct. By twisting my neck I could see out beyond the obstruction. Twenty feet away, pale in the moonlight, was a row of carved stone pillars. They were the pillars in the courtyard of the Temple of the Butterfly; and I was lying behind one of the matching pillars on the opposite side of the court.

The mazelike rooms and passages . . . the ancient sewage system . . . I was willing to bet Uncle Jaime knew ways out of that temple that even the archaeologists hadn't found.

My feet hurt, and my hands were numb, but the gag was driving me crazy. It was soggy from my inadvertent drooling, and it itched. I thought that if I couldn't scratch I was going to die. So I hoisted myself to a sitting position and began scraping my cheek against the stone of the pillar. I didn't have any plan in mind; it was discomfort, not heroics, that forced me into action.

Then I heard the eeriest sound I've ever heard. From far off, rendered ringingly distinct by some strange acoustical echo, came the sound of slow, advancing footsteps. It was like an old morality play—the offstage footsteps of Death, coming on remorselessly. And you knew that when the footsteps stopped, you would see the Thing that made them, and that would be the end—the end of the play.

It must be Mr. X, on his way to the meeting—walking slowly across the plaza, admiring the moonlit bulk of the pyramid; mounting the steps and crossing the vestibule in front of the courtyard. The allegory was valid; he was a harbinger of death.

It was an odd time for me to start developing a social conscience; and I suppose my feelings couldn't be explained so simply. But I knew, all at once, why Tom was in the job he had chosen. The attitude of men like this merchant of death was an insult to the poor innocents who try to get through life without hurting people any more than they can help. This man would barter a thousand lives for his expensive car, and ten thousand for his property, complete with swimming pool. It wasn't fair.

I pressed my face against the rough stone and moved my head. I scraped the gag off, together with a patch of skin. I put my back against the pillar, pushed with my sore feet, and stood up.

By that time the third member of the association had arrived. They were speaking English. I suppose Mr. X didn't know any Spanish. Men like that don't have time for lessons with Berlitz. They can hire all the language majors they need. But he wouldn't want an interpreter tonight, he would not want any witnesses.

So I would show him a witness he didn't know about.

I couldn't be any worse off. If I sat there and did nothing, Ivan would be back to collect me. He might kill me, despite his plausible excuses. (Rule one: Never believe the other guy.) The alternatives were almost worse than being killed. So I had nothing to lose. If I projected myself into the midst of this supposedly secret meeting, I might cast some doubts on Ivan's efficiency in the mind of his prospective partner. It would be some satisfaction to make the mastermind look bad.

Hopping wasn't easy. I felt as if I weighed a ton and a half. It made a lot more noise than I had expected. The voices stopped at the first thud of my feet, and I tried to hop faster, before Ivan could stop me. I lost my balance, and rolled into the courtyard.

What an entrance, as an actress friend of mine used to say. Flat on my back, fists digging painfully into my spine, I stared up at the faces that hung over me like dark moons. Ivan's face was livid with anger, Uncle Jaime's was a mask of disapproval. The other face really did look like a moon; pale, and luminous with a perpetual sheen of perspiration, it was as blank as the lunar surface. Nothing would surprise this man. He had seen everything.

I gathered that Ivan was getting seriously annoyed at my constant interference. The hands that lifted me up bit into my skin.

"My hostage," he explained. "An enterprising woman, as you see. Were you bored there alone, Carol?"

"Careless," the third man said quietly. "Is your nephew unable to do without his women, señor?"

Ivan's expression was murderous. Before he could think of a suitable response, Uncle Jaime spoke.

"That is not his weakness. Ivan, there is blood on the child's face."

"She fell," Ivan said.

"Untie her hands. She is in pain. You are worse than careless, you are clumsy if you cannot deal with such a small girl without vulgar methods."

Ivan let go of me and spun around. I'd have fallen, except for Uncle Jaime's quick hand. The third man stood at a little distance, watching with the courteous withdrawal of a stranger who has walked into a family quarrel. He lit a cigar; the smoke spiraled slowly upward.

"You see?" Ivan's hand moved in a gesture of appeal, not to his uncle but to the witness. "This is the old man's weakness; this is why you need me. In his way he is capable, yes, but he lives in the past; he does not admit that vulgar methods, as he calls them, are now part of the real world. Together we will do the job for you."

"A beautiful job," I said. "A charming job for a hidalgo, the descendant of noblemen. Corrupting children. But you'll never see that, you won't see them dying of overdoses and screaming when they can't get a fix. You won't see the people they gun down so they can get the money to support their habit. You won't ever see the corpses. How about María, Ivan? Have you taken care of her yet? How about Danny? You'll have to take care of him too; addicts aren't trustworthy. You did a great job with Danny," I said; and I looked at the bulky figure of the third man, silent and unmoving, the smoke from his cigar rising straight as a signal into the air. "You don't know about Danny, Mr. Whatever-your-name-is. You ought to know; then you'll appreciate what a prize you're getting in Ivan. Danny is a friend of mine; a guy who told me, once upon a time, 'Don't be sorry. Don't ever be sorry.' Today he sold me out to Ivan for a pinch of mescaline. He was mixed up and unhappy and in need of help, and what did he get? He got Ivan. You're going to make a marvelous corporation, the three of you."

"Okay, miss," the man in the shadows said. "You've got it off your chest. Now shut up. We have some business to discuss."

"No," Uncle Jaime said.

I can't imagine how he had hidden the gun. It was enormous—long-barreled, pearl-handled, like the Roy Rogers six-shooter I had yearned for when I was nine. It was pointing at Ivan.

"All along I have been in doubt," Uncle Jaime said conversationally. "I allowed myself to be persuaded. Now I have changed my mind." He inclined his head, in dignified apology toward the man in the shadows. "I make you my excuses, señor, for bringing you so far for nothing."

The other man said nothing. The ash dropped off the end of his cigar; and Uncle Jaime's voice had a new note as he added,

"In my day I was, as the Western films say, the fastest gun in Mexico. I do not think you would risk carrying a gun tonight; but please keep your hands in sight. I can still put a bullet in this unworthy nephew of mine, and another in you, señor, before you can move."

"You are mad," Ivan said, in a strangled voice. "Insane —"

"No, no. I have been mad, but now I regain my senses. My marijuana, it is a harmless indulgence, I see no wrong in it. But this game you try to bring me into—I do not play a game which hurts children and is rude to young ladies who are our guests."

I backed up, in obedience to his gentle tug on my arm, and I felt the ropes around my wrists loosen and fall. I was too dizzy to think clearly. It had happened too fast.

The knife dropped at my feet while I was rubbing my stinging wrists.

"I apologize," said Uncle Jaime in his most courtly tones, "that I must ask you to cut the ropes around your lower extremities. Then, I think, you will have to run, and go as quickly as you can. Go to the restaurant. There is a night watchman. He will let you use the telephone. You know the way?"

"Yes," I said, hardly feeling the painful rush of blood into what Uncle Jaime called my lower extremities. "I know the way. Uncle Jaime—"

"Go quickly," he said, in the same calm voice.

I looked from the grotesque old museum piece of a gun to Ivan's face, which was no longer young and handsome. I went—quickly.

When I emerged into the plaza, the moon was sinking. The long shadow of the pyramid stretched out like a finger, obeying the dictates of the god to whom it had been dedicated. Ahead and to my left, the higher pyramid stood. The restaurant was beyond it. I had to cover several hundred yards of the Avenue of the Dead, climb the wall, up one side and down the other, and circle the pyramid. It was a fairly strenuous walk, which would have taken me fifteen or twenty minutes at my best. I wasn't at my best, but I knew I had to make it in less time than that.

Time was my worst enemy; it had defeated me once before. A fat old man with an antique gun against two ruthless killers . . . How long could he hold them off? Then there was Tom. I hadn't worried about him when it seemed as if I might not survive to find out what had happened to him. Now I pictured all the possibilities. I saw him as a prisoner, being slapped around by a pair of resentful guards; I saw him sprawled out at the foot of a cliff; I saw him helpless in the dark, racked by convulsions. . . .

Then I heard the shots.

There were three of them, unevenly spaced; after an aching interval came a fourth. I couldn't help it; I stopped and looked back.

A figure separated itself from the shadows of the temple facade. A slim, dark figure, running like a deer.

Dust spurted up under my thudding feet like little wisps of moonlight. I knew I wasn't going to make it. I didn't have enough of a lead. I couldn't scream, I didn't have breath to waste. I reached the wall and started up the steps on all fours. I got to the top; and then that ungovernable urge grabbed me again. It's awfully hard not to look when you know something is closing in on you.

When I turned, his congested face was on a level with mine and his clawed hand touched my skirt.

My scream was rendered with real feeling. It was a gargoyle's face I saw, out of a dream of demons. I went down the other side of the wall faster than I had meant to, hearing cloth rip, but not feeling the tug. I was beyond that, I was beyond any feeling but terror. I ran, not toward hope or safety, but away from the unendurable.

When I saw the lights ahead and heard the voices, I thought I was having hallucinations. I went on running; I couldn't have stopped if I had wanted to. I fought the first man who caught me, kicking feebly and squealing like a trapped rabbit. Then another pair of hands came out of the darkness, and a set of features materialized; and I knew that, awake or dreaming, I didn't have to run anymore.

III

The hotel room was not the one I'd had before, but it looked very much like it. The bedspread was green instead of blue, and the pictures were different; but the view from the big window was the same. The Reforma was almost empty at this unearthly hour. An ugly gray dawn was spreading. Propped up on the bed, wearing my least sexy nightgown, I smelled like a pharmacy—iodine and alcohol and some kind of salve that must have been made mainly out of sulfur.

I was pleasantly surprised when I scraped off the layers of dirt to find that there was nothing wrong with me that those three medications couldn't cure. I still think one of my toes was broken, but, as Tom pointed out, there's nothing you can do about a broken toe anyhow.

Sprawled out in an armchair, he looked worse than he had before the doctor got hold of him. Part of his hair had been shaved off, and the bandage on his head looked like a big white egg. The shadows under his eyes were a bright purple, and his beard was deplorably darker than his hair.

My eyes moved from Tom to George, who was occupying the other chair. George was neater, but the marks of his hours of worry were as plain to see as Tom's bruises.

I was tired—to put it mildly—but not sleepy. There were so many things on my mind, I didn't know which to mention first.

"What about Danny?" I asked.

George's narrow, gray face took on a hint of animation.

"We'll do what we can. I'm not as optimistic as I once was—or as pessimistic as I was later. I think there's a chance for him."

His eyes met mine without evasion. He had decided he would live with that memory now—with it, and with my awareness of it. I wondered if he saw the past as I did—as part of the inexorable pattern of people and events. Few other men could understand Danny's need as he did. And if he succeeded, then one life saved might help to make up for the lives that had been lost.

"I think you can do it," I said.

Tom cleared his throat, and I looked at him critically.

"I still don't understand why you aren't tuned in."

"It wasn't LSD," Tom said. "I should have known that little swine was lying; all his schemes were overly complex. What I got was the usual, psilocybin or mescaline. They wear off in three or four hours instead of twelve."

"Even so . . ." I tried to calculate. "I don't know how much time passed, but it wasn't three hours. How did you get to town, alert the police, and get back?"

"Sorry to destroy my image, but I didn't. I was flat on my face fighting monsters when Lieutenant Ibarra found me. He broke into the local *farmacia* and shot me full of chlorpromazine."

There had been a lot of policemen at Teotihuacan, but I recognized Lieutenant Ibarra right away. The last time I saw him he had been trying to flag a taxi on the Reforma.

"But what was he doing at the pyramids?"

"You can thank yourself for that," Tom said. "Ibarra has spent the night at Teotihuacan ever since the last time you bought souvenirs from Carlos Mendoza."

"Then that was it—the new smuggling method you hadn't figured out."

"It was Ivan's idea. Followed logically from his job with the tourist agency—which is a perfectly legitimate operation, by the way. I didn't catch on till the day I was in Carlos's shop with you. It was such a wild hunch, I almost didn't mention it to the other boys."

"Ibarra wasn't able to get into the shop until last night," George said. "Carlos never left the place, and his sleeping quarters are next to the storeroom. We know why he was absent last night. That shed where you were held prisoner is on Carlos's property, not far from the shop. Ibarra heard the hullabaloo following your escape, and went out to see what was going on. That was why he was on the spot when Tom needed him."

"Me and my brilliant thinking," I said gloomily. "Do you mean that if I had gone the other way—"

"Your reasoning was perfectly logical," George said. "You couldn't possibly know that the police were nearby. If it's any consolation to you, we probably couldn't have arrived in time to catch Ivan if you hadn't bollixed up his arrangements. Ibarra called for reinforcements right away, but it took time for them to reach the place. Even then we didn't know the precise location of the meeting place. Carlos couldn't tell us that; Ivan didn't confide in him."

"You got Carlos then," I said, with some satisfaction.

"Oh, yes. Ibarra had found enough evidence in the workshop to confirm Tom's hunch. Some of the statue copies were hollow, and two of them were filled with marijuana. Apparently Ivan made some test runs, using pot, to make sure the technique would work before he got the heroin."

"It worked," Tom admitted. "The main weakness in our customs inspection arises from the sheer bulk of the traffic. When you think of the weird hiding places that have been used, it's amazing how much contraband we find."

"I thought you relied on informers to get most of it."

"Believe it or not, less than ten percent of the contraband is caught because of advance information. Those inspectors are good; they are highly trained and motivated, and they develop a kind of sixth sense, as professionals do after years of experience. They look for certain types, certain mannerisms. . . ."

"I can guess which types," I said. "The longer the hair, the longer the search."

"Everybody is legally liable to search," Tom said defensively. He didn't have much sense of humor about his job. Few people do. "And the poor, persecuted hippies are more inclined to be smuggling pot. That's what made Ivan's scheme so good. He picked out women whose appearance was a testimonial to their middle-class respectability. People like that are the ones who sweep straight through customs without having a suitcase opened. And since they were unwitting, their consciences were perfectly clear. All Ivan had to do was con one of these respectable females into buying a statue from Carlos. They're popular items; he might even give the lady one as a memento of their beautiful friendship. Damn it, the plan was practically foolproof. He didn't need a patsy very often; you can pack several kilos of snow into one of those statues. And before he selected the victim, he knew all he needed to know about her; any information that wasn't on the form supplied by the agency he could wheedle out of the lady in friendly conversation."

"He sure could," I said, remembering the ladies from Minneapolis. "Oh, my gosh—I wonder if poor Mrs. Gold is carrying around a dog filled with grass."

"We're checking on all Ivan's recent customers. Of course the marijuana wasn't in the statues on the shelves. Carlos made the substitution when he packed the lady's bag, in his workshop. He gave her the bag as a souvenir if he couldn't persuade her to buy one. They were ideal for packing those bulky statues, which take up a lot of space in a suitcase."

"The straw bags were part of the plan too," I said. "They're so distinctive you can spot them a long way off.

But I don't see how it worked. There was an exchange?"

"Right. Ivan's lady tourists traveled by plane; people who have their own cars normally don't invest in tours. There are some nonstop flights, direct from Mexico City to New York or Chicago or L.A., but many of the planes stop at San Antonio or Dallas for customs inspection. So there aren't more than six or eight cities through which returning American citizens are cleared through customs. We don't know yet whether Ivan had assistants in all these cities, or whether he chose only tourists whose flights were scheduled to stop at San Antonio. The plan worked the same way, wherever it was carried out.

"As soon as Ivan selected the lady and learned her travel plans, he sent a wire or postcard to his friend, who runs a curio shop in the city—a shop specializing in Mexican handicrafts. There are several types of statues that are used, and an equal number of different-colored bags. In his message Ivan indicates the statue type being used, and the color of the bag. The agent packs his bag, from a supply which has been brought in legally, as commercial imports, and trots off to the airport in time to meet the plane."

"He'd have to know which flight and which day," I objected. "Seems like a lot of information to put into one message."

"Not really. Suppose the wire says something like: 'Two more days, wish it were ten. Tell Ellen Sunday.' Ellen stands for Eastern airlines, the numbers give the flight number. 'Days' indicates that the statue is the one of the dancing dogs; the word 'wish' means a purple bag. It's a simple code."

"I guess so. The agent identifies the tourist by her straw bag, then."

"Right again. The lady will be carrying the bag, it's too

fragile to be tossed into the baggage compartment. The accomplice in San Antonio is an accomplished man—years of training in shoplifting and pocket picking. An exchange is simple, once you know the tricks of the trade."

"Suppose the agent fails, though, or doesn't meet the right plane. There's five pounds of heroin wandering around loose."

"No. Don't forget, Ivan knows the home addresses of his girl friends. The statue is perfectly innocent-looking, it has to be, in case some nosy customs man takes it out of the bag. Ivan can send someone to make the exchange later, after the lady arrives home."

"I guess it would work."

"It's beautiful," Tom said, warming to the idea. "We wouldn't have caught on to this one for a long time. Not without George."

"I had a hard time convincing you," George muttered.

"I believed you."

"You were the only one who did. I'm afraid it proves that you are still too naïve for this business." George smiled, but it was a weak smile. "And, you see, I would have failed you. Ivan's plans were, perhaps, overly complex, but in one thing he was brilliant. He had an uncanny ability to judge the weaknesses of other human beings. He played on the vulnerable point of every one of us—me, Danny, Carol—even you, Tom. You wouldn't have fallen into that clumsy trap if you hadn't—"

"Fallen for your daughter," Tom said calmly. "How true. I haven't even got the grace to be ashamed of it."

"Ivan did well with us innocent *gringos,*" I said. "Where he failed was with his own compatriots. María and Jaime."

"The old lady is much relieved," Tom said. "When Ibarra

went out to get your suitcases, María packed them for him, and she told him everything. She did her damnedest to warn you."

"He must have been her darling when he was little," I murmured. "She was wiser than any of us. She knew he was sick. That pitiful ceremony—it was his soul she was trying to cure. How did she get wind of what was going on?"

"She knew everything that went on in the house," George said. "Every whisper, every secret thought. Old women like that do. And she had enormous respect for Jaime. He was the true master of the house."

"I'm sorry about him," I said.

George stood up.

"You're exhausted. Did you take that pill the doctor left?"

"No pills for me. I'll never be able to look an aspirin in the face again. Don't worry, I'll sleep."

Tom pried himself out of his chair, groaning.

"I'll be down the hall," he said. "If you want me . . ."

"I do. But not right now."

"Okay." He kissed me, without even looking at George, and shambled out.

Left alone, George and I were silent. There were so many things that were waiting to be said. And so many that could not be said, now or ever.

George put his hand on my shoulder.

"Don't grieve for Jaime," he said gently. "It was a good death for him, he couldn't have imagined a finer one."

That started me crying. I mopped my eyes with the edge of the bedspread. He was right about Tío Jaime. He had given his life in defense of his honor, to save a woman—he was old enough to think of it in those terms. A lot of the old ideas are bad, but it's a pity we can't save the good ones when we throw out the rest.

I wasn't crying for Uncle Jaime. My tears were for the one person whose name had, carefully, not been mentioned. She had her faith. That was all she had now. Her own sense of honor had kept her from interfering when the man she loved set out to destroy her son. She knew he was evil, that he had to be stopped. But she could never go back to George, not even in the half-living, unsatisfactory way in which she had lived with him before.

Maybe she was one of the lucky ones after all. I don't know. We have thrown that out too, the old, fortifying faith in God. We don't even know enough about it to understand the strength it has for some.

George kept patting me and I kept snuffling—weeping for Ines.

"We'll talk after you get some rest," he said. "We have a lot to talk about, haven't we?"

"Yes."

"I'll be next door. If you get frightened . . . or lonely . . ."

"I'll be all right."

"Yes, I think you will."

He walked to the door. He moved slowly, his shoulders sagging. He was an old man—most of his life was gone. But at the door he turned, and he smiled at me.

"Tell your mother," he said, "that she has done a wonderful job."

And there was another name we hadn't spoken that night.

Poor old Helen, off on her cruise, little dreaming of what her innocent daughter had been up to. If she ever found out, she wouldn't agree with George that she had done such a great job of bringing me up. But she had probably done her best. There are some things that can't be taught. They must be learned through living.

I leaned back against the pillow and let my sagging eyelids close.